D1607704

SUFI

a commentary

SHARON MARCUS

Printed in Canada

FIN 05 07 06

Library and Archives Canada Cataloguing in Publication

Marcus, Sharon, 1934-

    Sufi : a commentary / Sharon Marcus.

ISBN 0-9737534-3-9

    1. Sufism. I. Title.

BP189.M338 2006   297.4   C2006-903326-9

          THE SUFI PRESS
       Toronto, Ontario, Canada

CONTENTS

My Introduction to Sufism 1
The True Islam Which Belongs to Us All 15
The Path 39
Prayer 63
Explanations 87
The Inner Qur'an 103
The Prophets...113
Ritual 133
Questions of a Searching Heart 147
Faith and Wisdom..165
Remembrance of God..187
The Beloved 207
To Be Forgiven 219
Good and Evil...235
The *Qutbiyyat* 249
States of Consciousness 267
Surrender and the *Alhamd* 287
Three Worlds and the Search for Truth 303
A Choice of Destiny...317
The Great Exchange 331
The Significance of Duty 347
The *Nur*..361
The Enlightened Master 375
Scripture and Revelation 389
The Divine Attributes 407
Community 423

PREFACE

This is a short book about an immense subject which has
occupied me fully for half my life, occupied my heart and every
level of consciousness I have been able to summon. From the
very first moment that I met M. R. Bawa Muhaiyaddeen, may
God be pleased with him, I was immersed in the depthless seas
of love and wisdom which surrounded his sanctified presence.
He was the great Sufi master who was the *qutb*, the divinely
placed guide for all in this era who long to understand the
mysteries of God and His creation.

The true study of Sufism does not begin in a book or in
scholarly investigations because this is an inner pursuit, a path
which lies within that must be examined experientially by
anyone who has had a hunger to know what must be known,
and that translated means a hunger for God and His truth.
Bawa Muhaiyaddeen has been both my truth and the
verification of my truth: I have learned the only things of

consequence in my life from him. This book then, presents a synthesis, a compression at my point of understanding, of the Sufi way seen from the inside by a student, a disciple who had the bliss and grace conferred by proximity to an extraordinary teacher, a saintly being who always described himself as a student. Not revelation, but the accent, the flavor of revelation, this commentary offers a description or analysis of the mysteries at the heart of the Sufi experience.

God is One and the truth His immanent totality. The essential precepts and practices described here are presented sequentially, then repeated several times from different perspectives as that oneness and the totality are explored. May the merging of the heart with that One, union, return to the source which alone can satisfy our deepest yearning and love be granted to us all.

MY INTRODUCTION TO SUFISM

Bismillahir-Rahmanir-Rahim

It did not begin at the beginning, it began before the beginning, before I had any concept of beginning, when there was only the urgent recognition of the need to know. And from a Sufi perspective, even before that, surrounded by the divine embrace in the kingdom of souls where a ray of light exploding in the presence of God became a sacred flame for my existence, this was the point of origin. There has always been the need to return to that divine point, His presence, to merge with the totality, One, and that need was translated into a passion for finding my way to the truth no matter how difficult or improbable the way. This is an outer simplification of an inner process which cannot be described except approximately, what happens in there resonates non-verbally, nevertheless, it can be told.

1

There is also a more conventional narrative rooted in historical events, and although I find these details less exhilarating some account is useful, if only to document certain conditions contributing to the rapid spread of Sufism throughout North America late in the twentieth century. The story to be told, a lyrical sketch rather than a finished picture, is typical in specific ways while still profoundly individual at the anecdotal level, and clearly on this path, the path to God, we all have a story to tell because the individual threads wound together make a single golden fiber of exquisite grace and strength. It is this spun gold, God's story told as our own, which distinguishes the Sufi chronicle from theology, from doctrine and religion, it is the exploration and the light of revelation before the accretion of anything like institution, even the institution of Sufism itself, this collection of paths and forms, orders, teachers, disciples, which have all come and gone over the centuries, perhaps from the very onset of what it means to be conscious and human.

In pursuit of the formless we find ourselves locked within the paradoxes of dualism, boxes with an inside and an outside, when we want nothing other than to merge in the pure open space, the monism of One. How we solve this puzzle is not so much a matter of doctrine and theory as disposition; for some this means a renunciation of form, for others a dive into form, while for others still, the path lies through the structure of form to the formlessness beating at its heart. These are outlines, contours, shade and variation, nothing more, yet they have become the grist for mills of controversial debate. Did Sufism begin at the time of the prophet Muhammad, may the peace and blessings of God be with him, or have there been Sufis since the time of Adam, peace be upon him; is Sufism under the great umbrella of Islam, the original Islam of light and purity to which we were all born or does it emerge as a manifestation of mysticism in any religion or divine context; does it exist within the definition of orthodox Islam alone? Another question, are Sufis required to perform the ritual prayers and ceremonial rites of the orthodoxy whether that orthodoxy is Christian, Muslim, Hindu or Jewish?

To answer any of this, to look at the white hot revelation which thirsts for God's cool water, first find wisdom, follow the truth born in absolute faith, nourish the attributes of God Himself alive in every human heart, annihilate the sense of self, ego insisting upon distinction and individuation, because without wisdom to ignite it, the quality we aspire to is not that quality.

The transforming purity of love, yes, burning in the fires of love, yes, but if we hug a tiger we are devoured. Where does this divine wisdom come from, can we expect to encounter it along the routes defined by intellect or even intelligence, is it merely a byproduct, the residue formed by an accumulation of useful data and reasonable, truthful information, or must we develop new pathways? The access lies through faith, an axis so pure, so mysterious, it leads us to gates which swing open and doors with no locks, faith which is born and grounded in the knowledge of right and wrong, true and false, a recognition which constitutes the first step on our spiritual ascent.

We have books which give us the history of this or that Sufi movement or group, an analysis of theory and practice, but Sufism is not *about* something, it is the experience itself, our own, the critical exploration of who and what we are. If we hunger to know God we have to know ourself because He exists within us and we exist in Him, He is our reality and we are His. But how can we discover this power which cannot be detected in space or time, cannot be conceived by linear dimension or known in comparison to anything else, how is it possible? We have to examine ourself with a merciless exposition of flaws and faults, we have to look at our strengths

4

and weaknesses, disposition, karma, mistakes, failures, and extract every minute point which does not resonate as His quality, we have to eliminate every thought or word or act which does not come from Him and end in Him. Only when we succeed in removing these impediments, these obstacles, can we begin to approach that truth.

We must explore the nature of our own experience, forwards and backwards in time, and use the understanding we derive correctly. Sometimes in my life things have happened that I didn't understand and I missed a great opportunity, sometimes I did understand and still missed the moment, either accidentally or deliberately; only once in awhile did I manage to connect the inner and outer in exactly the right way, at exactly the right moment. A Sufi, a true Sufi is always in the right place at the appropriate time, has no accidents and sees what must be seen from the top of the mountain, with a perspective on before and after which transects what happens now with clarity.

The superb invitation of the great, true teachers, the saints and divinely wise beings, has been the offer to stand watch, to guide us through the dark woods of mind and desire where all the flaws lie buried, half hidden or fully exposed, guide us through all that and take us to our goal, our destination. If we are presented with an invitation like this we should accept it with unconditional gratitude, God is answering us, revealing that our prayer to Him is His prayer to us. Nothing in western thinking prepared me for the idea we cannot undertake this on our own, nothing in our philosophy or psychology, nothing in our art, music or literature presupposes the eastern assumption there are things which can only be done in the company of someone who has gone on ahead and come back to show others the way. Here in the west we search constantly to validate and even enhance the self, popular jargon trills routinely about self-esteem, while eastern doctrine insists upon obliterating that clamoring thing begging for recognition or comfort or support. How do we choose, how do we know we have chosen correctly, how do we know we have the right to be sure we've chosen the true posture, the correct attitude, the indispensable assumption?

One approach to finding an answer comes through understanding the nature of suffering, what is it, what causes it, what gets rid of it? Suffering is caused by wanting what we don't have, not wanting what we have; another way to say the same thing is desire and the consequences of desire cause suffering. Attachments, prefering our child, our friend, our spouse, our family, our country, our religion, they all cause suffering. Hunger, disease, old age and death, four inescapable human conditions cause suffering, and the demands, the righteous clamor of ego, that sense of individuation which separates when we want to be in unity, also causes suffering. If we want peace, if we have that pressing insistence to know God, we can begin by discarding the avoidable, removing what can be removed, starting with the separations caused by mind and desire, those architects of illusion. Once we understand that illusion is responsible for the presumptions of duality, of other, mine and yours, we lay the basis for the recognition that all suffering rises in the separation from God.

This is not something I grasped during the years of ignorance and suffering when I tried to understand the pointless futility which circled my days and emptied my nights. The path given to each of us is different, some have the supreme bliss to be born with the truth, some find it easily available, while others grope and stumble down every dark laneway and unlit corridor, uncertain whether there is such a thing as truth, and if there is, whether it possibly can be known. In my own experience, I can verify the horrors of this route, yet given the sort of person I am, was and have become, the significance and inevitability of every difficulty is accounted for. In any case, every story which ends in God is a story with a happy ending.

Raised as a Jewish child in an atheist household, I was always conscious of otherness, individually and collectively. In public school we recited The Lord's Prayer and read from the Old Testament to start every day, but not susceptible to the ecumenical persuasions of those who set this policy, I always knew it was theirs, not ours, and felt embarrassed if not resentful, not to mention disbelieving. Then later, as a passionate undergraduate, superficially confident, overflowing with the arts, attitude and opinion but made distraught by the uncertainties of existence and a suicidal shroud, I flirted briefly with Christianity. They looked good, all those beautiful churches, rituals, even exquisite prayers in Latin at some. It was the majority, this was the west, we couldn't read the literature, look at the paintings or listen to music without a deep immersion in Christian symbols, and I shopped around, Anglican, Catholic, Unitarian, Presbyterian, Methodist, I tried them all, nothing happened. Nothing happened because no one knew, no one had heard the voice of God, no one talked to God, no one knew Him well enough to say who we are in relation to Him, and so I kept going.

Philosophy I thought, philosophers must surely have the answers, it's their job, what they're about, but I was let down badly, first by Descartes whose proofs depended upon the faith I didn't have, then by the rationalists and the skepticism of Hume which swept up everything from the path, then by the existentialists who didn't seem to have a cogent structural base, until finally there was nothing left but the positivists who disallowed everything but the analysis of language and logical propositions. Still dissatisfied yet profoundly entertained at the level of intellect, I played this game for some years, but I also studied Blake and wrote poetry, a little, not much. One day while I was living in England, I mentioned to a friend that it seemed likely I would have to give up either poetry or philosophy because there was such a conflict between the inner processes they entailed, and she said without hesitation that I should drop philosophy. I didn't comment although I heard my own unspoken assent.

All this time, and the years that followed, I look upon retrospectively as part of the search I had no idea I was on; it's

9

not always possible to say where we were until we arrive. During the philosophy years I learned something about intoxication, everyone drank in those days, and since moderation was not my strong suit, I drank to excess, always in pursuit of pleasure, and more particularly, in pursuit of that brief instant defining what I took to be overwhelming clarity, before the overwhelming darkness and confusion which inevitably followed. I noticed however, that I couldn't write, that I often felt unclean and that the demands of this life were beginning to intrude upon the routines of everyday existence, including job, study, family and friends who were doing other things. And so it was easy enough to give this up altogether, as a matter of preference, not necessity, when I began to study music more seriously. Later, as the intoxication of drugs became psychotropic interventions leading only to paradise lost, I clung eagerly to the illusions they fostered, haunted by the suspicion, no the expectation, this would run out, would come to an end, and then what, where would I go from there for the illumination I now eagerly sought, and which always seemed to elude me?

This was very late in the sixties and into the early seventies; a comparative avalanche of translated texts from the east had arrived in the bookstores, the knowledge and wisdom of eastern philosophy and religion poured out simultaneously from travelling gurus, musicians and books. Hooked on the concept of instantaneous illumination and immediate transmission I practised yoga and various forms of meditation, visited gurus, adopted a mantra or two and read as much as I could grasp of the mystifying texts and every first hand account of the spiritual life that came my way. Becoming vegetarian just at the beginning of the seventies was an interesting leap across a great divide for me, it was an open acknowledgement that I was the subject of my investigation, not the investigating object, that I had thrown my hat into the ring by accepting the assumptions of change, of changing myself.

But of course, I had already made signicant alterations before the recognition for the need came, and that is often the way it is, things fall away on their own, God helps us discard what we don't need without a sense of wrenching sacrifice. At this point I was critically aware that it was time for a teacher, a flesh and blood being, not a book or a travelling act or a compelling presence, a real teacher, someone who had the goods, as I liked to put it, someone who knew what it was and how to distribute it, how to teach the transformation. Of all the things I read,

11

encountered or studied during this initiating period, there was nothing about Islam, in part I suppose because there was little that interested me available in translation, except of course for Rumi whose discourses I found pure, revealing, and the Qur'an which I could not penetrate because of the translator's outmoded language. In addition, I have the impression looking back that I might also have been subject to the influence of the unfavorable, even hostile press Islam has always been subject to in the west.

Still, this is what I was plunged into with the first luminous words coming from the sanctified being who became my teacher, my guide, my father, who was so much more than that. Muhammad Raheem Bawa Muhaiyaddeen, may God be pleased with him, was not only the reviver of true faith, as his name indicates, he was also the *qutb* of our era, the primary guide for the life of the soul on this earth. He had the gift of pure wisdom, the capacity for direct communication with the divine, and evidently permission to offer what he knew to anyone who asked. The day I watched him speak at a radio broadcast in New York, answering questions from callers on the most esoteric subjects, things which had been kept secret in the past and only passed from master to disciple under rare circumstances, I understood he had been given license to explain the great mysteries to us all.

Why we should have been brought to such an exalted master remains something of a mystery for many of us who had the grace to remain in his presence during the final years of his life, but when I asked him about this once with bemused persistence, his reply, without much elaboration, was that we had been given what we deserved, what we had earned. Later, much later, after he had left his body behind and returned to God, it occurred to me that his disciples, like the companions of the prophets, had been chosen at the beginning, in the world of souls—but that is more or less speculation.

And what is this Islam which I walked into so comfortably, so naturally, with the first loving words of greeting I heard him say how many, many years ago, what happened to bring me into the most improbable realm I could have imagined? It was not conversion, not in any sense of the word, it was more like a declaration of what I had always known but had never been able to find, restoration of the original vibration which comes before sound and well before speech. It was the final, the ultimate act of revolution. With everything he said I was aware of a resonating affirmation coming from each level of consciousness, a yes from the level of the cell, from every pore and follicle. His words were deliberate, they reached into my body like hands touching my heart, inviting me to the presence of God whose existence was announced and confirmed for the first time. There was no need for mantras and yoga, no need to climb to the top of a mountain or retreat to the jungle, God is here, in each human heart, and even more astonishing, we are within Him. All the details of everything he taught, everything he explained is derived from this basic fact.

THE TRUE ISLAM
WHICH BELONGS TO US ALL

As members of one human family descended from the same parents it makes no sense to divide ourselves into race, religion, language, class, caste or any fine subtext of these categories, not even into gender for that matter, since the soul is neither masculine nor feminine, and it is important to balance the perspective of this world with the perspective of the divine kingdom which circles around and permeates our lives. We are all born in the state of Islam, a purity which proclaims the state of His perfection, something we knew and affirmed in His kingdom before coming here. It is our passage through the world, the karma, desires, the ties, prejudices and attachments engendered by the world which obscure the original state of our birth, and it is our work here in this world to clear the way back, we come from Him and return to Him. This is an obligation laid upon us all without reference to whatever religion or language or position is engrafted on that pure state, this is the answer to the haunting why of our existence, the why was I born and why am I here, that destroys our peace unless it is answered correctly.

The word Islam has two components, *isk* which is love and *lam* which is light; in Islam we are in loving surrender to the light. Through the purification of loving God we surrender to the grace and wisdom of His presence and His truth, we surrender the things of mind and desire, we surrender the self, the ego, the persona so completely it is obliterated, lost in the totality of One. This is the death to the world, the death before death which marks the goal, the destination of the Sufi path. How we get there is the commitment to God we are prepared to make, a commitment which might surge at different times in our life in different ways. I have, from time to time, spoken to individuals describing my life, how I spend my time and what I do, and they have said that is interesting, but I'm not ready for that, I still want to have fun, I still have things I want to do in the world, things I need from the world, I have my business, my family, I need a big house, I want children, and of course this makes sense to them. The only problem with this careful reasoning is that God's timetable is significantly different from ours; lives hang from such a fragile, unpredictable thread we can never say with certainty whether our time is short or long.

What we have to manage, what we have to figure out is the balance between the left, the world, and the right, the divine, how do we stay in the world and serve God with every breath? The answer is given in different ways at different times in our lives, and certainly there was a long time when I would have given the same response to this observation about my life that has been given to me occasionally. The path opens for each of us as God determines, when the time is right. I can no more regret the years I spent wandering off in every wrong direction than anything else in my life, it is as it was and God alone knows why. Nor can I decline the invitation to remember Him, love Him and serve Him now, what's past is past, what's gone is gone. This is not some subjective quietism, this is the muscular recognition that we need to exert ourself, the best and wisest way possible in whatever circumstance we find ourself, but it is God's show, the outcome is His, the ultimate responsibility is His.

And what does this mean in terms of the functional opportunities we encounter in our daily experience, how do we

17

discover or walk what may be a very fine line between right and wrong, how do we preserve the truth if it is all up to God? There are two parts to solving this equation summed up in the well-known saying of the prophet Muhammad, trust in God but tie up your camel. In other words, we are required to do our part, we can't just lie down at a busy intersection and expect God to divert the traffic away from us in every direction. There is nothing God does not know, but if our destiny had already been determined there would be no need for us to come here to work it out—there is a record and a balance sheet which must be made to come out correctly, to come out even, without mistake. The way we survey our experience is relevant to our understanding of the things and people we are confronted with; this means if we perceive each event as something which has been given to us by God, nothing that happens is either bad or irrelevant.

The misfortunes and disasters which fall into our lives, they seem to come on their own, must also be seen as coming from God, sometimes only to strengthen us, to strengthen faith and determination, sometimes as a blessing we cannot recognize because we don't yet know the end of the story, although God does. He knows what we cannot know, and that is a rather obscure blessing as we continue to pry into a more clairvoyant view of what lies ahead for us, but who would endure what must be endured if we knew the outcome in advance, who would bear the uncertain burdens we have thrust upon us or we willingly undertake if we knew the end before the beginning? If I had seen the number of years it would take and the ardors of this path at the outset, I doubt whether I would have accepted it, the mere weight of years alone might have discouraged me. I see now it could have been otherwise if I hadn't made that choice in a state of peripheral blindness, for which I truly thank God. We do make a great effort to see down the road, as we should, but we should also remember the implications of the curse laid on Cassandra.

To see a disaster as a blessing, or at least an opportunity to come closer to God, is not always easy, except in retrospect. Developing the muscle, the tough inner reserve to experience a difficulty as a gift is certainly a major assignment, not something I have begun to master, yet I do elect or choose to do this, and the choice, the conviction that this is a way to end suffering is a significant avenue to the peace we crave like a drug. Some years ago, there was a brief but intense period in my life when all the horrors the world can inflict seemed to

19

converge at once upon me. A year or two later when life had put on the mantle of the normal and usual again, a sympathetic although injudicious friend inquired curiously, wasn't my faith affected? Startled because I hadn't expected such an innocently rude question I said, "Well I didn't really expect to live through it, but my faith was all I had, don't you see my faith was all I had left?"

During the actual events we referred to, I didn't perceive it that way, I was aware only of the presence of God sustaining my life in spite of the painful situation which seemed ready to destroy me altogether, and I knew that God's protection was extended even in hell. The faith which was the only thread from which my life had hung so precariously was not an affectation of piety, it was the only living thing in a dead landscape, a dead universe, and it was there because I had chosen to believe, to accept the reality of God's existence while rejecting the impermanence of my own; I had chosen and God saw my gesture of choice, reinforcing it with His gesture of grace. From the Qur'an we learn that God Himself must initiate the need for His guidance, nevertheless, choice remains an esentially human characteristic. Animals cannot choose to change their nature, tigers are naturally rapacious, dogs are faithful, cows are benign, they all worship God as their disposition and condition dictate; it's just the opposite for the human condition, we can change ourself. We may not be able to change anyone else, no matter our fondest expectation to the contrary, but the truth is we can certainly change ourself, we have to come to the understanding if we love God and want to return in a state of purity, we must begin by choosing to assess and change who we are to become who we must become.

Islam starts with an instruction course in right action, good manners, good behavior, respecting and treating all living things with the same respect we expect for ourself, sharing the joy and the suffering of everyone else as no different from our own. Islam is a kind word, a good thought, a generous act, feeding someone who is hungry, clothing another who cannot clothe him or herself, Islam is making peace and being just, fair, not treating your child differently from mine. If we have that longing to know God, we must realize He is a formless power who can be known only through His attributes and the actions these qualitites give rise to. To know these qualities we have to look at our own heart where the imperfect, human version is lodged like seeds in the ground waiting to be fertilized and nourished, waiting to be born. And what are they? They are all familiar to us, they are aspects of the good we have always been aware of, the patience, truth, love, compassion, tolerance, contentment, mercy, forgiveness, equality, peace, purity, justice, faith, sincerity and generosity which are absolutes in His immaculate existence and shadows in ours. Since we cannot describe God by listing our own qualities, we recognize that His love is the love within love, His patience the patience within patience, His compassion is the compassion within compassion, and so on.

Interestingly enough, these good things that must emerge from us are often preceded by things which are less lovely, less desirable on God's path; like weeds in the garden they come first and have to be removed by meticulous cultivation. This weeding process is also a little like muscle building, it can't be done all at once, it happens slowly, with great patience, the first step needed for this process to unfold. Looking back on my own experiences in this difficult arena, I think my struggle with a nasty temper is relevant. I had learned as a child that the hot anger and fits of rage I was subject to, in conjunction with the dismissive contempt this anger implies, was a controlling instrument which I did not hesitate to unleash. Since it didn't seem to occur to anyone that I could moderate my behavior, this bad quality acquired a little life of its own, I was even rather pleased with my own ability to launch such an avalanche of terrifying emotion, proud of my anger and its effectiveness, as if it were an ally I could count on. The self is fond of its lesser aspects.

Eventually, I did begin to notice the effect on myself, the days it took to recover from this onslaught, the devastation of my own nervous system, and finally it seemed to me, although still unconcerned about what my anger did to anyone else, that it was not such a good idea. It took years to begin the disengagement of this entrenched bad habit, it was rather like trying to stop a freight train in its tracks. I discovered that the intention to stop it, thinking about stopping it were not enough, it was only when I felt the tides of anger begin to rise within myself that I could unlearn what I had accumulated so carefully over the years, then slowly, slowly I could push it back, push it away, keep it down and under control. Progress was slow but evident and I kept working at it, even if I sometimes felt like Sisyphus. Now I don't often find this response percolating up as a spontaneous reaction to a variety of situations, although I am affected by someone else's anger, especially if it is directed at me. Now there is a deeper, a physiological level like blood pressure which must be harnessed.

This is the inner struggle of Islam, this fight within ourself to improve and correct the horrors we find there is the battlefield of the prayer mat. If we let the weeds flourish indiscriminately in our garden there is no room for the flowers, they cannot grow side by side, the weeds will always take over; a bad quality will not slowly be replaced by a good quality, it must be eradicated. It doesn't matter who we are, what religion or lack of religion we are born to, this essential reclamation of the purity we brought with us is a necessary first step, the introduction to understanding who we are in relation to God, in relation to the meaning of being here, it is a step we have to repeat again and again until the way is clear of the obstacles we create even as we climb to higher levels of wisdom, as the consciousness of wisdom matures. We are forgiven for the things we do in ignorance, and we know we are forgiven when we no do not find ourself doing those things any longer; we are also rewarded in ways that need no verification for the things we do wisely.

Since purification of impulse, desire and pointless mental action are so necessary, we have to consider the value of prayer as a primary instrument put directly into our hands to help us with this transforming process. There is a *hadith,* a saying of the prophet Muhammad that has been handed down, which resonates with authenticity: there are three things we are not entitled to ask each other about, money, travel plans and our prayers. Money is a private matter, travel at the time of the prophet had its own hazards, discretion was important for safety, and prayer is also a private matter. There are literally millions of different prayers and approaches to prayer, no one person or group or religious entity can claim to possess the only effective access to God, the only route to His attention, whether we pray once a year, once a week, five times a day or with every breath.

We don't necessarily pray the same way at each period in our life as faith and wisdom develop or mature. Changing the way we pray from time to time, both the form or formlessness and the content, is useful, first to accommodate changes in our capacity, and next so that our prayers are not just put on automatic, so that we don't fall arbitrarily into the unbroken rhythm of a routine which does not begin and end in a fusion of love and light. This is not to say that ritual prayer cannot be done except routinely, on the contrary, it is entirely possible to

25

be carried through form, step by step, stage by stage, to an exalted place we might never otherwise find. Positions, postures, words and intention have a specific reference to phases of our praise and worship, to the understanding which can soar as God determines to enlighten us. We can have nothing to say about someone else's prayers, God alone knows the heart. Al-Ghazali said that God has the keys to every heart and opens each one with whichever He chooses.

We don't have to visit a mosque, a temple, a shrine or an altar to pray, but no matter how we choose to pray, first we must build our own inner sanctuary, our own synagogue or church in the heart. We should start on the inside and work our way out, begin with a sincere dedication in the depths of our consciousness, let the vibration which comes from God as a light and a sound resonate in that space without dimension where we can meet. Know that God exists within us and we exist within Him, accept this, believe it without reservation then consecrate the inner church, build that private place beyond form and come to the understanding that prayer is not only a word or posture, a thought or attitude, it is the way we live as well, what is called in Arabic the *din,* the faith manifest in our life, the path of purity, the *dinul-Islam* we all share

26

equally. It's easy enough to talk about the beautiful qualities, the absolutes of God we aspire to discover and uncover in ourself, however until these attributes are evident in our conduct, the things we do, how we behave, it's only talk, nothing more.

Since we know that God sees every part of our lives, we can't confine our approach to a few regulated moments at intervals during the day or the week, everything we do or say should be done with the conscious need to make that word or act acceptable to His presence; the text and resonance of our experience should witness that presence. My understanding, from the beginning of any understanding about prayer at all, has been that God sees and knows our situation. He sees and knows what we need and want, there's no reason to ask for something He is about to confer, something that was prepared for us long before we arrived in this world, there's no need to ask because it has already been given or denied. Prayer is not concerned with asking for this or that, saying I want, I need, please give me this because my life is otherwise incomplete, insupportable, I can't go on like this any longer. He knows, He knows. Instead we offer our love, we offer our gratitude, we offer our praise and surrender the outcome of our desires and dramas to Him, His disposition of our affairs, not ours, His will and determination, not ours.

Doctrine, theology, the dogma of my religion or your religion have little to do with the sanctity of true prayer. They might have much to do with the consolidation of truth which ends in an institution that might or might not be relevant to our understanding, but there is no reason to place any structure or hierarchy between God and each soul reaching out with longing and sincerity to Him; for this soul there is only absolute faith, wisdom and the qualities ignited in the flames of that faith and wisdom. The orthodoxy of almost any sect or group has a problem with such institutional exclusion from private or public prayer, while the mystic might have little or no use for all that apparatus except perhaps as an interface at critical junctions with the world, like birth, marriage and death. There are Sufis and mystics however, who function quite happily, sometimes quite visibly, like Thomas Merton for example, in the context of an established religion. In the west, it seems to my limited range of observation, most who are born in the west and come to Sufism at some point in their lives, tend to identify themselves with a community of likeminded people rather than a religion, while the farther east we go, or for those who were born in the east and moved to the west, there is a closer connection to the ritual practices of Islam.

Although the Sufis, the mystics, are characteristically tolerant of divergent practices, with the encompassing understanding there is a truth at the core of each religion, this courtesy is often not extended to them by the larger religious communities, afraid of losing control, afraid of controversy, enmeshed in the business of their own structures. In different parts of the world at different times, today as well, because Sufi organizations represent a powerful force in a small or tightly controlled state or nation, there has been open and sanctioned hostility between governments with an invested connection to an established religion and the Sufis in general, as a movement, in addition to specifically targeted groups. It is also true historically that sometimes Sufis have been very active politically, at the time of Mansur al-Hallaj this was certainly so, and have represented a genuine threat to established authority, both ecclesiastic and political. Even today, Sufis travelling to Saudi Arabia have been warned not bring any books or paraphernalia readily identified as Sufi in origin or context.

But in Islam, the Islam of purity which belongs to us all, there is nothing in attitude or actions towards each other which denies freedom, which is repressive directly or indirectly; restraint yes but repression no. The four cardinal virtues God has bestowed as a gift for every human life include restraint or reserve, along with modesty, sincerity and concern about doing something wrong, inappropriate, something incorrect in God's eyes. To begin with modesty, a founding principle, what does it mean, why is it signicant? Verbal modesty about individual actions or accomplishments, on whatever level, follows automatically from the need to diminish the spoken clamors of ego, easy enough in the company of a genuine saint. But certainly the inner voice which longs for recognition is more difficult to quiet, attached as it is to that urgent sense of self, I have done this significant thing, I presented that distinguished analysis, I know these important people. Only the genuinely humble, self-effacing lack of concern or pride or arrogance about things we might have said or done constitutes modesty, only the scraped ego can be described as modest, only the annihilated ego can truly fulfill modesty's ultimate requirements.

I think I learned everything I needed to know about modesty in dress from years in the physical presence of the great master who was my teacher, a being who radiated purity and manifested the proximity of God so unquestionably, it was impossible to be indecently dressed around him. Like Adam and Eve after the fall in paradise, we were conscious of a nakedness that needed to be covered, but there were no extremes, nothing that made us excessively conspicuous, either for the men or the women. The women wore jeans or long skirts, loose, comfortable clothing, no *hijabs* or all-covering outer garments, and for most of us in the early days not even a headscarf; the men wore jeans and a tee shirt or a shirt and trousers, but no shorts. They were advised not to wear *kufis,* the skullcap headcovering, in the street; we were occasionally reminded to be invisible in a crowd for our own protection.

There was a dress code, more or less unspoken, but it was never repressive, it came from our own sense of what was correct or appropriate under the circumstances, it came from an awareness of the sanctity of the human form, God's light impressed on the forehead and in the heart, it also came as direct instruction from the *qutb* once in awhile. This is a difficult concept to convey without sounding prudish, it has to rise up in each heart along with an awareness of the body as a sacramental thing to be protected and used correctly, along

31

with the profound recognition, as the Qur'an affirms, there is no compulsion in Islam, no one has the right to impose unwelcome or unwanted restrictions on anyone else.

Restraint is another first gift or principle to recognize because it implies the discipline and control of our thoughts, words and acts. We try not to shout out the first thing that comes into our mouth, we try not to rush impetuously into a reckless action, we try to marshall our thoughts and emotions so that they do not wander aimlessly in worlds we freely improvise. The reserve side of restraint manifests in respect for each other, caring for each other in ways which are acceptable to God, treating each other with courtesy, as brothers and sisters of one family. Sincerity lies close to purity, meaning what we say, saying what we mean, no false sentiment or emotion, a constant search for truth, no hypocrisy or meanness of thought, the constant acknowledgment of God's uniqueness and His totality. Concern about the correctness, the appropriateness of our conduct in every situation, in business, professionally, at school, among our families, with our friends, wherever we find ourself, means the constant remembrance of Him, knowledge of His omniscience and omnipresence. This overwhelming sense of awe in His divine presence will keep us from doing things which might not be wrong but possibly might not be right, it will purify our sense of right and wrong, make it more exacting and scrupulous as we move from step to step, level to level.

These four precepts, a lightly sketched code of behavior at the core of Islamic purity, are merely prescriptions for a healthy framework, conditions on which prayers can rise, laying the foundation for a solid structure to be built before God, a structure composed of the translucent thoughts and actions we live blissfully in here and inherit later. Heaven and hell are not only the condition of some remote afterlife, they are also in evidence here; there is a direct connection between what we experience here and what we experience there, we keep the peace or the torment we acquire in perpetuity. Bawa Muhaiyaddeen said more than once that the house we build here is the house we receive there. Since this is so, it is imperative to assimilate the truth, the wisdom and the qualities flowing from that wisdom into the structure of our lives, we have to live in the attributes of the reality which is permanent, the essence not the ephemeral.

Islam offers both an outer and an inner map to pursue that path, guidelines which can be interpreted quite literally to establish

33

the treasures of our existence. The orthodoxy describes the outer map as a set of obligations, prescribed duties; looking at this from another place however, we can see these things as obligatory only if we accept this map as the right one for our unique journey, because they can also be understood symbolically, they can be fulfilled at a much higher level than the outer description implies. On whichever level we choose to understand and practise them, they are to be understood as valid and necessary human accomplishments, known in the outer, conventional way as the five pillars of Islam.

The first thing is we are to have absolute faith in God, an unswerving faith that believes without question, to the depths of our being, in God. This *iman,* as it is called in Arabic, is the only thing we actually need, but if there is a drop of imperfection in our faith, other things follow which might compensate, which might bring us to this level of complete belief, believing that we believe. An inner understanding of this initial requirement is the total acceptance of God as the only reality, denying our own in the totality of His, the self, the ego obliterated, subsisting in Him alone, His words, His actions, existing in the divine radiance of His essence.

If we do not find that exalted state within ourself we must engage a level of prayer, *salat*, to raise us to it. The outer instruction is to pray five times a day at prescribed intervals in a specific way, as Muhammad himself outwardly prayed. Praying five times a day will obviously get us there faster than once or twice, although it is admittedly not an easy thing to adopt if we are not born into a community committed to its practice, the times of prayer have a way of occurring in the middle of life, business, school, family, swirling around in directions which pull us away from God and into the world. If we can turn our attention to God in the midst of the demands made by the world, this focus will purify our capacity to devote ourself to Him exclusively while we care for the things in the world as well. Inwardly, we recognize that this formal requirement is not enough, to pray adequately we have to fix our every thought and intention upon Him, we must worship in a state of loving surrender with every breath, negating everything that is not God with the out-breath, affirming that He alone exists with the in-breath.

And if this purifying state of prayer eludes us, there is charity, *sadaqa*, to open our heart, the charity of sharing what we have with those who have nothing or less than we do, of feeding the hungry, clothing the poor, housing the homeless, helping someone who is troubled or in difficulty in some appropriate way, even with a kind word, a sympathetic gesture. There are so many ways of helping, of supporting the good things around us in a meaningful way, not only giving money but our heart as well. This charity is feeling the sorrows of other people as if they were our own, a compassion which melts at the sight of suffering and responds with love in the best possible way. A full inner understanding means sharing, giving it all away, so that by the end of our life on earth nothing material is left, and we leave taking only the good we have done.

Then we have fasting or *saum* to take us to a deeper place of devotion to God, to that praise of Him which engages the purest surrender in each cell of our being. Fasting teaches us to experience the hunger of those who never have enough to eat, whose poverty means constant physical deprivation, the exhaustion which depletes even the possibility of health, being well, happy, at peace. For us the fast is only temporary, undertaken to feel closer to God, to the suffering of others everywhere; we break the fast at sundown, but those who fast involuntarily have no relief from their pain. The fast traditionally enjoined and made obligatory is for the month of

Ramadan on the Arabic calendar. This is a lunar calendar, significantly different from the Gregorian one we commonly use, but there are many other regular opportunities for fasting as well, optional days like the three white fasting days in the middle of each month and certain holy days. There is a larger, deeper understanding of the fast which takes us even farther, the essential, the inner fast means abstaining from every wrong thought or act, from every quality in the heart which is not God's, the ultimate eradication.

Finally, there is *hajj,* pilgrimage to the holy places of Islam once in our lifetime if we have the financial resources to undertake it, an outer obligation to pray at a place of accepted sanctity in the monotheist tradition, consecrated from the time of the prophets Abraham and his son Ishmael, and rededicated by Muhammad. This is the great opportunity to die to the world. As pilgrims we approach the sacred place in a burial shroud, all worldly obligations resolved or severed, announcing again and again with absolute conviction, "I have come beloved Lord, I have come." A ceremonial observance of significance to millions and millions, for the Sufi this rite is an outer verification of an inner Sufi precept, the death before death conveying the utter annihilation of self, the transcendence of night by light which means an end to aging and death.

In addition to the five pillars of Islam, Sufism recognizes six inner duties or obligations, making a total of eleven, an interesting number, which lift the very concept of duty or obligation to a higher plane. On the level of the soul, the inner path of progress towards the Beloved, towards God, a duty resembles an act of prayer and purification teaching us how to come close to God, the surrender both physical and beyond the physical, how to know Him, how to become the slave serving Him with love. These inner obligations related to how and what we perceive are a key unlocking transitions from outer observances to inner transformation, necessary changes which make it possible for that union with the Beloved to take place. We cancel what we see with the physical eye and look with the inner eye which sees only what God sees; with the inner ear we hear only the sounds of God, putting aside the sounds of the world; the tongue tastes only the taste of God, utters only His words; the nose catches only the fragrance of God, no longer engaging the scents of the world; and the melting inner heart, an imperishable piece of flesh which houses the soul stands in the presence of God.

THE PATH

Actually, there is no path, not anything cut and ready made by religion, philosophy or a system of mystical approach, there is ultimately nothing except our own effort to carve a passage through the dark woods of the world. The perilous route which lies across a dense undergrowth and the misleading overhang of illusions erected by duality, by the functioning of mind and desire, can only be made safe in the company of a wise being who has come this way before, but the truth of our journey must come from the clarity in our own heart and the determined purification of our life. Nevertheless, we are told eventually we come to a place where there is only room enough for one, a route which lies beyond our understanding, beyond the known and available, where we must be absorbed into the heart of our beloved master, the sheikh, the teacher, the guru of our wisdom, and this sanctified being must be completely suffused within ours because from this place on, we go alone.

There is something known as the *siratul-mustaqim,* a bridge or tight, narrow causeway of faith and right action to take us through the world to God. It has been described as the mere seventh part of a seventh part of a hair in width, a filament slung high above chasms of raging fires, up where furious winds toss it from side to side and in every direction. This is just the way life in the world is, we are not to be discouraged by every difficulty coming our way, we are not to be deterred by obstacles, we must persist, we must never give up. And since there are navigational aids, devices to help us make the journey, maps to show us how to find our way, we fill ourself with the courage and strength flowing from God's grace alone, we take refuge from the pain of the world in His qualities, His wisdom, His truth. That narrow bridge, so subject to the storms of the world, each of us must erect alone, no one can do it for us, no one can transform our qualities and actions but ourself.

In some ways it's harder than it once was, the world seems to have been in a less corrupted state at certain other times, but in other ways it's easier now as maps of the esoteric, once kept secret and passed judiciously from master to disciple are readily available to all who come thirsting for God, hungering for His truth with an open, melting heart. Perhaps it's a sign marking the terribleness of the times we live in, our survival as a human species suspended from a fragile thread dependent on props from beyond, or perhaps this is God's timetable catching us at last, one final effort to keep everyone safe. As the darkness increases, light to find our way mysteriously increases too. The so-called maps are neither diagrammatic nor visual, but paradigmatic, they offer clear patterns for the development of understanding, to help us change our qualities and learn the nature of surrender, to open our hearts so that God can change our capacity to come closer and closer to Him. The secret truths from those who present themselves as beings of light and wisdom are available publicly, privately, from books, in person, on radio and television, on the internet, so available because we have a clear need for the subtle wisdom to distinguish brass from gold, trivia from truth.

To begin with, we need to reperceive our experience, past, present and future, examine the past for flaws in understanding, weakness in performance and carelessness in our relations with others. We turn to the mistakes and failures of the past with sincere regret and beg God to forgive us for the things we did in our time of darkness, our time of ignorance, we beg forgiveness for what we did before and form the determined intention not to repeat our errors, not to act again on the misconceptions tied to an old habit or belief. It might take some time to ransack all the old files, to scan our records with a critical, repentent eye, but once it's done we're finished with the past, no reason to wallow in the things we did wrong, no point in endless sorrow or misplaced guilt. It is equally important not to linger over the wrongs done to us or the things we have seen we would rather not have seen, important not to allow warp and distortion at the level of the merely psychological because that makes it impossible to proceed.

The way is hard enough without the emotional unrest projected by remembrance of a disturbing childhood, it is necessary to relinquish the past, necessary to start with a clean slate if we are to assess the present correctly. Remembrance of things past works for literature, not for spiritual ascent. Since life itself is inclined to administer all the pain we can endure, self-inflicted suffering is only an indulgence and an obstacle which obscures what we need to see about ourself. Mental and emotional problems should be dealt with before undertaking the progress of the soul where the intensity of concentration, the focus of prayer can burn the house to the ground if the structure is already unstable. When we engage the present, perceptions which transect all levels of consciousness between before and after, a fleeting concept hard enough to grasp by itself, if we are preoccupied with thought, emotion, confusion, a lack of clarity, or if we focus on an obstacle rather than the reality which is God, we lose this moment and all succeeding similar moments, taking us farther from our goal instead of closer.

As for the future, we have to be careful not to project our own will and let God's will determine how or whether to take the next step. Have a plan, yes, exert ourself to the limit of capacity, yes, but know the outcome is in His hands. If the next step is very clear, we take it trusting in God; if the next step is unclear or even uncertain, we wait until there is clarity and the way lies open. If the way is blocked, sometimes it is better to turn around and go another way, sometimes it is better to wait until the gate opens, sometimes we are to hammer on the gate with our prayers in a state of complete inner patience. Wisdom alone can determine for us which choice is appropriate, the wisdom which emerges from the faith of pure certitude and a determination to persist in truth. We have to consider the totality of our experience as the individual instruction course designed specifically for us, for who we are, so that we become the most enlightened version of who we are.

We study and learn step by step, passing, failing, repeating whichever grades we need to repeat, coming eventually to the understanding our whole life is a student's life, we never stop learning the things we need to know. And yet there are moments when we have to recognize it's time to finish a particular lesson and put it into practice, we cannot sit in the same place repeating the same experience again and again, we must keep moving, changing, improving. What point in staying in the same place or making the same mistakes consistently? If we don't take what we need from what we are given and assimilate this, incorporate it into the way we behave, we have missed the point. What point in saying with satisfaction that an experience we've had is a lesson, a teaching, if we've said the same thing about a similar episode any number of times? We do remain students, but we graduate from time to time as well. It's important not to get stuck, to be immobilized at a certain level of understanding or accomplishment and stay there, with or without the complacent acceptance we're not going any farther.

Some of us, in the urgent recognition that the world is falling apart, the world needs saving, contemplate how to help, how to stop the imminently destructive tendencies we see all around and realize the only way to begin is with the only thing we have control over, the only thing we actually can change, ourself, but somewhere along the line, enchanted by the inner progress, we forget and find our attention distracted, diverted before we have completed the work that needs doing individually, before we can take on the world or even a small part of it. If we are serious about saving the world then reperceiving ourself, the context of what we know in relation to who we are, this becomes an important step, a giant step that can't be turned around or halted midway. The exhausting and sometimes tedious work of reclamation and reformation must continue, must not be interrupted by the siren call of everything out there, because the truth is, there is nothing out there which is not in here, whatever we perceive outwardly exists within. If we become that shining, irresistible example of the good, the pure, the slave of God, others will be inspired to do this work on themselves and they in turn will inspire others. That is the direct method.

To save the world we must begin by saving ourself, by initiating the process of emptying ourself, everything we once thought valuable, worth saving or hanging onto has to be thrown away, probably for good, because the criteria of value have now been radically transformed. The treasures of yesterday are today's trash which needs to be packaged, wrapped and tossed, whether it's a system, a method, a concept, a conceptual construct or even the very understanding of what constitutes analysis, since for wisdom, analysis may be quite a different thing. Why do we need this disposal of so much just for starters, what is the reason beyond the obvious for the ritually empty cup? The truth is the opposite to what we expect, it is an absolute of imperishable purity which cannot be mixed with anything else or it loses the resonance that makes it pure; the truth is a jewel which can be examined from each of its exquisitely faceted surfaces, according to the conciousness, the subtle wisdom of the understanding which contemplates it, but every facet reflects only the light at its heart, the totally luminous presence cancelling everything except the One.

We empty our heart and our understanding to start again, to learn like a baby producing the first tooth, taking the first insecure step, only this time it's not the things of the world we have offered to us, thrust upon us, this time it's the truth of God and His kingdom which alone can build the enlightening structures of wisdom and peace. If we take one drop of God's truth and try to make an alloy of it with anything that comes from the world, we destroy that drop, we make something which might seem palatable when we taste it for the first time, yet in the end, it becomes a foul taste we reject altogether or else it rejects us in disgust. There are reasons why it is imperative to find the right teacher and the right instruction course, someone who can teach us to distinguish truth from fiction, fact from fancy, so that we develop our own capacity to know the difference, so that wisdom matures from level to level as we leave behind the frivolous presumptions and the ignorant darkness of the world. The sweeping generalities promulgated by arrogance as truth are worthless, and that trumpet which rings not with humility, not with the strength of pure silence is a sound that warns us, not this, not this.

Once we have cleared the playing field by leveling the ground and ridding it of the debris accumulated through the mistakes and confusion of poor judgment, wrong assessments, misconception, we see that we can all be called believers. This is not a term to be reserved only for those who believe in God, His truth, His omnipresent existence, the difference is what we believe in; we all believe the earth will accept the weight of our next step or we are unable to move, we all believe the fire will cook our food or we starve, we believe the water will hold us up or we drown, we believe the medicine will cure our illness or we die, and that is the belief we are to have in God, the unquestioned certainty He exists, His reality is the truth and the permanence, that is the matter-of-fact, unquestioning level of belief we are to have. What we reserved earlier for the acceptance of the illusions substantiated by a duality we now shrug off, is the belief we focus on One, not just the usual belief in one God that monotheism profers, but the totality of One, the affirmation of One, the *la ilaha illallahu* denying the existence of anything but Him.

Now we begin to understand the qualities and attributes we aspire to, now we begin to comprehend the instruments made available for the journey we have undertaken, and how to use them. This inner patience, the starting point for prayer, for study, contemplation, any work on the inside, or the outside for that matter, why should this be the first thing we need, why should this quality among all the beautiful divine attributes be the indispensable starting place? There is a Sufi maxim that the successful outcome of anything presupposes turning to God at its inception, and if we turn to Him in that unquestioning state of absolute patience which accepts and acknowledges His supremacy in all things, whatever the outcome we are necessarily satisfied, we leave resolution to Him alone, we do the work trusting His guidance. We might think we know how we would like a certain thing to turn out, then perhaps it does and we offer thanks; still, there is every possiblity it turns out some other way, and we offer thanks knowing that He knows what we do not. We are sustained by the patience which finds the perfect symmetry of His, without dropping into distress or disappointment, without consulting preference, and in doing so we bring the event to a successful conclusion.

We don't have to think in terms of success and failure to be alive to the real nature of patience, we can see that patience is the divine eraser to wipe away every petty dissatisfaction which haunts the ego, the wounded self, even after the great reclamation begins. Determining to do a thing is not the doing; the way is long, the road unpaved and filled with ups and downs which patience alone can level. While patience is not the antidote for qualities like anger, greed, jealousy, hatred, intolerance, because the good qualities do not replace the bad in that way, it is part of the mechanism to help focus on their elimination. We use patience to help dismantle the walls of anger we have spent so many years constructing, we use patience to reduce these walls, brick by brick, a gesture or impulse at a time, and simultaneously we use the same patience to fertilize the garden of new growth which the walls have enclosed, and which, with God's grace and a perceptive, meaningful intervention, we can take down. Two things are going on, the undesirable is being eliminated and the things we need are being fostered, but it's not a continuous loop one thing implying the other, each process demands specific attention.

In the great unraveling of things we know to be knotted obstacles along the way, we resort to other props in the battles of the self, we go more deeply into the resources which open up as we become aware of their use and availability. As patience spreads its cooling shade above the fires of temperament and disposition, we find, if we dig beneath patience, a companion for this engagement against the forces of mind and desire, against illusion and ego, and that ally is contentment, absolute contentment, another of the precious qualities of the divine to be sought and used. Now none of this sounds like a secret, like revelation, these ordinary, known characteristics of the human condition without reference to the divine, what makes them extraordinary however, is their recognition and introduction to service, what makes their

50

acquistion revelatory is accepting the need for change, accepting that these are routes to a change which will transform our experience and our perception of experience.

Discontent is a most potent disturber of our peace. We are not satisfied with our job, it's not the important work we trained for, we are not paid enough for that discouraging position besides; we don't like our house, it's too big, too small, too cold, too hot; we don't want to be alone any longer, we want a husband, a wife, a partner, and if we have one, that person is not quite right for us, doesn't understand us; we want a child, children, and if we have one or two they continue to let us down, they fail to satisfy our expectations; we don't like the way we look, we're not tall enough, not thin enough, not smart enough, not young enough, not quite handsome or beautiful enough. In fact, if we examine our life in detail nothing actually makes it, nothing is right, as it should be, and a mountain of small dissatisfactions becomes a whole mountain range we have to destroy if there is ever to be peace in our life.

On the other hand, if we look for contentment, not a supine inertia but a radiating joy in the presence of God, knowing that He has given us everything, bestowed each gift upon us in every way, our life is wrapped in the mystery of perfection, the right wife or husband, a good job, excellent children, a body that functions well and never lets us down, a comfortable place to live, all this to let us contemplate Him with praise and thanks. This is the contentment allowing us to receive whatever comes as an opportunity to work on ourself, to improve, to change, whether the situation is something we might have chosen or rejected, this is the contentment lying at the feet of patience which understands the mountains are nothing more than illusion, subtle manipulations of the mind in submission to the dictates of desire. When we grasp the nature of contentment we have an introduction to the limitless nature of desire, the things we want, either the trivial longings or the towering passions, and then we perceive profoundly, in an inner way, that desire will never leave us in peace until we start to say enough, my dearest Lord this is enough, You fill my wants, You alone can satisfy the soul wandering in search of You. This will not put an end to the maneuvers of desire, nothing will, yet it can open an avenue to pure peace if we are ready to go that way.

If we cannot master patience in a given difficulty, or if we fail to grapple with the roots of contentment, we can turn to an even deeper level of respite, even restoration, in what can only be described as total trust, the absolute surrender to God which is the opposite of giving up. Our patience is gone and contentment is nowhere in sight, at that moment we have to turn to God, our supreme Lord, acknowledging we have come to the end of our own capacity, done all that we could with His help, and take refuge in Him alone, surrendering ourself, the difficulty, our whole life to His disposition. And it's not just in moments of sorrow or difficulty that we surrender in pure trust, although such moments might precipitate this posture of devotion. When we search deep within to find that place where He exists in us and we exist in Him, we recognize perfection and surrender to it, we recognize purity and surrender to it, we recognize the divine attributes and surrender to each of them as we simultaneously perceive the gulf between His excellence and our frailty. We live in a body that rarely gives us peace, we have demands made on us by the world that rarely gives us peace, we live finitely, He lives infinitely. Enough my God, enough, we offer everything to You because nothing competes, nothing compares, You are supreme.

In the fourth and final phase of this transition from the world to the divine kingdom, from the body to the soul, from hell to heaven, we move beyond surrender to praise with every breath, we transcend both difficulty and resolution in a place where nothing but praise resonates, where the majesty of His presence is so overwhelming, so dominates the levels of consciousness, of the wisdom which experiences His truth and acts upon that cognition, nothing remains but praise ringing through earth and all the heavens. We come to this state of resonating praise when God lifts us from pure surrender to His immediacy, when we know that He is all we know, all we can know. Sometimes we are taken directly to this place from the depths of despair, the wretchedness of loss, the only route which carries us from selfhood to painless non-existence, sometimes this can be our escape from the pain of the world. Nevertheless, by freeing ourself from the praise and blame of the world, by accepting that the responsibility all belongs to Him, and therefore all the praise as well, we can find an access not lined with pain or suffering, we can make the deliberate ascent in consciousness. It is possible to taste this from time to time, the trick is to remain there, stay in the resonating state of praise and not come back.

There is another map, another group of four routes converging on perfect illumination that we can study. The four roads are simply named surrender, concentration, balance and wisdom, each one to be understood as action and attribute. Surrender, now the first step, is the total capitulation of the self which means relinquishing everything, body, mind, persona, spirit and soul to God. We say yes, this is Yours, not mine, take it, take all of it and do what You choose because I know my whole being and my essence are governed by Your will, not mine. Then we focus, we concentrate on changing our qualities into His, we concentrate our prayers and our praise, longing to be one with Him, merging with His qualities to know that One. At the same time we maintain a balance, one foot in the world, one foot in the divine kingdom, no escape into solitude here. If we are to live perfectly with Him, we must also live in the world where He manifests His existence for us, gives evidence of His existence in all created phenomena. The fourth road, wisdom, is the match igniting our qualities, leading us beyond any difficulty to the enlightenment which is our destiny, our goal.

As we proceed with this analysis of who we are in relation to God, as we start to understand the encompassing state of being which includes everything and excludes nothing, we need to know where we are on the inner map, a map that indicates level, capacity, function, availability, access and direction. This is a map which plots states of consciousness, gives a specific characterization of wisdom's ladder, a scale to ascend correctly and in tune, rising from the primitive sensory perception all living things possess to the divine immanence, His light in totality. We begin with the primary sense data received through sight, sound, smell, taste, stimuli of the outer senses which function for us in approximately the same way they function in the rest of the plant and animal worlds, with the startling adjunct human life possesses, the possibility of inner sight, sound, taste and smell when the sensory vehicle is focused on God alone. From the first level, the reception of data, we move to the recognition that information has been received, awareness, a simple consciousness, a level of comprehension or wisdom rather like an undifferentiating catalogue or record, imprinting, a duckling to its mother.

With the manipulation of data found in this imprinted record, we move up again to another level of consciousness, the reasoning ability which lets a bird build its nest, an animal care for its young and lets us solve an algebraic equation, the level of problem solving essentially no different for us than for animals. This level of intellectual performance is usually held in sufficient esteem by the human creature to cast doubt on whether his or her mental experience is no different from that of an animal's, but from the perspective of divine wisdom, the gymnastics of intellect at whatever level are merely exercises. These exercises of the mind bear no reference to the functioning of the spirit, of the soul, and are for that reason at least, classed together as a lower level of consciousness. It is only with a purely human action, assessing the actual performance of intellect, that we rise above animal consciousness.

When judgment operates we find ourself in the human sphere, when we begin to distinguish right from wrong, good from bad, we enter the exclusively human realm, the first step of spiritual ascent. Animals make no such distinctions, they forage, they eat, sleep and reproduce, they pray in their own way, but they have no ethical capacity, there is neither right nor wrong for them while they merely do what they do. For the lion or the tiger it's not wrong to kill, for the fox it's not wrong to steal, and they do these things only to eat or feed their young, not with the wanton carelessness of the human species when we undertake such acts. When animal characteristics emerge in us we behave with a depravity unknown among the animals, but we certainly have the ability to recognize the good and aspire to it, and we do have the ability to understand the nature of evil and reject it. Although this capacity to assess, discern and choose does not represent a particularly high level of accomplishment, it remains the dividing line which indicates what is human and what is not. This also suggests that the face and body of a human being do not necessarily make us human. If we act with rapacity, cruelty and voracious greed, taking, consuming more than our share, ignoring the equal justice found in the needs of others, we forfeit our human description.

From this first level of wisdom which manifests human consciousness, we begin the ascent to more specifically exalted levels fed by grace and nourished with faith. If God is the only truth, the only reality, then wisdom flows from knowledge of Him, of His existence in us and ours in Him, from the affirmation of faith, the *la ilaha illallahu,* nothing exists but God, You are God. How do we acquire knowledge of this mysterious power we cannot see or touch, this power which has no voice except through ours, no formal manifestation except through ourself, how is it possible to know Him? We know Him because we have access, within ourself, to the qualities which identify Him, we know Him because His light has been impressed in our heart, at the crown of our head and on our forehead, we know Him because He has created us to be like Himself, because He has revealed His essence in our essence. If we long to return to Him as the source, the origin, like a river running down to the sea we look within to find His likeness and discover Him there, and then we find Him everywhere, in the trees and the grass, in the sun and the moon, the earth and the sky, we find Him in every living or inanimate thing and every living being.

The key is the search within our own qualities, His love on fire within ours, His patience a radiant stillness beneath ours, His tolerance a gracious open space, His justice a pure flame of mercy. When we taste the intimation of His totality cloaked in our finality we begin to understand certain things about who we are and about Him, we begin to find the seamlessness of His existence subsuming ours as we ascend from divine explanation to divine explanation. Progress from this first subtle level, wisdom with its face turned to God, depends on the grace emanating from His divine presence and the deepening purity of our faith. Such knowledge comes directly from irrefutable revelation, possibly to ourself, more likely through an impeccable source, a teacher of excellent wisdom whose connection to God is absolute, whose purity and wisdom sound the perfect note, the divine intunement, an existence which is nothing but the presence of God. The grace of being found, even sought out by such a teacher we can take as confirmation of our own intention, capacity and God's pleasure with our search.

There are a few rare beings who represent, who embody the luminous wisdom of the next level, a level we are all, in fact, born with but few learn how to approach, contemplate or exist in. This is a level of consciousness, of knowledge which both lives in and understands the complexities of revelation, direct access, the immediacy of communion, the ascent known as *mi'raj,* conversation with God. Although most of us are not usually allowed to stay in this exalted state, we do have glimpses of it in certain kinds of experience, especially the outer limits of pure prayer reached by a combination of effort and grace. Our best knowledge of this state, for most, comes through the association with someone who actually exists in it all the time, an enlightened being described in Arabic as an *insan kamil,* a perfected human being. There are those who proclaim themselves to be such, but in my experience, those who announce themselves this way are missing at least one essential characteristic of this state, humility, and probably several others as well.

As a member of the small, vibrant community which coalesced around the physical presence of Bawa Muhaiyaddeen, I did have the opportunity to live with and observe such a person who was more than just a perfected being, he was the principal spiritual advisor to a company of spiritual advisors, both seen and unseen. What I can report of this state then, comes from a careful, loving examination of the sanctity of his life that consistently manifested the qualities, the words and actions of God. In him I found nothing of ego, self or persona, nothing which did not reverberate the presence of God, he was invariably wise, loving, compassionate, just, tolerant, forgiving, playful, subsisting in God alone, filled with the intoxicating joy of intimacy with His creator and the ability to dispense all this, make it available. His invitation to us was to accept what he had to offer, do that hard work of personal reclamation which culminates in the luminous divinity of God-man, man-God.

When Bawa Muhaiyaddeen left his physical body behind and returned to God, he had already long since ascended to the seventh and highest level of luminous consciousness, perfection merged with perfection, the qualities of a human being penetrating and being lost in His qualities, water merging with water, a seamless reunion, God returning to God. There is little more to be said outwardly about this state of divine transcendence, except to note for the correspondence of outer with inner, on the night he passed beyond this world, a new star was sighted and reported in the press, while he deposited the light of his own existence in the hearts of his beloved followers.

PRAYER

Pray for me we say to each other, pray for me, as if my prayers were better than yours or yours were better than mine, or the swelling, more impressive crescendo would have a greater impact and produce more effective results. We need to remember that God has reminded us again and again, if we turn to Him, if we call on Him, He is there; we may not hear Him, but He always hears us. Although it is true that sometimes we do need to ask for a specific intercession, there is no real reason to implore His special favor when He has seen what we need and made it available before we were born into the world. God who has no dimension, no spatiality, no time, might have a calendar which doesn't operate on the tight time frame we would prefer, but we have to have the trust and absolute faith that He knows, He knows. Prayer, praise, worship, devotion, remembrance, those are not things God requires, we do. We might even pray fervently to God asking for His protection while we do something we know to be wrong, yet prayer is still a primary instrument of purification He has placed in our hands.

The truth about prayer is that it is a subtle thing, only God can pray to God, everything else is just an echo of some desire which falls back into desire, illusion or the crashing of the elements responding to the elements. To understand the significance of this means looking at the old Aristotelian idea of substance or matter which shares something with the ancient Chinese analysis. Historically, western philosophy has always inquired into the nature of reality by examining substance, both material and non-material, ideas and language. The components of the material and spatial worlds have been identified as irreducible entities called elements, but this is philosophy, science subsequently broke these elements down, each system of analysis defining new generations of the irreducible while never dislodging the umbrella of each category. The traditional categories then, are earth, fire, water, air and ether, as it was once known, but we can think of as outer space where colors and illusion exist.

Everything which has form, everything which exists including the human body is made up of these elements; still, there is something in the human form, a sixth component which is not elemental, not derived from matter or substance, and that is the soul. There is an imperishable, physical place in the body which houses the soul, yet the soul itself is a ray of light which comes from God and returns to Him. Once we understand that everything belongs to God, that nothing is ours although He has made everything in existence available to us, we begin to grasp the implications of prayer rising from the elemental aspects of ourself rather than the true prayer of the soul in direct communion with Him. A prayer that begins at the level of the cell is a prayer for the creation of another cell, a form to worship, to ensure its rebirth. When a prayer rises from earth it necessarily returns to earth, it does not go to God, when a prayer has its origin in fire it rises from fire and necessarily returns to fire, and so on. These prayers are not connected to divine wisdom even though they might produce happiness or sorrow; since they begin in darkness they inevitably end in darkness. Only the thing which begins in God can go back to Him, only the voice of the soul can address God directly, only the inner ear of the soul can hear His response as our eye sees Him alone, as we offer the inner heart to His mystery, His complete light.

All the different forms of prayer, the ritual prayers of any of the religions, anything we chant or recite, the mantras, tantras, yogas, visualizations and meditations, all the things we call prayer do not ascend to that exalted state of true prayer because they are housed in our own karma, in the conspiracies of illusion rooted in our baser self. When mind and desire are involved in our prayers, we acquire the things of mind and desire, when the elements speak for us, we can only acquire the ordinary things of the elements, but when we have reached a state of pure wisdom we can be one with God and God addresses God. The only thing separating us from God is the mind and the worlds created by the mind, the place we choose to live, the place which keeps us from dealing with all the things binding us to the world, which keeps us from rejecting the impurity of this world and transcending the limits of time.

How do we come to that absolute purity, the remembrance of God with every breath, how do we learn to live in the resonance of the *hu?* Before we can know God, we have to know all four major religious groups which constitute the human story divided into four parts, we have to study the path of each religion, extract the truth at its heart and proceed along to the path without a path. Since each religion is conjoined

66

with levels of spiritual ascent, there is an implicit hierarchy which seems distasteful to ecumenical cordiality and the equality of faith, but when we recognize there are lateral steps within each religion that correspond to the religions above them on the scale, lateral steps which also move upward, this should dissipate some of that concern, there is no reason to look upon any one of them as higher or lower. Whatever the religion, it can only take us to an institutional destination, not to the truth itself, not to the mystical reality of union, merging with God. The religions do what the religions do, and for those who are satified with them, it is enough; for the few who do not find completion there however, there is more.

The first of the four groups includes every religious entity that uses any kind of form to focus our attention on God, whether it's an image, an idol, a mental image, a picture, a painting, a song, a dance, any religion which projects a form and worships it belongs to the first group which has been called Hinduism. Because the religions compose the human story, each group is identified with a place in the human body—for Hinduism that place is the area below the waist, the generative area, the producer of form. At this first level called the *shari'at* in Arabic, sometimes translated as divine law, knowledge of that law, every form presented by the mind, every thought and intention including art and psychology, takes an outer form. Like Abraham's father who created idols, we create a form inwardly and then copy it outwardly, two forms of worship. When desire creates a form this is Hinduism, the things of creation, things that may be created. In our understanding of spiritual ascent, this is the first step, the ability to distinguish good from bad, right from wrong, the ethical capacity, a purely human characteristic.

If we look laterally to the steps of ascension within this level itself, we begin to perceive the exalted nature of the first step because it is in that place we come to know ourself and to know God, the earth, the angels, the prophets, the truth, absolute faith, wisdom, purity, justice, prayer, worship, fasting, charity, compassion, restraint, patience, love, the purification of the senses, correct and appropriate behavior. At the second level called *tariqat* in Arabic, which translated means the path, the way, not incidentally, referring only to God's path, it means the route to anywhere, we know where to put our faith, we know the difference between right and wrong, we adhere exclusively to the good, to what is right and avoid what is wrong. As the first level corresponds to earth, the second level corresponds to fire where the sun and various forms of light are worshiped, this is Shinto, Mazda, the ancient Persian Zoroastrianism, this is the heat of fire where we examine the the causes of destruction, hunger, disease, old age and death, we examine the fires of hell where everything burns.

In terms of our human form, the area around our navel is the second level. At this place we have to destroy all the fire within ourself, the fires of anger, jealousy, rage, envy, greed, intolerance, injustice, bigotry, the hell of mind and desire, we have to destroy all this and accept that only God exists, nothing else, and be one with Him. We accept there is no other God but Him, nothing can be compared with Him, identified with Him or even associated with Him because He alone is without end, the indestructible treasure. The prayer of the *tariqat* cannot be prayed if the elements still reverberate; what must be sounded here is the resonance of a true human being perfectly in tune with the divine. Next is *haqiqat*, the third level represented by Christianity, the level of the heart in our body where formless vapors or spirits exist along with formless animals, those animal qualities we nourish which consume good thoughts and intentions. When all the animals and spirits have been destroyed, when all the artful games and the music of the body have been vanquished or controlled the pure note of the body becomes *la ilaha illallahu,* nothing exists but You, O God, You alone are God. Everything, all the flesh, nerves and cells reverberate with this music of the soul. The *haqiqat* level of the heart is the level at which conversation with Allah, with God begins, this is our *mi'raj,* our ascension, our mystical journey when all the forces of mind and desire are under control and we mount the winged creature who represents their submission, flying up to heaven.

The fourth level, *ma'rifat* or gnosis, is the head, the face which distinguishes us, the level of divine knowledge, divine wisdom, the place of union with God. The elements, karma, illusion and all the unwelcome propensities of mind and desire are completely overcome, we exist in perpetual light, in a state of absolute surrender to God. In *sufiyyat,* the Sufi level above the head, the fifth and ultimate state, there is no alternation of light and dark, of day and night, there is no aging, there is only the timeless purity of subsistence in God alone. This is the state of death before death, the permanent *mi'raj* when we are constantly in communion with God, we see with His eyes, hear with His ears, catch only His fragrance in His nostril, taste only His taste and say only His words with His tongue, the inner heart merged in His totality. This is the state of silent prayer with every breath, when knowledge of the divine and absolute faith are so in love with that endless beauty, they are one, Sufi devotion, one within One.

There is another correspondence for each of these five levels, they are also to be understood as the Sufi explanation of the five daily prayers performed in Islamic orthodoxy. This means that at *fajr*, the predawn prayer, we examine the first level of the body, the earth and all it holds, we analyze our birth, discarding what is neither truth nor wisdom, we distinguish right from wrong and choose God alone. Then at *dhuhr*, the midday prayer, we destroy all the fires of our existence, the anger and jealousy, the hells that pursue and torment us, establishing with certitude in our heart that God alone exists. By *'asr*, the late afternoon prayer, we subdue the formless beasts and spirits alive in the heart and begin the prayer, the conversation in His presence. When *maghrib*, the evening prayer comes, we resonate *la ilaha illallahu*, negating the existence of anything but God, the true song of the soul resonating from every cell in the body, uniting with Him. Finally, at *'isha'*, the night prayer, we have died to the world, we exist in God alone, God prays to God.

71

This whole process of scraping away the debris, the residue of the world from our heart so that we can offer a house filled with light and purity to God, a house where He can live with us, this process can be completed in a single instant of revelation, this can happen. For most of us however, purification proceeds slowly, one step forward and possibly one or two back, the lazy student who puts off the assignment until something triggers a last minute, desperate response. It is so difficult for the human being whose life is filled with distractions and secrets to recognize the need and act upon it, it is so difficult for the intelligent to give up the life of the mind, to realize the inherent sadness and futility in the life of the mind, so difficult for the athlete to give up the muscular life of the body, so difficult for the artist to give up the life in art, for the entrepreneur to give up the life of business, so difficult for us all to cut our attachments, abandon the desires which lead us by the nose. It is the focus and the attachment to that focus which are replaced by a focus on God.

The necessary first step to be taken in the life of prayer, the actualization of the ethical capacity in a new consciousness, comes in different ways. For some it might come with exhaustion, sorrow and suffering, for some it might be discovering the end, the limits of the senses, knowing that the satisfaction found in taste, sound, sight, smell is about to end or has ended, for others it could come with the recognition that techniques, practices or intoxicants which promised fulfillment would not deliver what they seemed to promise, for others it might be restlessness, a lack of peace which seems out of balance with our inclination to inner poise, serenity. The need to pray, the longing to be in a constant state of prayer is not something that can be taught, it must arise individually, from within, awakened by God but swimming into focus through our own situation, our own despair. Of course, there are some who have the great happiness to be born with that certitude already in place, and for them the walk through the traps and traumas of the world is less devastating, more manageable and comprehensible, but no one is exempt from our inner work, the rectification of an infant's purity dressed in the wisdom of experience.

Just as taking the first steps of prayer varies from person to person, the development or failure to develop is also subject to unlimited variability. The levels of spiritual ascent already described are maps indicating what is to be found where, yet there is no time frame with any map, we have to travel in our own way, in our own vehicle at our own rate of speed, without any guarantees that we will reach our destination, if we choose to have a destination. Nevertheless, we have to think, why would God deny us, deny the attempts we make to do the very things we have been sent here to do, why would He not encourage us at least as much as any indulgent parent would? If we stretch out our hand to Him He stretches out His to us, if we take steps in His direction He moves closer to us. It is said if we take one step towards Him He takes ten towards us, if we recite His name with praise He recites ours, and then the angels and unseen beings recite it too.

A primary obstacle along our way may be inertia, losing the impetus of the search, failing to double the effort when our input flags, or even suddenly deciding, well this is good enough, I've done as much as I can, this is as far as I can go. Or we might be so content, so fascinated with what we have already discovered we feel no need to continue. Then again, there may be times when we find ourself marooned on a plateau with no way up and no way down, stuck, in spite of all our efforts. We do have remedies for all these situations, although it might take time and a lot of that essential patience, first, to realize we need a remedy, and second, to find the right cure. Something that never fails, if we can find the inner strength and resolve, is to work harder, harder than we can imagine, as if we were drowning and gasping for one last breath of air, as if we were trying to run from some immediate threat to our life, a wild animal, a man with a gun, because that is the intensity we need to escape.

There are alternatives as we try to deepen our faith, alternatives like change, change of prayer, change of the routines of prayer; we do not necessarily need to pray in the same way forever, without ever changing the prayer itself, the methods or practice. Recognizing the need to change must come from wisdom, not the arbitrary restlessness which haunts the mind and awakens desire, it must come from a pure analysis grounded in faith. When we begin with the understanding that to know God we must know His qualities, must eradicate from ourself the things which do not belong to God and acquire only what is His, it could seem that this completed transformation is all that will be required. And it is true, if we can jump into that purifying bath which removes all the filth accumulated in ignorance, in arrogance and illusion, wash ourself clean in a single or even a repeated series of deliberate acts that keep thought, intention and performance absolute and true, this is what we need to do. So we work on our qualities, we study our faults, analyze our successes and failures, keeping the pure vision of that spotlessness before us in everything we do, holding up the words and example of our master, the teacher, as the light in our darkness.

Some have insisted on this, the most formless, the most pathless path as the only acceptable route to God, to truth and wisdom. It may be a combination of disposition and experience which makes it impossible for us to perceive the value of specific prayer, or the prayer mat, as a way of speeding up the reclamation, perhaps even making it possible to finish the process. Initially, we are so dazzled by the revelation, the radiance and splendor of God, we walk in a paradise where anything is possible, nothing too difficult, then as faith and wisdom deepen and intersect with that point of revelation, we might open ourself to the availability of practices which are helpful. In my own experience, I found myself always ready to change what I did as Bawa Muhaiyaddeen, my Sufi master, offered new directions to explore, and always puzzled by those who refused, briefly, indefinitely or permanently to accept new invitations from the being they called the father of their wisdom. Some, a few, might have been given different instructions although I cannot be certain of this, others might have been merely reluctant to move on, move away from something they found satisfactory for the understanding they had, many simply left our community when they found the changes unacceptable. In retrospect, looking back over the years of Bawa's instruction, it seems to me now, as it did then, he never let us stay in one place for too long, he taught us the value of change as a remedy for the spiritual problems we encountered on our journey, as well as a way of introducing new avenues to enlightenment.

Prayer is such a private, individual matter there is the *hadith*, described earlier, from the prophet Muhammad concerning the inadmissability of asking individuals about their prayers. Three things, we have only three things we are not entitled to inquire about, a person's money, travel plans or prayers, but there is no prohibition restricting voluntary disclosure, and some of the patterns in my evolving experience of prayer seem relevant. The subtlety with which I was taken from one conviction to the next reflects the grace and wisdom flowing from the teachings of our *qutb,* the human embodiment of divine explanation who led all those willing to follow his instructions in a similar direction. Unlike most of those in the small community which formed around that compelling presence, I had come from a place of no prayer, nothing resembling prayer or any form of religious education had been offered to me as a child, and in the face of available mockery and derision, it did not occur to me to look around for any such thing. Later, there were yogas and meditations which did not focus on God, merely on some dim perception of something I could not quite identify, and so I discount these, although possibly I learned something about attention and concentration.

As the first explanations washed around me in a purifying stream, conveying both a clear destination and travel instructions, I was so in love with the truth being taught which now focused on God, His unicity, His omnipresence, I sometimes could not speak or breathe, I was lost in the transforming slipstream of revelation and wisdom. Still, when I considered how I had lived for most of my life, even in the preparatory years before meeting a true teacher, I was eager to start reciting the first formal prayer given to me, the *subhanallahi kalimah* or third *kalimah,* as we called it. I learned it from a transliterated Arabic script, the fact that it came in Arabic presented no difficulty for me—it was simply the language of prayer being offered, and since I had no other it was easy to accept. Aside from which, it was made quite clear that God understood every language, that we could recite this prayer in English if we chose, nevertheless, there is a certain resonance in Arabic that can be useful. Later, much later, listening to the movement of the breath in spoken Arabic, it seemed to me there is a direct connection between the language and a form of prayer I was soon to learn.

But first, the third *kalimah* is a prayer of sacrifice, the prayer recited when animals are slaughtered for human consumption. For vegetarian Sufis however, the sacrifice is of the animals in the heart, symbolizing the imperfections and impurities lodged in an unclean place. This prayer which recites the praise, the glory and majesty of God is intended to slaughter these animals, these qualities that keep us from the presence of God; it is this prayer which also helps to remove illness from the body as well as the mind. I sat quietly, by myself, as often as I could, reciting this brief prayer hundreds of times each day. One morning when I was sitting by myself, repeating the prayer, eyes closed, legs crossed, hands lightly cupped in my lap, my sheikh walked past me, glanced at me with approval and smiled. If I had needed confirmation, that was clearly it. Within a few months however, a copy of his collection of discourses on the *dhikr* was put into my hands, marking the introduction to my study of this most exalted, most purifying method of prayer. But I see the necessity of beginning with the third *kalimah* to clean the house, to clean the heart and heal the physical and spiritual wounds. It remains a prayer to be repeated, recited or sung regularly, frequently.

Dhikr or the remembrance of God can take many forms, some quiet and internal, others recited, intoned, chanted or sung, others performed with certain kinds of outward physical action like whirling, gyrating movements, hyperbreathing, and still others accompanied by musical instruments, different drums often being used for this. Silence and outer stillness characterize the highest and most profound of these practices, although many of the more physical *dhikrs* induce very blissful, very exalted states which those who perform them believe bring them close to God. It is now nearly half my life since I began the study, by which I mean the practice of the silent *dhikr,* a practice undertaken for the purification of the heart, the body, the essence, to remove all the barriers between multiplicity and unicity, to forge the intimacy of merging, becoming one, the divine presence annihilating separate and other.

On the one hand, it is a relatively simple prayer, on the other, its complexity and subtlety are such that beginners often wonder whether it is possible at all. Many years ago when I was encouraging a friend to work on this prayer, he complained that he was having difficulty with the breathing, was he to be denied the sanctifying grace of this practice because of a deviated septum? My immediate response, motivated by amusement as much as affection, came equally from ignorance and certitude when I laughingly explained it wasn't like that at all, the *dhikr* would find its own way, establishing in my own heart with this comment the living nature of the prayer itself and the conviction that its performance is self-correcting, there is no wrong way, eventually any necessary refinements evolve as part of the practice. Quite recently, I gave a description of the prayer to an interested acquaintance with a good understanding of certain other practices, and his observation was that the description made it seem easy, but he doubted the possibility of doing it at all. It does take some time to become comfortable with this prayer, but once it is rooted, established, nothing else will take its place. In addition to the book of discourses on the subject, much more powerful and instructive were the three weeks of daily practice, at about four-thirty in the morning, in the prayerful presence of the *qutb* guiding us each step of the way.

In spite of the difficulties my account implies, I would like to outline the nature of this fundamental instrument. First, after ablutions, four verses from the Qur'an and the third *kalimah* are recited, and then the prayer begins; it consists of the silent recitation of the first *kalimah, la ilaha illallahu,* in conjunction with the out-breath and the in-breath. This affirmation of faith not only asserts a pure belief in one God, it denies the existence of anything but God who is the only reality, the only permanence, everything else is merely the illusion of duality, a dream which is the product of the illusion that things have reality outside their existence in Him. All the negativity, all that is not-God is drawn up from the lower body with the *la ilaha* and exhaled through the left nostril, without touching the nose, and this includes every thought, quality and action which is not of God. Then through the right nostril, with the *illallahu,* we breathe in the existence of God alone in a stream of light which goes first to the forehead, the eye of wisdom at its center, then to the crown of the head, the throne of God, then down the back of the throat to the heart where it is distributed to all parts of the body. The out-breath follows immediately making a continuing loop, with the breathing carried on at its usual, normal rate. The raising and lowering of both the eyebrows and thumbs to help guide the breath are especially helpful, particularly in the early stages of this practice.

After a couple of years our focus was shifted to certain other *dhikrs*, chanted or sung communally, individually or occasionally in small groups much later on, *dhikrs* which were introduced to improve our capacity since we were not making sufficient headway with the difficult, silent *dhikr*. These new out loud *dhikrs* were profoundly helpful, they were like light baths reviving light, but after some years, when I believed I had come to the limit of what I could take or be given from this form of prayer, I returned to the silent *dhikr* with gratitude and relief. The years of bathing in the peace and light conferred by singing the beautiful names of God, by invoking blessings on the prophets, the saints and angels were their own reward; nevertheless, impelled by the urgent conviction it was imperative to reach a level higher than peace and comfort, and it was therefore important to explore a form of devotion whose limits I had not seen, I took up this silent prayer again. Of course, there was a sense in which I had never given it up because I had continued, over these years, to try to make this the prayer with every breath during my waking and sleeping hours, but I had not sat in periods of intense practice.

To build the inner house of prayer, the mosque or church or temple where we can be in silent worship all the time, this is a significant part of the instruction, preparing us for the outer, the external prayers we do together to bind the community, to promote the integrity and unity housed in so much diversity. The introduction of *salat,* the formal, ritual prayer of orthodox Islam, came later, a couple of years after we had begun the out loud *dhikrs,* an introduction which came as a great surprise to many, although it should not have. If we had listened carefully to the explanations which had been given from the beginning, we might have understood there was something here to learn too, but we were not ready. Initially, our fervent, small group was a miscellaneous collection of aspirants, eager for God, unprepared for routine and discipline, formal or informal; it took some years in the presence of undeniable sanctity until, in the sun of his luminous example, we began to have a little idea of both.

Our sheikh was back in Sri Lanka when word reached me that he had begun to encourage the performance of *salat,* and I was so moved by this I tried to find someone to teach me these prayers at once, but it took at least another year for that to happen. Curiously enough, the Sufi meaning of each time of ritual prayer had been carefully explained to us in my first few days of listening to Bawa Muhaiyaddeen's discourses, but most rejected out of hand what many of us now consider to be a special gift. Still, you have to know that to know that. A few years later, when I reported to a member of our Fellowship who lived at a distance, whom I had not seen for a few years, that I included the five daily prayers as part of my regular practice, he was shocked, as if this conventional act had been some kind of heresy.

The Sufi canopy is broad, although it seems to me now that the most comprehensive stance, offering avenues for every capacity and every level of understanding, is the most useful. Just as there are necessary outer manifestations of good thoughts and qualities corresponding to their inner beauty, there are outer performances of prayer which manifest the continuing devotion, the worship and endless praise which can happen only in the inner mosque. True prayer is a subtle thing, it must not be a chant or an echo of the things mind and desire dictate, it must not be the song of the elements to which only the elements can respond, it must be the single pure resonance which comes from God and returns to Him, the *hu* which is His sound ringing through this world and all the heavens.

EXPLANATIONS

At certain times in our lives there are questions we inevitably ask ourself about the nature of reality, questions we really need the answers to if life is to have any meaning for us, the who am I, who is God, what is our connection, range of questions. For some, answers fall easily and comfortably within the context of our understanding, God exists or He doesn't, I certainly know who I am, this is my name, my job, my family, my state in the world, my relations with God are important when I am in trouble and I call on Him, otherwise I don't really think about it too much. I go to the church, the mosque, the temple when I have to, or once in awhile when I feel like it. I feel connected to the faith I inherited from my parents, but I don't pray much, if ever. Easy, laissez-faire answers, a protective covering over the implications posed by these questions which have been asked again and again by the human generations. For those not content with routine answers, the search can sometimes be profound, even agonizing if the right answers are not readily forthcoming.

How we ask these questions, how deeply the answers are directly relevant to our lives, what we think, what we feel, what we spend our time doing, all determine the nature and value of the investigation we undertake. It might take a whole life of inner examination to find satisfactory answers, or, as it happened to Ibn 'Arabi, God might reveal everything between *fajr,* the predawn prayer and the first light of dawn. Whether we recognize it or not, it is our connection to God which inspires the questions and ultimately reveals the answers, but the work is our own; the effort we make in conjunction with the gift we've been given, His grace, establishes the kind of answers we receive. We can choose to live without God, we can choose to dedicate our life in service to Him, we can sit astride the fence, we can be filled with gratitude, we can be miserable, what we choose is what we get. For anyone with an open, melting heart who is moved by the need to search for the truth, God will always provide answers which go beyond the merely worldly, the merely psychological, the merely religious. He will not refuse a pure, sincere request, an inquiry inspired by the longing to know. He is the knower who has filled us with the need to know, and He alone can give answers to satisfy that need, all it takes is a single drop of His light.

When the right answer comes we will recognize that it is the truth because it will vibrate irresistibly with the truth we already have within ourself, even though it might be buried beneath all the veils and illusions of the world, even though it runs against everything we have learned to accept as true in the past. The truth of God sounds a specific note which always rings in tune with itself, always knows itself and responds readily, like the sympathetic strings on a viola d'amore which lie directly beneath the bowed strings. This instrument makes a nice analogy for some understanding of our relations to the Sufi master, to the perfected human being already merged with God. If we want the explanations of the wisdom he has already acquired, if we want access to his love, his mercy, grace and compassion, we must merge with him as he has merged with God, and this means we must learn to vibrate sympathetically with him while he is played by Allah. Then we must go beyond that and become the string beneath the bow.

It is essential to find a truly wise being, a perfected being who can open the book of our life for us and show us how to read it. This is not something we take from a printed book, it comes from a living connection, and living might not always imply a physical, outer, visible being, it could be a presence who has gone on ahead and returns to help in intimately mysterious ways. For the most part though, a physical teacher will find us when we are ready, when we have come as far as we can on our own and still hunger to know, still find deep dissatisfaction with the world and what it offers, with ourself. Relations between master and disciple are individual, private, demanding, based on love and service which flow both ways, based on the recognition that the student wants what the master has and the master knows how to dispense it.

There is nothing egalitarian in this association, nothing which permits the disciple to pick and choose what he or she accepts or rejects, we are dealing with absolutes here. When we go to a great violinist for lessons and we are told that we must place our finger exactly here to get the note in tune, we cannot deviate by the thousandth part of an inch, if we are told to play certain notes upbow we cannot play them downbow, if we are told the only way to finger a passage is this way, we cannot play it that way. We do not dispute, we do not debate since we have the overriding conviction this person knows what we do not. The student accepts the virtuoso's word implicitly because he knows from the experience of listening to the teacher play, or seeing the results of that teaching, this is what has to be done to learn, to improve, to master the instrument.

Similarly, when an aspirant comes to a teacher, a sheikh, a guru, the disciple has to accept the totality, everything the master offers, if the instrument which is the self is to be mastered and played in tune. In part from listening to what the teacher says, from experiencing the sanctity, the purity of the teacher's presence, and in part from the mystery of his or her fusion in the divine, the disciple chooses or, more accurately, is chosen. Here the similarity to the music teacher more or less ends because the soul and the self are more subtle than an instrument and more difficult than an orchestra.

The relations between master and disciple will vary from disciple to disciple as the teacher determines what each student requires; to some he will seem to be aggressively demanding, to others generous and lenient, but this has nothing to do with favoritism or preference, this has only to do with the needs of each soul. To the extent we push ourself, make demands on ourself, do more than is required of us, the master will look on benignly, guiding us when we ask, correcting us gently if we make a mistake. However, if we continue to duck and hide, if we take one step forward and two back, the teacher will keep after us, toughening our resolve, chastising us for faults and errors, stripping down what must be removed and scraping away the qualities which cling to us like barnacles.

All this seems reasonable, comprehensible, but what does it mean for one being actually to merge with another, how are we to understand what this entails? Think about falling in love, we think, breathe, sleep, eat and exist for the beloved, we are obsessed, our reality consists of the beloved, we are blind and deaf to anything else, material or non-material. This is the starting point, the beginning of our connection to the Sufi master which grows as our qualities, thoughts and actions are modified in the scorching sun of his presence, the overwhelming availability of the divine in his existence, the purifying bath of instruction. When we understand that the attributes of a perfected human being, the patience, love, wisdom, compassion, mercy, tolerance, contentment, justice, truth, the surrender, purity, sincerity, gratitude and trust, when we understand that these qualities are what make him inseparable from God we acknowledge the importance of developing them in ourself, qualities which might be dormant or embryonic but there. As they mature within us, slowly or quickly, we initiate the convergence which at the point of intersection will be called merging. In practical terms, it might mean years and years of sweat, study, faith, prayer and diligence, but nothing in our life is more worthwhile, nothing is more important.

As the wisdom of the master wakens ours and begins to percolate up through the inheritance of ignorance, we exclude any style of prayer or thought which does not emanate from him, we discover the poisonous irrelevance of other systems, of analysis with a vocabulary other than his, we find it difficult to read other explanations because it has become necessary to translate into the language of understanding he has given us. His grace and wisdom must remain unmixed with anything else to sustain its purity while we move closer and closer into the totality and oneness of his being, light flowing into light, essence converging with essence. Every thought and action, like the music student, is underwritten by the inner inquiry, how does he do this, how does he say this?

In the same way that the teacher has taken us without reservation into his heart, his being, we eventually discover a place within ourself which is not separate from the sheikh, not other than the sheikh. Spontaneously, we recognize certain thoughts, words and acts are his, nor ours; this is the business of merging in action, we identify aspects of who we have become as no other than the teacher. We do not look outside ourself for his guidance, his presence, we know he is already there, functioning within us. The identification can be complete when the transformation of qualities, ours into his, is complete. It is imperative that the sheikh, the teacher, the guru be a truly enlightened, truly perfected human being for the process to be valid, there is no reason for it other than merging with God. Merging with the sheikh who is merged with God, a being whom we can touch, see, hear and speak directly to, is an avenue which leads more easily to the oneness with God which satisfies that longing, that hunger of the soul.

To understand the urgency of this longing we have two primary images which are not in any sense metaphors, they are direct transcriptions of the reality our existence needs to encompass, creation and ascension. If we are to know God we have to know Him from the moment of creation, His creation of everything from Himself, the beginning of the beginning, and we have to know how to rise in ascension, to communicate with Him directly, no one in front, no one behind, no one above

94

and no one below. Sufi means knowledge of the divine at this level, the purity and annihilation of the self, the obliteration of ego and persona leaving God alone, the totality, nothing exists but Him. Why creation? Because what God did at creation we must enact within ourself, we must eliminate all the darkness, the negativity from ourself so that only light remains. Why ascension? Because we must do what Muhammad, what the prophet of God did when he harnessed all the forces of mind and desire to make his winged flight to God.

First creation. There was a period which cannot be described correctly as a period of time because time did not exist, there was an extension of darkness enclosing everything. God was a timeless, spaceless, vibrant darkness housing everything which roamed and clamored restlessly inside Him, the non-material waiting to be born, the truth unmanifest. For unimaginable ages He existed alone in that state, the totality praising totality immersed in its own completion; then He wanted to be known, and from that intention to make His truth and justice known, all that is emerged. A light began to stir within Him, the *nur,* the radiant light of His plenitude, kept resonating in luminous praise within Him until it emerged, reciting the splendor of His grace and wisdom. When God looked at this in amazement He asked the spreading light who it was, and the *nur* explained how it had always existed as His light within Him, identifying at the same time all the living entities waiting to come into existence, the heavens and hells, the angels and unseen beings, Adam and his progeny. In His delight with this pure explanation, God told the *nur,* whom He called *Nur Muhammad,* He would create all this through his light. The *nur* returned into the source once more, then eventually emerged again. This time a shadow came from the *nur* which became another light, the *qutb,* the divine luminous explanation.

Now the darkness was totally dispersed as the contiguous light of the *nur* and the *qutb,* touching each other, caused a shower of particles, rays of light that fell everywhere in the universe and the world of souls as living things, embryos which consumed those rays of light. When Allah looked at these entities vibrating with the consciousness of His existence, He understoood the nature of His causality and His totality, proclaiming then that pure consciousness and light together would always see Him in this world, the world of souls and the hereafter; if the *qutb* and the *nur* resonate to make the luminous presence of Allah known, that living being recognizes Him. Then God created all the forms, forms made of the five elements, each beautiful, each made in a specific way with a certain place to exist and food to nourish that existence. Finally, He created Adam, man, the most exalted of His creations, pressing the light of *Nur Muhammad* on his forehead, announcing that human beings would know what even the angels would not know.

This Sufi description and explanation of creation is an emblem for the awakening of human consciousness, an injunction to eliminate the darkness of unknowing and a static consciousness which does not know what it knows. We can choose deliberate ignorance if we do not respond to the light stirring within our heart, we can choose not to know God and His truth, we can accept the limbo defined by misery, despair and hopelessness; or we can examine our heart with the light of *Nur Muhammad,* the light of prophecy, plenitude and creation, we can let that sixth level of wisdom and consciousness, the *qutbiyyat* which is quintessentially the human level of wisdom, take root and flower. We designate our own condition, we are not compelled, we are free to make what we want of this radiant gift of light, we can have a life that is blissful devotion, a search for perfection and the penetration of mystery. If we do not follow a path of light, the sombre desolation culminating in an empty life of the mind, the vacant life of the body is all we can aspire to.

But we can understand the entirely human counterpoint to this stunning act of creation from which all life began, we can engage the light impressed on our forehead and the wisdom endowed in our consciousness to illuminate the life we live and the light we spread. By selecting the path of perfectability, an Islamic concept recognizing the origin and destiny of what it means to be human, we abandon the existential dread hovering over a life of the senses and the mind, a fear grounded in uncertainty and ignorance which seem poised to engulf not only individuals but whole societies as well. There is a terrible darkness brooding over our lives today intimately associated with the deliberate avoidance of light, there is an inability to come to grips with the causes of sorrow and the consequent pointlessness so many of us experience. Once we turn our face to God, to Allah, sorrow begins to dissolve, understanding fills the receptive heart as meaning occupies whole deserts of emptiness.

What emerges from the ashes of emptiness, the mythical bird of regeneration and rebirth, is the need to ascend, to rise up, soar beyond the life of the senses which includes the arts and sciences, to a level of communication with God, *haqiqat,* the level of the heart where such communication begins. Once the ethical persuasions defined in the *shari'at,* the first step of spiritual ascent, are firmly established, fear is obliterated and the certitude required by the second step, the *tariqat,* is in place, that is the absolute adherence to the good and total avoidance of the bad, we move up to that place which is revelation, we speak to God and He speaks to us. If we want to understand how this ascension is possible, we look to the experience of the prophet Muhammad whose mystical night journey, the *mi'raj,* which happened more than once, is described in the Qur'an and *ahadith,* accounts that conceal as much as they reveal. But from the *ahadith* we learn that *mi'raj* is *sunnah,* that is, an example we are encouraged to emulate.

This complex journey, events which occurred simultaneously on more than one plane of existence, has been pieced together in exquisite detail; here we need refer only to an outline however. On that night of *mi'raj* Muhammad went from his home in Mecca to Jerusalem, up through the rock where all the prophets prayed, the immense rock now housed in the Dome of the Rock, accompanied by the angel Gabriel who was his guide up to the fourth heaven, after which he had to proceed alone. And how did he go, how did he travel on this journey which seems to have had a material dimension defined by light, as well as a non-material one functioning in the soul? He is said to have travelled on a mysterious creature called the *buraq* which Gabriel made with seven distinguishing characteristics: the jewelled wings of a peacock, like the five colored bird whose form, the five elements, was placed among the four main branches of the tree called religion at the time of creation; the back like a donkey which carried the burdens of the world; the tail of a horse which flew like the mind, faster than the wind; legs like an elephant, trampling the world with its karma, its arrogance; the strong, bursting chest of a tiger; the heart of a rapacious tiger; and finally the face which looked like the face of a beautiful woman, but was actually the face of maya, of illusion.

After going beyond the fourth heaven, Muhammad continued on by himself, received certain instructions from God on prayer, on his relations with his followers, talking to Him behind a curtain or veil, then he visited the baby in an emerald cradle who was the *qutb,* his grandson who would be born fifty-one generations later. After more conversation with his

Lord, the prophet returned to earth. No matter how we choose to interpret or understand this remarkable event, we are to realize that the *buraq* represents the forces of mind and desire which have to be harnessed for the journey to be possible; no matter how we choose to interpret or understand this remarkable event, we are to realize that this is what each of us is expected to accomplish, we have to subdue the qualities and attributes which are not God if we are to speak to Him, commune with Him in a meaningful way. This is the meaning of the *haqiqat* prayer, the third prayer of the day, the late afternoon of our life when every pore, every nerve, every cell resonates with that one pure note which is the song of the soul, of God in love with God.

Sufi

THE INNER QUR'AN

We have an inner and an outer for everything; anything which can be identified externally has a counterpart, its inner original, although it might not initially seem primary as we face the constant bombardment of sensory data which makes the out there world seem more persuasive, more present to our experience. Yet we grasp easily that any form is temporary, that created things have a limit, if something has a beginning it has an end. We know that God alone is permanent, that He alone is without limit and has neither beginning nor end. We also know that the ray of light from Him which became the soul is only housed by the elements, by earth, air, water, fire and ether, as it was once called but we can now think of as outer space. We know that the intangible, invisible soul has its own ascendant, distinct life in a realm quite separate from these elements, and since it does not die it shares in that permanence. The interior form, from which the external form is projected like a movie, is the thing that gives existence to and validates the outer—it is only because there is an inner that we are then able to recognize the outer. This is the reason we are admonished to admit that when we identify a fault or flaw in someone else, we must acknowledge it as something we know, something we also have or else we would not be able to perceive it.

When revelation comes from Allah, it comes first as a vibration which is translated into a wave, a light that becomes a sound, then a sound which becomes a letter, a letter which becomes a word that can be written down. The pageant of revelation demonstrates a procession from inner to outer, the sequencing of experience from which we can take our understanding. There are seven different kinds of sound which come from God, five sounds connected to the elements, one to the human being and one to God Himself, the last two in unison. The Qur'an was sent to the prophet Muhammad with these seven sounds which became the letters of this holy book, the words of God. He also made the form of Adam, the first human being, with the twenty-eight letters of the Arabic alphabet that we will discover when we investigate our inner form. Each life is its own book, a story written with letters of light in a language we must learn how to read, a story we have to write, direct and act, our most important production.

We have the Qur'an on the outside, a difficult enough series of revelations to comprehend since its speaks to all of us for all time in language which is alternately direct, metaphoric, historic, symbolic, admonitive, instructional, covering so many aspects of the human experience it is often elusive, obscure, but still immediate and poetically available. To help us interpret the depthless reserves of the divine in this mysterious book, we have great works of Qur'anic scholarship which are immense, subtle, diverse, building superstructures of supposition on a few fragments, some helpful, some misleading, some quite fanciful and diverting. The inner Qur'an, inscribed on the heart of every human being, has no written supports, no guide to its understanding and interpretation except the light of the heart and the wisdom of the *qutbiyyat,* the sixth level of human consciousness. Until that level functions fully in the individual heart, the illuminating presence of a fully realized teacher is indispensable.

It is a recurring Sufi theme that to know God we have to know ourself. In the same way, we have to know ourself to read the inner Qur'an, to read the inner pathways, learn what each element is, where they function, learn the correspondence between the angels and physical locations in the body. The archangel Gabriel, manifesting the grace transmitting the revelation of wisdom, is the leader of all the angels both in the presence of God and in ourself. The four archangels, Michael, Israel, Israfil and Adam, who were mixed into the clay of human creation, materialized as water (Michael), fire (Israel), air (Israfil), and earth (Adam), in our human form. In this context, when Adam is associated with earth he is also an archangel. These five archangels are found in the five Arabic letters, the *alif, lam, mim, ha'* and *dal* which together make the *alhamd,* the heart of all praise within the inner heart.

There are more specific locations for these angels as well: Gabriel in the spleen, Michael the liver, Israel between the liver and the gall bladder, Israfil the lungs and Adam, the earth, the earth which houses desire and the creation of forms is connected to birth. Iblis, the discarded angel, lives in the bile. There is a relevant account from the traditions here, telling of angels coming down to open the chest of the prophet Muhammad as a baby, removing the bile from his body. The *Nur Muhammad* burns at the center of the forehead, the essence of light and wisdom. It is also said that the element of ether or outer space, with the quality of lethargy and fascination, makes the head; that air, characterized by desire, makes the neck; fire which has the quality of anger makes the heart; water, with the characteristic of lust makes the navel; and earth which has the attribute of fear composes the *chakra* at the base of the spine.

In cosmological terms, seeing the reflection of an orderly system of worlds within the human form, we look again to an ancient catechism which grasped the nature of the universe in sweeping realms of understanding. This understanding has the universe arranged into fifteen spheres or realms, seven above the center point and seven below; these fifteen outer worlds correspond to the existent fifteen realms within the human form, seven above the center point which is the heart, and seven below. In the outer cosmology, the world we know presents itself as if it were the center, containing all the things of the world, while in human terms the heart is the house of *alhamd,* the five letters, filled with the radiant light and wisdom flowing from the *Nur Muhammad.* Such esoteric information is not readily available through introspection alone, it must come, one way or another, from the illumination of pure wisdom passed through the chain of masters sent to inform and advise us.

To read the inner Qur'an we need special glasses, we need the eye which looks at all human beings as receptacles of light, the eye which sees God's qualities in every human form. When we discard the sensory data of outer sight and use our inner vision, we see the way God sees, when we put away the sounds of the outer ear and listen with God's ear to the sounds of God, taste with a tongue that knows only the honey of God's taste and speak with a tongue that pronounces His words, when a tiny piece of flesh in the nostril catches only the fragrance of His scent and when the inner heart vibrates with the wisdom of the *Nur Muhammad,* the light and grace of His creation, then we know the meaning of the seven heavens in the body of man. From another perspective, we notice these heavens correspond to the inner *furud,* the inner obligations of Islam placed beyond the five outer prescriptions, the pillars of Islam, and so we can infer that the Sufi who masters these so-called obligations lives in a constant state of multiple heavens, paradise in this world. If we find paradise here there is no need to fall into the trap of searching for paradise there, we are not enclosed by even the highest desire and the soul can return to the source, merge, be one with God.

The seven lower worlds in the human body, the netherworlds cosmologically, are the navel, two lower openings, two legs which trample the surface of the earth with arrogance, fulfilling the obligations of karma and illusion, and two arms which seize the things of the world because they are what the center point of the lower worlds demands. These are the hells we construct for ourself in this world, this is the experience we acquire. What we build for ourself is the very thing we receive; if we choose to live in hell in this world, it is all we know, it is all we can aspire to and all we can have. The importance of learning how to read the inner Qur'an is quite clear. We start with the book of life which God grants with His divine imprimatur, "Be!" and He lets us be, born into the world in a state of purity known as Islam, then we have to make the journey through the world, see what we see, hear what we hear, assess it, learn what we have come to learn, acknowledging the things of the world but dismissing them as not good enough.

The delicate thing about functioning in the world is the need for balance, we have to avoid the yawning pits of dualism just waiting for us to trip and fall. On the one hand there is the immanence of God, He exists within every aspect of His creation, in hills, mountains, trees, rivers, all the plants and animals, birds, insects, heaven, hell, there is nothing and no place where He is not. We look at something, a sunrise, a sunset, a tiny flower or the jewelled wings of an insect and know that God alone can be the creator of such marvels, yet on the other hand, if we look at this as separate from ourself, as out there, other, then we are in danger of losing it altogether. Because we have to realize His totality, we have to know everything has existence only because it is meshed in that totality, and He exists in us just as we exist in Him. Whatever we see, whatever we identify in terms of separation instead of identity, oneness, unity, has to be deposited back where it belongs, inside, within, a chapter of that immense inner Qur'an which we have to decipher and read.

The book of our life is the book we write; He gives us the materials, the pen, the ink, the paper and tells us to write the truth, write the story of our own destiny. If it had all been transcribed in advance there would be no need for us to come here, work it out, discover how the story goes, how it turns out in the end. It is the effort we make here, with whatever we are given or not given, walking the direct, open path to God without being distracted by the seduction of the senses, without entertaining the separations of self, ego, the clamor of desire and the howling complaints of the mind, it is our pointed search for Him which is the flesh of the story and our love of Him the bones. If we spend the long, empty nights in prayerful meditation we find the book opening before us, the pen in our hand, the truth flooding our heart. If we focus on that One in our breath and our blood we find the mistakes are analyzed and eliminated, the errors in the script are erased.

It is only with the radiant light of the inner Qur'an that we can learn the hidden meaning of the three worlds, this world, the world of souls and the next world, that we can learn the secrets of all the human arts and sciences, of good and evil, truth and falsity, faith, mercy and justice, and it is only with the purity we have earned and His grace that this light is switched on, made available, since perfect purity and the light of His grace compose the inner Qur'an. It is the *Nur Muhammad* who is the prophet of the inner Qur'an, the light and grace of His divine wisdom; it is with this inner Qur'an that we will understand the heart of pure faith, know ourself and know God because God made everything with the *nur*. How easy it is to talk about this, how hard it is to do, so hard that God sent all the prophets, saints and wise beings to convey these messages to us.

Sufi

THE PROPHETS

There is a tradition that God has sent one hundred and twenty-four thousand prophets to the world; the Qur'an tells us there has never been a people to whom God did not send one of His representatives so that the truth of God would always be offered, always be open to discovery. Clearly, our commonly held western perception of the prophets as an interesting collection of ancient Hebrew men has omitted thousands and thousands, and I cannot help wondering who some of these deliberately or accidently obscured individuals scattered through time and the world might have been. What we do know is that not one of them came to start a religion, not one of them said forget about God and worship me, yet this is the way the story has sometimes turned out—institutions tend to venerate their founders. It is hard to know what we are to make of these extraordinary beings who stood with one foot in God's kingdom and one foot in ours, hard to reconcile that mixture of the human and the divine so evident in one being, even with the knowledge of God within man and man within God.

When a Sufi looks at the religions and their practices, one of the most difficult things to understand is their consistent refusal to accept each other's prophets, Jesus and Muhammad not accepted by the Jewish people, Muhammad not accepted by the Christians and Jews, others unknown to Christians, Jews and Muslims. The prophets, may there be peace and blessings upon them all, came to remind us who God is, who we are, what our connection to Him is, how we should live in the light of this connection and what the ethical implications of this connection are. Theology came later when we tried to incorporate a body of revelation into a binding universal code whose relevance diminished as time passed. And yet the core, the imperishable core remains; at the center of each religion's doctrinal utterances, sometimes specifically obscured, sometimes inadvertently buried, there is something of immense value, something we need to learn. If the four major religions constitute the human form, symbolically, literally, however we choose to read it, and we are required to know ourself, then we must also know the essential truth of each religion.

The primary understanding of those religions which correspond to the lower levels of the body, which invoke or introduce a form to summon up the love or remembrance of their deity, is the principle of worship, surrender of individual capacity to a power beyond the human level. Then fire centered religions, associated with the area around the navel in the human form, worship of the sun, the moon, the stars, acknowledge the need to burn away whatever is displeasing to their deity. Historically, with Judaism comes accountability, we are responsible for our actions, if we have injured another being, if we have caused pain or harm we must make restitution in a way to restore the balance of good and evil. Christianity, at the level of the heart, introduces the pressing need for love among human beings, the love thy neighbor as thyself conception of love which means treating all living things as we ourself long to be treated. Islam, which functions symbolically with Judaism at the level of the head, has at its center the need for each individual to examine his or her own heart, to correct the faults, flaws and errors found there rather than looking at someone else's mistakes. Sufism, the crown of light above the head, distills and synthesizes the wisdom of each tradition, using whatever is necessary to bring understanding to completion.

Culturally, we indicate the important role of the prophets in our collective human consciousness, which pays little or no attention to the lines religions draw, with their importance in music, art, sculpture, literature, drama, poetry, even television and movies, a significant inclusion since they represent the largest, the only mass audience. Whether it's Michelangelo painting the creation of Adam, the first prophet, on the ceiling of the Sistine Chapel, John Milton describing the fall of Adam, Donatello's David, a movie about Moses and the Ten Commandments, or David and Bathsheba, a novel by Nikos Kazantzakis about Jesus, or the film based on that novel, a film about Muhammad or a novel by Salman Rushdie about him, they all keep the prophets alive in our experience, part of the human apparatus, although the specifics in terms of biographical detail might be limited to non-existent. The stunning exception to this is the life of the prophet Muhammad about whom much has been recorded and written down; however imperfectly or late in the day this information was transcribed from the oral to the written tradition, there is still much more known about Muhammad than any of the others.

Of all the thousands and thousands of prophets the Qur'an mentions twenty-five, with eight of these singled out for special attention. For the most part, the Qur'an assumes a knowledge of the Jewish and Christian scriptures, the other 'books' it refers to so frequently, and for that reason the information given there tends to be more like commentary rather than linear narrative, although there is some of this too. The great source of information on the life of Muhammad comes from the *ahadith,* the collections of teachings, sayings and stories about his life which were passed orally from generation to generation until they were written down, one to two hundred years after his death. This of course, presents enormous problems of reliability and accuracy which the Islamic scholars have dealt with by assessing their reliability in the trains of transmission. Since I have, in my own experience, seen the unreliability of reputedly reliable transmitters reporting on the life of the *qutb* for this age, with whom I had the bliss to spend a number of years, I allow myself reservations about the accuracy of *ahadith* concerning the prophet Muhammad's life.

Nevertheless, reservations aside, we still have an astonishing portrait of an extraordinary man, whose attributes as a messenger of God and a leader of a growing community during difficult times in a difficult place, give us an approach to understanding something about the life of a prophet, a man chosen by God to direct the lives of his followers with precepts and injunctions flowing through him from God. He was not required to interpret these vibrations that came as words to him, only to convey them: *qul* the Qur'an says again and again, say this, tell them this, pronounce these words. And that is the task of the prophet, to tell the people exactly what God tells him to say, nothing added and nothing taken away. When these revelations first came to Muhammad he was terrified, did not know what to make of it, this was his human side. When he was persuaded the revelations were genuine, that they actually came from God and not some other agency, his fear diminished as he took on the responsibility of spreading the exotic, terrifying, beautiful admonitions and explanations, then accepting the need to protect those who recognized the truth, the validity of what he said. Protection was certainly necessary because truth is never easy, it always comes with a price and a burden of opposition from those who are unwilling to endure the need to change, to be wrenched away from the ideas and beliefs they have always held as the way things should be.

Not every prophet was required to establish a new community, build a new state or nation; most of those we know about were given messages of inner reformation for a people who were losing the truth, losing the ethical wisdom they once had. The eight prophets singled out for specific emphasis in the Qur'an however, Adam, Noah, Abraham, Ishmael, Moses, David, Jesus and Muhammad do have that in common, they were either directly or indirectly involved in a wider communal responsiblity for the human condition which would evolve following their presence on earth. Inwardly, mystically, each of the eight prophets is related to one of the eight spans which compose or make up the human form—nothing exists outwardly which does not have an inner origin. There are certain *kalimahs,* prayers asserting the oneness of God and the nature of prophethood for each of these eight.

Adam, whose *kalimah* calls him the pure, the one who was chosen to be the first man by God, was sent as father and progenitor of the entire human community. He and his wife Eve, also a prophet, are said to have had twenty-one sets of twins from whom the rest of mankind was born. What kind of society they might have produced we can only speculate, but the darkness that seems to rise generation after generation was made known from the beginning when one child killed another, when Cain the hunter, blinded by jealousy, killed his agrarian brother Abel. At a time when the world was destroyed by water, Noah and his family who had kept their purity although it was lost all around them were saved. Noah, whose *kalimah* describes him as the one saved by God, was given the ability to control all the animals kept within the ark of his body, the ability to start everything again in a new home, a new society with a supreme belief in one God.

We came as the children of Adam and Eve, but for faith we belong to Abraham. This prophet, the great monotheist patriarch, is epitomized in the *kalimah* as the friend of God whose faith was so complete he smiled in a pit of fire. Rejecting the multiple deities worshiped by his father and his father's people, as Muhammad was later to reject the idols worshiped by the Arabs, Abraham's belief in the God who neither rose nor set, who was neither carved nor created by human hands, was so complete, absolute, his name is still invoked in blessings by Muslims today in every cycle of ritual prayer performed at each of the five daily prayers. His son Ishmael, whom the Arabs look to as the first of their line, was ready to sacrifice himself to God when it seemed to Abraham this was what God was asking him to do. While Abraham was still struggling to understand the sacrifice he was to make was the attachment to the child and not the child himself, Ishmael, called the sacrifice of God in the *kalimah*, held the knife to his

120

own throat, insisting that if God was ready to receive him he was ready to go.

Moses came to release his people from slavery, but we are all his people, and the slavery is not merely outer bondage, it is the slavery to cravings and passions, the binding greed, envy and desires of the flesh and the mind we have to be released from. The commandments God gave to Moses were to free us from ourself, and he is honored in the *kalimah* as the prophet who spoke to God. David, whose *kalimah* names him the prince of God, seems to have been a different sort of man, a warrior and strategist, yes, but sent with his songs for the unity of the human community, and Jesus, the prophet of love whose *kalimah* calls him the soul, the soul which exists as light, is said to be descended through the lineage of David. Jesus, who never claimed to be anything more than a man, is the son of God in the same way each of us is the son of God, created by Him, light of His light, children of one Father.

With Muhammad we come to the final prophet, there are no prophets after him. He is called the seal of the prophets because with him the message is made complete, he is sent as a prophet for all the people, to unify the religions, bring them together as one. His *kalimah* which simply calls him the messenger of God implies no other prophets will appear, but God's representatives, the saints, the sages and *qutbs* are always with us. The principal difference between a prophet and a *qutb* is that the prophet can say only what God commands him to say, while the *qutb* is permitted to comment, offer an explanation or clarify. The light of *Nur Muhammad,* which is neither male nor female, impressed by God on the forehead of each human being, is the prophet or guide for our inner Qur'an. The light of the *qutb* which is the sixth level of consciousness or wisdom in the inner heart knows itself, has always identified and known itself as God's unchanging truth.

Preserved in an assortment of legends and stories from different countries we have word of a mysterious, eternal prophet whose name, Khidr, means green, the living freshness of a permanent truth. He seems to be identified biblically with Melchizedek in the Book of Genesis, and Paul, without naming him, apparently has him in mind in the Epistle to the Hebrews where he is described as a being of no known lineage, with no father or mother, and no beginning or end to his days on earth. He appears unpredictably at different times in different places to teach some aspect of the truth, usually to an exalted being who is deeply searching for God. There is an account of the role Khidhr played in the life of a well-known eighth-century Sufi whose name was Ibrahim ibn Adham, a truly moving story worth repeating one more time.

Ibrahim was born a wealthy prince who became king in Balkh, Afghanistan where he lived a life of endless luxury, yet buried deep within his heart was a love and a longing for God. One night as he lay asleep among the jewels and splendor of his great palace, he heard a noise on the roof above his head. "Who's there?" he called out.

The answer came, "O I lost my camel and I've come here searching for it."

"You must be a fool to think you'll find your camel up there on the roof!"

"No more a fool than you if you think you're going to find God lying there on silken pillows in a bed ornamented with precious gems," came the reply.

This episode made the king thoughtful, something inside him changed as he ordered his guards and retinue to allow visitors to his palace without the grovelling and gifts he had previously insisted upon. One day soon after, a ragged old beggar appeared among the crowd, but this was too much for the guards who tried to prevent him from going in. When they looked at his face, when they saw what was in his eyes they were powerless to stop the old man who kept walking through the astonished courtiers until he reached the king. "What do you want here?" demanded Ibrahim ibn Adham.

"O I've just come to this hotel," came the innocent reply.

"This is no hotel, how can you say this is a hotel?" indicating the magnificent palace with a sweeping gesture.

"Make no mistake about it, this is just a hotel."

"This is the king's palace, my palace," insisted Ibrahim ibn Adham.

"If you really think so," said the beggar, "Then tell me who lived here when it was first built." The king gave him that name. "And where is he now?"

"He died long ago, he is no longer here."

"Well then, who lived here after that?" The king gave him that name. "And where is he now?"

"He died long ago, he is no longer here."

"And who lived here after he was gone?" The king gave him another name. "And where is he now?"

"He died long ago, he is no longer here."

The beggar went on asking the names of those who had lived in the palace until he came to the king's own grandfather and father, each time inquiring, "And where is he now?" The king was obliged to say they were no longer here. "Well you see, it is a hotel after all. They came, they stayed here awhile, they ate, they rested and they left, just as you will. You are all travellers stopping briefly on your journey to somewhere else." Then the beggar disappeared.

The king was so upset by this exchange he ordered his servants to organize a hunt for distraction, to forget what he had heard.

He went in hot pusuit of a beautiful deer, an arrow poised and ready to shoot when the voice of the deer rang across those silent woods, "Wait Ibrahim, wait, think for a moment. You are trying to kill me, you hope to eat my flesh, but have you stopped to consider what is pursuing you, what will devour your flesh?" So distraught by now, the king abandoned the hunt and wandered off until he met a poor shepherd, exchanged clothes with him and went in search of his perfected master, Khidr, who had already appeared to him three times, once on the roof of his palace, once as the beggar in his court and once as the deer in the forest. Ibrahim found him again and spent some time studying God's truth with the eternal prophet.

The wisdom or knowledge to be learned from Khidr is not conventional wisdom. Without referring to him by name the Qur'an describes him, in the 'Abdullah Yusef 'Ali translation as:

> . . . . . one
> Of our servants,
> On whom We had bestowed
> Mercy from Ourselves
> And whom we had taught

Knowledge from Our own
Presence.

Although he is not named in the Qur'an, it has been generally accepted that Khidhr is the prophetic being referred to in this chapter, *Kahf*. Here we see the eternal Khidhr as the guide and teacher of the prophet Moses who has a longing to learn the higher, the esoteric kind of teaching we turn to a perfected master for. What Khidhr demonstrates for Moses is the futility of accepting the perceptions provided by our normal outer vision; it is only by grasping the inner truth that we can understand the nature of any situation, the reality of any situation or person from God's own perspective. First of all, Moses and his attendant are supposed to meet the teacher they have been searching for at the intersection of two seas, an actual physical location as well as the symbolic intersection of two streams of knowledge, worldly and divine.

They have a fish which they are to observe closely to discover the specific meeting place, but somehow they are distracted and fail to notice the point when the fish ". . . . . took its course through / The sea in a marvellous way!" We think we are ready for divine wisdom, and we are, but the world still

127

pulls us this way and that; Moses is forced to retrace his steps until he finds Khidr at last and humbly asks if he can go with him to learn the things he needs to know. Khidr is a little skeptical of Moses' ability to be patient enough to wait for the wisdom to understand what he will be shown, but Moses promises to follow his teacher in silence, be obedient, study and learn. Khidr then takes Moses through three separate situations, each one so shocking that Moses forgets his promise of patience and silence, openly accusing and questioning his guide every time. In the first episode Khidr scuttles a boat manned by certain desperately poor men, and Moses is horrified, thinking that Khidr wants to drown them.

Contrite when his failure to keep his word is pointed out, he promises again to be quiet, observant, but he becomes angry once more when he sees Khidr kill an apparently innocent young man. Then they come to a town where the people refuse to give them food, yet Khidr repairs a wall for them, just on the verge of falling down. Exasperated, Moses has something to say one more time, letting us see the very human side of one of the greatest, most important prophets. Now Khidr rebukes his pupil for the last time, explaining to Moses, before he leaves, the inner meaning of each episode Moses has misinterpreted. By sinking the boat with minor damage, Khidhr has saved it from being commandeered by the king's men, and by doing so has saved the livelihood of these poor people. The apparently innocent young man is guilty of terrible crimes he is about to commit, and the wall which was ready to fall down would have exposed a treasure that belongs to two young orphans in the town, a treasure they will be able to claim later on as rightfully theirs.

The teaching Moses receives bears a striking resemblance to the instruction Khidhr himself had received from the angel Gabriel, when God sent him at some unknowable intersection of time and eternity to instruct this living prophet of wisdom who had searched long and deeply to know God. Gabriel shows him how all the prayers and rituals of purification he has subjected himself to are all part of the world defined by the mind, not by the ocean of grace where he longs to bathe, he shows him this by allowing him to observe, as Moses will, a series of events in which the reality is different, opposite to the way it appears outwardly. One of the many stories handed down seems the most telling.

On his journey in the company of the angel Gabriel, Khidhr sees a small lake with a group of eleven boys swimming and playing happily together, except for one little blind boy who sits by himself on the shore. Khidhr, distraught with concern for the child begs Gabriel to ask God to restore his sight, but Gabriel refuses several times until Khidhr's insistence wears him down, and the child, able to see, joins the other children at play. A little later, on their way past the same lake, Khidhr sees with shock eleven slaughtered boys lying on the shore and the once blind boy playing in the water. Now horrified, Khidhr sees what he has done and begs Gabriel to ask God to take back the boy's sight. The boy becomes blind again and at the same time, God brings the eleven boys back to life. Aside from our obvious inability to read the face or heart of another, this incident functions on many levels, illustrating the divine compassion which pardons our ignorance, our failure to know or behave with wisdom. And since the number eleven is a number we associate with the *qutb,* we are also given the understanding that the qualities and wisdom of the divine can be slaughtered by one quality of the world, that we have to blind ourself to the world's wisdom to have the grace of the divine.

We must recognize that all the prophets were sent for everyone, no one people can claim exclusive rights to any prophet, they came with a message relevant to us all. Ultimately, we are also to find the place within the body, within the heart, where each prophet exists. Adam is the creative energy of the body, Jesus is the soul, Abraham is our faith, Moses is our wisdom, Noah is the controller of our animal qualities, Muhammad is our light, David is the spontaneous song of God's grace from the heart and Ishmael is our surrender.

Sufi

RITUAL

Just as there is no path there is no ritual either, not in the sense of an outer obligation or performance of duties carried out without a profound penetration of their inner significance, without a recognition of its relation to this pathless path. If we constantly evoke God's protection by saying *bismillahir-rahmanir-rahim,* in the name of God, the most compassionate, the most merciful, the creator, sustainer and nourisher, perhaps this gives the appearance of ritual, and in a sense perhaps it is. Nevertheless, when we use these words as we step outside our house, right foot first, we are opening the umbrella of His divine presence while we try to escape from or are caught up in the dramas of the world. When we utter these mysterious, powerful words turning the key in the ignition, we ask Him to guide and steer us safely to our destination on this small journey and on the larger journey of our ultimate destiny. Before we eat or drink anything we say these words so that the divine grace of His food will merge

133

with our bodily existence and nourish our intention to be one with Him.

In fact, before we begin any piece of work or business, study or prayer we begin with Him, His presence, His guidance, His protection because we have the understanding that only God can pray to God, only God can nourish God and only God can protect God. At the same time that we try to expunge the self, the ego or sense of 'I,' we divert out dualist despair with the energy we must bring, the effort we must make on the material plane. The balance needed between the human and the divine is part of a pattern to develop the wisdom which can ignite the truth, the qualities and actions liberating the soul. This illumination or liberation can of course, be approached with ritual as well, the repetition of prayers, whirling or turning, techniques which may be thought of as the *shari'at* of Sufism. But the method which takes us from the desert of doing, from the compulsion to remain at the psychological level where we are obliged to investigate each sin, each minute imperfection again and again, this is the pathless path. Here, if we absolutely believe we are not in the desert, we can live in the oasis of grace, in the place where that wisdom which knows itself and has always known itself can be our guide.

Disposition, experience and capacity, all summed up or contained in the idea of karma, and that indefinable whisper of God's grace play a role in the attitude and approach we develop in relation to ritual. Those who crave order, authority and a visible manifestation of effort will be more readily drawn to the routine discipline of structure, while those who are more comfortable in the quiet chaos of disorganization will probably, although not necessarily, prefer the borderless continuity of unprescribed effort. Ritual obligations, like the five daily prayers, fasting, pilgrimage, become obligations only if we accept them as obligations, then they are not optional, they are necessary.

The Sufism practised in North America where aspirants have come through a variety of spiritual investigation like different yogas, Zen, the practices of American Indians, Buddhism, a multiplicity of religions disguised as therapies and therapies disguised as religions, rather than the traditional monotheist religions they were born to but were not always raised in, this approach to Sufism is less likely to be anchored in ritual than the Sufism which has its origins in the Middle or Far East. In this eastern Sufism the practices of the orthodoxy are more usually combined with their understanding because it is what

Middle and Far Easterners have grown up with. Once when I was in Jordan some years ago, a friend asked why I had picked Islam when I had been born to such a nice, easy religion, I think he meant Christianity, and that seemed like an interesting perception, especially coming from someone who had no special interest in religion, except what he had acquired in his upbringing. The answer to such a question may not have as much to do with what we pick in this world as with what we chose in the world of souls. The specific form our practice takes depends also, to a certain extent, on whether we believe in a broader definition of Sufism which includes mystics from the time of Adam, or choose the narrower definition which confines it to the conventions of Islam.

Whichever we choose or have chosen in a consciousness we are no longer in touch with, sooner or later everyone comes to the mosque, the church or the temple for one of two good reasons. We come first to confirm the inner mosque, an action rather like the legitimizing stamp of a marriage certificate. At least in this culture we marry for private, inner reasons, but admit the judicial procedure to make it legal, binding beyond preference and inclination. We come to the temple as well for that interface with the world, the sacraments of birth, marriage and death which require a location for enactment, receiving the newborn into the community, marrying within the community and dying, taking leave of the community.

With the word ritual we have to come to grips with the relations between inner and outer, we have to contemplate whether actions performed regularly, routinely, can transcend their available outer significance and have relevance to travellers of the pathless path. There are three answers here, yes, no and possibly. Those who say yes firmly accept that the steady pressure of the forehead on the prayer mat keeps the fires of intention and inspiration burning hot, burning high, allowing progress on the inner transformation which takes us to the immediacy of God. It is difficult to reach that state of remembering God with every breath, at least we turn automatically to thoughts of Him, to our love for Him with the regular performance of prayer. Those who say no insist that any form is an intrusion between the formless soul and the formless One, there is no access to formlessness through form. It is God alone who can change our capacity; we do whatever we do, but only His grace can rip away the veil between us. And those who say possibly, savoring the purity of these two responses, cling to the inner meaning of each act, each posture, each word during their performance or utterance. By confronting the meaning of each time of prayer at the time of that prayer, we make it possible to cut the things we need to cut, change what needs to be changed. By circumambulating the outer Ka'bah we do *tawaf* around the heart, the house of prayer cleansed of every impurity, standing in the presence of God.

Truth is a very fine line, sometimes we find ourselves astride it leaning into the wind which blows us one way, then the wind is at our back and we lean the other way; in the end it is hard to accept or reject either stance, or the balancing act in between. God will not deceive us; as long as we undertake what we do, or choose not to do, with the certainty that our permanent remedy is deeper faith, faith that builds such strong roots it is impervious to the wind or the direction from which it blows, we keep going. If we know that hunger of the soul, the longing to return, to be one with Him again, if we can sustain this imperative without being overcome by inertia, the listlessness of apparent failure many succumb to as the years unfold and change seems unaccountably delayed, we stop wondering about relevance, perceiving only the need to persist no matter the obstacles we must still overcome. When a door opens we walk through it, when a door shuts we go another way, secure in the divine understanding that He knows, He knows. He sees our vulnerability and imperfection, yet beckons us on with such love.

There is no conversion in Sufism—it is rather more like a fast or slow process of discovery and recognition, it is faith and revelation. There is no formal moment, being baptized or taking *shahada,* before you weren't and now you are, although some might understand that acceptance by a sheikh or teacher is such a moment, but that can also be protracted, even casual, not immediate. Not everyone who wants this acceptance necessarily receives it the first time around, it can take years of being blown through the world, going from group to group, engaging in one form or other of exoteric practice at the level of the merely psychological, possibly going from religion to religion. Sometimes letters of light are immediately inscribed on our forehead, a binding covenant between sheikh and disciple, a non-refundable gift.

Whatever the initiation or lack of it, the instruction proceeds privately, inwardly; there are no classes, no doctrine or catechism, we begin with right conduct and qualities, *adab,* the

139

transforming recognition of what to keep and what to throw away, especially throw away. It's not a question of studying the life of Ibn 'Arabi or reading everything of his that has been translated, it's not a question of reading Rumi, al-Ghazali, 'Abdul Qadir al-Jilani or Bawa Muhaiyaddeen, it's not about studying the history of this order or that, or reading everything we can on the mystics of Islam. We can do all that and still be on the outside looking in, like Massignon who spent much of his life writing a study of Mansur al-Hallaj with such majesty and devotion. There is a line we have to cross, the object of our study is ourself, we are the subject, ourself in relation to God, and if we are too timid to take that step, the leap from object to subject, we will never get wet, we'll only dream about what it must feel like to be wet.

When we begin the first steps are easy, bathed in a paradisal light, the certainty of being home at last, truth and revelation continually exploding in the heart, overwhelming love filling us with bliss. As the work continues and time accumulates like mist around the light, we find it harder to carry on, each careful step more guarded because now we are responsible. If we make a mistake we are subject to instant correction, God does not let His devotees linger in error, we are chastised at once. If we are praised threefold blame will follow; if we rush we fall, if we trip we fall hard. During the later years when we begin to grasp the enormity of our undertaking, the fragility of our personal resources, most of us find ourself more open to the usefulness of practices associated with ritual, the daily prayers, the charity, fasting and pilgrimage part of the unfolding drama locked onto perpetual transformation. Perhaps this was the reason why, in my own instruction, the mosque and pilgrimage were the last things given to us, aside from the fact it took some time until we felt sufficiently comfortable, at ease in such exotic surroundings with such bizarre practices. We were not ready for this at the beginning, would not have stayed for this at the beginning.

Those who were raised in the traditions of the Islam practised in the Middle or Far East sometimes wonder about the nature of Islam in America, unable to distinguish the merely cultural from the essential; sometimes the line between ritual requirement and a purely cultural consideration can be blurred, a little hazy. We dress the way we dress, modesty equally enjoined on the men and the women, no prescribed style of covering for either. Be inconspicuous we were advised, if we want to escape from the world, don't draw attention to ourself in the way we choose to dress. Some of course, might want to think of themselves as converts, take pleasure in announcing their inner change with an outer proclamation, don't take me for the person I used to be, look at me, you can tell. This phase often comes and goes. If we don't cover our head except at prayers, this is Islam in North America, it is not our culture and certainly not our understanding of the precepts of true Islam, the surrender to light. Any custom which has a repressive appearance, like insisting upon women covering all or parts of their person except in the privacy of their homes, their family, we instinctively omit as not only unacceptable but incorrect as well.

Some years ago I remember reading and hearing it is not advisable to go near a mosque if we do not know how to do the prayers, do not know how to perform ablutions correctly, and this might still be the case generally, although there are mosques in America which specifically invite in vistors, students, the merely curious to see what it's all about. This is not so much from any proselytizing fervor as an attempt to make Islam more familiar, more mainstream in a suspicious society which does not readily tolerate otherness. Explanations about the inner meaning of ablutions do much to make the bizarre ordinary, or at least as ordinary as anything on the inner planes can be; when the meaning of an obscurely complicated ritual act is clarified, in any tradition, it begins to make sense.

All the religions preserve some aspects of ritual bathing, although it has become less familiar in a largely Christian milieu where bathing, changing our clothes before going to church and baptismal practices are the most evident remnants, but there are specific ablution rituals, among others, in Judaism, Hinduism and the American Indian rites as well. In Islam, we can understand the primary outer obligation to present ourself clean for prayers five times a day. When the prophet Muhammad taught his followers how to cleanse themselves before offering their prayers to God, they were living in a hot, dry climate, mostly desert, little water, no such thing as hot and cold running water, not even any soap until after the time of the prophet. It was important to scrub as efficiently as possible, being as economical with the water as possible, and since everything he taught has been handed down and scrupulously adhered to as *sunnah,* as his custom to observe, we traditionally do our ablutions the way he did, without reference to the daily, luxurious, total bathing practices of today.

While the outer necessity for such detailed procedures might have diminished as our water supply and plumbing improved, the inner relevance remains unchanged, by cleaning ourself for prayer we also clean our heart. We wash our hands, face, forearms, head and feet to free us from the desire for the things of the world, to maintain a state of unblemished purity when we present ourself to God in prayer, and if we think only of God while we wash, the whole body becomes pure. We wash our hands to remove the wrong things we have done with our hands, the blows we have carelessly administered, the hurt we have caused, and reach out to do good. We cleanse our eyes to remove the stains, the sights of the world and see with His eyes; we rinse our mouth to clear away the taste of the world and expunge the thoughtless, ill-considerd words we might have used which caused harm or pain to someone. With that pure, clean tongue we recite only the *dhikr* in remembrance of Him, the *la ilaha illallahu* which means there is no other God, nothing exists but Him, He alone is God. We take water into the nose to eliminate pride and desire, to be free of the vile scent of the world and receive only His fragrance, and then we wash the forearms to cut our attachments to family, to be strong in prayer.

Cleaning the ears means not listening to the sounds of the world, sounds that hurt our heart, that affect our faith and distract us from God; it means listening only to the sounds of God with the ears of God. When we wash the back of our neck we wash away injustice and unkindness, when we wet the top of our head we rid ourself of anger, inherited or acquired imperfection, all the illusions of the world. As we clean our feet and ankles we direct ourself not to be led around by mind and desire, to walk the path that leads to Him without hurting any living thing. This repeated cleansing makes both the body and the heart pure, it brings us close to God if we perform our ablutions with an uninterrupted inner understanding that eventually takes us to a state of permanent ablution, light bathing light.

If we look at some of the other ritual obligations from this inner perspective, the charity, fasting and pilgrimage described in an earlier chapter, we see the splendor of the kingdom of God, a kingdom in which we care for each other, share what we have and learn what it means to live in His world and die to this one. Whether we offer someone a glass of water, our love or help in a difficulty, we are acting with His compassion which is the meaning of charity. When we fast and experience the deprivations of poverty and suffering, we are moved to relieve the suffering of others, and that is the purification of fasting. When we go on the pilgrimage of the heart, circling the place of His truth in surrender, knowing the death before death, this is the meaning of pilgrimage. An outer act is just an outer act, this may do a certain amount of good in and of itself, but if we can penetrate the hard shell to touch the soft living core, the essence, we move from ritual to reality, we move from this world to His.

QUESTIONS OF A SEARCHING HEART

For a Sufi the spiritual journey, a highly personal and completely individual matter begins in different ways and culminates, not as separations of the individual search, but in a unified field, identity, where we recognize everyone and everything that exists as one, merged in the totality which is One. Whether we begin in the context of a specific religion or principled idealism the search, as a conscious, deliberate search, seems to have its roots in a restless dissatisfaction with the nature of the questions proposed by our own tradition because the answers they offer do nothing to quell the unhappiness rising from uncertainty, or the longing to know whatever it is we need to know, whatever it is we are supposed to know. The wrong questions never yield the right answers; learning to ask the right questions is a necessary preamble to discovering answers that open the way before us, answers that resonate the truth which is the only thing that can calm the mind enough to allow faith to discover new depths.

147

When the first true questions arise we might even dismiss them at first, irrelevant, metaphysical, not to be dealt with in a carefully structured system of rational thought, and that is certainly so; nevertheless, they might persist in a new, slightly disconcerting way, they cannot be shoved aside. What can we do with thoughts and assumptions that clearly fall outside the range of what we have determined to be competent mental processes? It usually takes some transfiguring event to dislodge the presumed ascendance of the mind, some experience which catapults us into wisdom's realm where intellect is the servant, not the master. With our world now turned upside down, though we might not immediately perceive it that way, we can begin to search using the mechanisms of the heart which are not to be thought of as feelings, emotions, intuitions or even inspiration, all these are mental products quite irrelevant to the truth we are looking for.

Divine knowledge is not accessible to the mind; we can only discover this kind of knowledge through surrender to God who has provided us with every technique we need to find the understanding, the knowledge which grants peace. It is deepening faith alone which points to wisdom, which is the fertilizing effect for wisdom. God and His grace can change our capacity, but He does not ignore our effort as He draws us closer and closer; although to some that grace may seem to arrive quite spontaneously, in fact we always receive what we earn, what we work for, and for that reason we must put the resources we have into our faith, work hard to purify the heart with our prayers, our words, thoughts and acts. When we begin to resonate the patience, forbearance and at least the first intimation of the ninety-nine beautiful attributes of God, we accept the validity of a few primary questions we need to ask, need to have a way of finding answers to.

The questions we have to respond to are simple and basic — who am I, who is God, what is our connection, where did we come from, where will we go when we leave here? The who am I question usually comes first, a question that does not seem to originate in Islam, but it is posed frequently in the Hindu and Buddhist traditions where certain aspects of Sufism find their origins. In fact, all the religions can hear echoes of their own sound here if they listen for it because a Sufi characteristically extracts the essence from each of them, constructing in their place a transcendent altar of pure thoughts and intentions in pursuit of the formless One. This first inquiry,

149

an attempt to understand the nature of existence, the reality of our own existence, is a pivotal first question because we can begin to reperceive the immensity of what needs to be investigated and known with a new set of instruments, finely tuned instruments which measure the inner universes, different standards, new criteria.

This is something like the leap we have to make between Newtonian and quantum physics, what applies in one realm does not apply in the other, our world is genuinely turned upside down inside the electron. To study the kingdom of God we need new rules, and this is more than just a revolution, a thing that goes round and round ending back where it began, this is an axis transecting that circularity which carries us, like a rocketship, to a new world where nothing we ever believed to be true can be accepted without examination by these new rules. For a time it is necessary to throw away everything that came from the mind, at least until wisdom can make sense of the new world; but we have to be careful here, we have to discard with discretion making sure that nothing and no one is hurt during this dismantling. It is easy to let the zeal of discovery wipe out patience, mercy and compassion, the very things we want to foster. We must do this restructuring in the presence of a competent guide, someone we trust, someone who can warn us not to throw the switch before the house is properly wired, so we don't burn it down.

Usually the first thing we look at in this process is the body, and we notice with surprise we are not our body, this entity we identify so closely with ourself, that is not who we are. We can lose an arm or a leg, even more, we still think of ourself as ourself; evidently the body is not who we are because we see the changes from year to year, decade to decade, yet we experience uninterrupted continuity. If it's not the body, is it the history of events attached to this body, this elemental composition of flesh and blood, is it the memory of what has happened, where we have been? We know how unreliable memory is, we see how quickly history dissolves, becomes irrelevant often in the passage of time, memories can't account for that identification we automatically assert and cling to. We recognize that this material presence is not the indefinable we are searching for. Yet we are not to discount the body altogether, the body is primary, necessary transportation, our indispensable vehicle for the voyage of our life; we can't do without it, but this is not what it's about.

Wondering why we are here in this world at all becomes a part of trying to figure out who we are, is there a point, and if so, what is it? If we have lived with any sense of pointlessness, futility or frustration, the resolution to this speculation will fall into place around the answer to who am I if we find the right answer. Once we are able to admit the essence of ourself is not going to be found on the physical plane, we might stray into the thought-feeling-emotion construct looking for clues about the nature of our existence, but here again we are stopped by their ephemeral qualities. Our thoughts are impure, they fly around the world without provocation; sometimes they might be profoundly important, more often than not they are merely silly, the lyrics of an old song bouncing on an endless loop. We are not our thoughts.

Our feelings are also temporary, they come and they go: I feel happy; I feel sad; my feelings are hurt; I feel good; I feel bad. Our feelings merely describe a passing state, nothing to do with permanence, nothing to do with the essential being who experiences these transitory states. Emotions are sometimes indistinguishable from feelings, they seem to represent an extended feeling, one that stays around for awhile: I am in love, I can't stop loving her; this person is my enemy, I can't

152

stop hating him; I will always be bitter about certain things that did not work out as I wanted them to; I am heartbroken, he stopped loving me; I am grief stricken because my mother died; I am jealous of that person who always seems to get whatever she wants whenever she wants. Some emotions are noble, others are not, they are as much a product of the mind, whose ascendance this new playing field has determined to disallow, as our thoughts. In any case, changing emotions are clearly not our essence.

What about the 'I' which is the subject of all this diversity, is the ego the source of our sense of continuity, is that sense of selfhood the thing which specifies myself and no other? Are we ready to attach our identity to the very thing which separates us when it is unity, oneness we are looking for? Not only that, we take the ego to be a flimsy thing, subject to all the ups and downs of life in the world, sometimes vivid and muscular, sometimes weak and cringing. We know as clearly as Abraham knew, looking at the sun and the moon, that his God did not rise and set, we know that our secret, our treasure does not live in the fragile and perishable house of me and mine.

If it's not the body and not the mind or all its adjuncts, what then, is there actually something called the soul even though every sophistication of science has been unable to locate this mystery? But science can only bring verifying instruments that rely on measurement and quantification to something which exists out of space and time, which is without dimension; and it is unlikely that science will learn how to develop a mechanism to identify the soul because science, by definition, relies on methods, on experimentation which deliberately excludes revelation, mystery and wisdom. These are nevertheless, what God has given us to know and understand the soul; only with the divine wisdom acquired through faith and the stages of spiritual ascent can we begin to know who we are, understand the soul and its immaculate connection to God. When wisdom touches the soul, the soul responds, holding tight to it, and we know that the soul exists.

The soul is that unchanging ray of light from God which has existed from the beginning, which will persist when the elements composing the body have returned to their origins. It is the soul that is our continuity, before and after, and it is the soul that keeps the hunger for our return to God alive, awake and demanding. What is connected to the soul is the light of the

Nur Muhammad, the light of creation impressed on the forehead of Adam at the beginning, and connected to the soul as well is the light of the *qutbiyyat,* the divine explanation which emerged from the *nur* itself at the beginning of the beginning. When we contemplate the soul from God's perspective, we see it as a mirror of Him; we see the ray that comes from Him, the *alif,* the unique, the One; we see the light of the *nur,* of *Muhammad,* that comes from His essence; and we see the divine wisdom, the explanation, the *qutb* that emerges from the *nur* at the time of creation. It is the joint action of the *nur* and the *qutb,* pressing against each other in the presence of the One, which produces the shower of souls filling the universe.

When we contemplate the soul from the human perspective we understand who we are, we came from God, we are a mirror of His light which will be reflected back into Him one day. In the meantime, while we are here we have certain obligations because of this divine origin, this connection and destiny — we are the reflection of a formless power whose existence we must manifest in what we do, what we think, what we say, what we believe. We do this by studying and acquiring His attributes already invested in us, a shadow form, the reflection in the

155

mirror. The inner universe, where everything is upside down in relation to the outer worlds of illusion we are so familiar with, has absolutes that we tend to disallow out there, and these absolutes compose the formless continuum of His reality, His existence. These are absolutes we might once have accepted without any hesitation or doubt, naturally and intuitively correct in the world of a child, we have to dig up that garden of innocence once again because if we want to know who God is, we have to know, understand and practise these attributes, His qualities and characteristics.

Among the three thousand gracious attributes traditionally assigned to Allah, to God, are the ninety-nine beautiful names which are a way of describing the actions, the service and duty God performs, His formless form. These names are His formless manifestation in action, His power, the way He allows Himself to be known and understood. If we open the inner Qur'an within the heart and read what is there we will find these names, and if we take that form for ourself, we will know God, we will merge with Him; our sight, our speech, our sound and our heart will be lost in Him, we will give up everything in the service of His compassionate qualities. These ninety-nine names, as they are revealed in His actions, include everything,

His grace, His essence, the divine knowledge, His manifestations, the good and the bad, heaven and hell, everything, the totality. The beauty of the names is their permanence, a mystery; the attributes are what has acquired form within the human being with the divine knowledge to understand the mystery, the essence, that inner Qur'an.

The names include the One, the merciful, the compassionate, the enduring, the just, the supremely exalted, the mighty, the patient, the living, the witness, the truth, the self-subsisting, the first, the last, the manifest, the truth, the witness, the glorious, the wise, the loving, the reckoner, the sustainer, the preserver, the resplendent, the gracious, the aware, the all-hearing, the all-seeing, the exalter, the humbler, the all-knowing, the opener, the creator, the king, the guide, the righteous, the pardoner, the indulgent, the living, the witness, the generous, the forbearant, the judge, the impartial. There are of course, others which are a little more difficult to grapple with, a little harder to penetrate, but even these more manageable names give only the surface intimation of depths we will never be able to explore fully, never come to the end of. The immensity of His grace and His protection, of the limitless mercy, the infinite waters of His wisdom are fathomless attributes to contemplate.

It has been said that if we take any one of the ninety-nine names or powers of God, divide it with the fine edge of divine knowledge millions and millions of times, and look at any one of these electrons we will find the ninety-nine revolving around each other without touching, the powers, the vibrations, the sounds, all revolving around each other. Then if we repeat this process, take one of those electrons and divide it millions and millions of times again with that wisdom, we will find the ninety-nine revolving in perfect symmetry without touching each other. This subdivision of particles can be repeated many times, the actual number of divisions reducing each time from millions and millions, to millions, then to hundreds of thousands, until eventually, taking a single particle and dividing it with that divine wisdom a thousand times, we still see the ninety-nine revolving perfectly, and the immense intensity of that power consumes us as we consume it. I like to think of this explanation as Allah's quantum physics.

When we look at the soul once again from a human perspective, trying to grasp its connection to the body, how it arrives there, we see that it functions as the witness, as the instrument of wisdom, the voice of conscience observing our conduct, assessing our actions. This is right, that was wrong it proclaims without hesitation, and it is up to us to listen or discard what it says. When wisdom is in command we pay scrupulous attention to the dictates of conscience, we rectify what must be corrected, make amends wherever necessary and carry on with the issues that have been approved. When mind and desire are in ascendance we might not worry too much about the voice of the soul, we might persist in error indefinitely, ignore warnings, premonitory flashes that could save us from the consequences we bring upon ourself. If the mind usurps the master's authority, trouble is brewing because the mind is connected to our selfish desires, to the world which never leaves us in peace when once it is admitted. Then wisdom and our faith, our trust in God alone can restore the balance, put our affairs into wisdom's pure perspective again. A Sufi works hard to maintain balance, to avoid the up-down syndrome of life in the world.

We are told the soul does not enter the body immediately, what does arrive on the third day after conception is something called the *anma* which is the essence of the senses, the power of the five elements. Here again we are looking at an analysis which is both Aristotelian and classically eastern in its focus; the *anma* works through form, the form of air, bile and phlegm.

Eastern systems of medicine assess the viability of the *anma,* which corresponds to Adam, with the pulse. In the second month after conception the *avi,* corresponding to the angel Gabriel, enters the embryo. This *avi* which works with the soul is pure spirit pushing the soul into place from above. Like the *anma,* its condition can also be determined by the pulse. The soul itself, the *ruh* in Arabic, is present at the end of three months; it is the light, it works through the power of light and cannot be detected by the pulse.

We know that the soul comes from God, we understand that He has given us, within the embryo of our being, qualities identical to His, the very attributes by which He can be known. We also have the body which we have to look after well with its insistent intrusions, demands, complaints and equally distracting joys; and it is important to give this body what it needs, feed it, clothe it, house it, provide it every requirement necessary for its thoughtful maintenance, but always with a clear sense of balance, the certainty we are not the body, not our thoughts, not our feelings. Yet it is the body which describes the dilemma of duality, of knowing that God, the permanence, the totality is One, still having to function through something which is, by definition, separate, other,

160

something driven by the dictates of mind and desire which are attached, not to the oneness but to the separation.

If we want to know God, be one with Him, merge in that ecstatic reunion, the body and its companions, mind and desire, must be transcended. To do this we have to harness the forces of mind and desire then climb up to Him in a body of light, as the prophet Muhammad did on his *mi'raj*, begin the communion, the conversation at the level of the heart, the *haqiqat* level of wisdom. From there we have to keep going, this is just a platform for the I am not of *ma'rifat*, the place of merging, where God alone exists and any sense of separate or other is obliterated in His consuming presence. When nothing other than those qualities of the heart, the love, compassion, mercy, truth, tolerance, forgiveness, justice, generosity, patience, forbearance, when nothing but the qualities and attributes of God remain, when all that is an obstacle has been transcended or obliterated then we can say that merging has occurred. If nothing other than God is present in every word, every thought, every act, this is a perfected human being, this is the human manifestation of the divine.

We have been brought to this world to learn who we are, to bring conscious knowledge of the divine into existence so that God can be known, so that God can know us and we can know Him. Once we know we remember where we have come from, it is possible to contemplate the destination, where we go when our time here is finished. When the body returns to the elements the light, enhanced by its passage through the world, merges with the source of light once more. If it has not been able to discover light during its time in the world, if it has persisted in darkness and separation here it will know only the hell of darkness and separation there. What we build for ourself here in this world becomes our residence in perpetuity, a palace of light or a degradation of darkness.

Our destiny is not predetermined, if it were there would be no reason to be here, no reason to put out a great effort, to strive and endure. God has bestowed His plenitude upon us, given us everything with the assurance that we would have the capacity to know, to understand things even the angels would not know. He has whispered His secrets into our ears, He has shown His beauty to our eyes, He has poured His wisdom into our open, melting hearts; it is up to us to examine the mysteries, allow them to unfold and be revealed in the meaning of our lives. If we do not undertake the opportunity to be His message bearers, to act as His representatives, we have lost the gift of truth and its revelation.

FAITH AND WISDOM

Faith and wisdom are profoundly intertwined; faith provides the solid root for wisdom's growth and wisdom nourishes the soil in which faith can grow. They are inseparable and necessary to each other, conjoined twins. For any number of problems an aspirant or seeker on the path will encounter along the way, the doubts and confusion which spring up spontaneously in a lack of clarity, the remedy is often to be discovered in deeper faith, the trust that God who knows the beginning and the middle also knows the end of the story, the remedy is deeper faith and the absolute gratitude for what has already been given and for the perfection of the outcome, no matter how it turns out. If wisdom falters faith can shore it up, and if faith is inadequate the tools of wisdom can refurbish it. Faith and wisdom together build the house of light for our soul, a house for this world and the next. What can we do to make our faith stronger, are there techniques or practices which will increase our faith? What are the instruments of wisdom, what is it that makes us wise?

We should remember first that God can do anything, if He wants us in a certain place at a certain time, make no mistake about it, we will, against every expectation, be there. We might be living in one country, but a great sage has arrived where we once lived, where we never expected to return, and yet we find ourself back there in the place where wisdom will be offered. If He wants us to find the person who will be our husband or wife, continents and oceans will not keep us apart, we will meet in some country or city neither of us thought we would ever visit or see. Since there is no doubt He can easily do these things outwardly, we should be persuaded He can just as easily do the inner things.

Many years ago as a teenager, when I was still looking for answers to the questions that burned my life, I would follow a line of reasoning with great anticipation, hopeful that truth would soon be revealed and made available, only to be stopped when faith was introduced, the necessary next step. Descartes in his oven was a stunning example for me, his method was so pure, so convincing, yet he left me behind when his argument appealed to faith; that finished me because I could not go there with him, faith was not any part of my existence or understanding. For me to have come from that absolute

166

negative to this absolute positive is neither evolution nor revolution, it is removing the oceans and continents which separated me from Him, it is the divine transaction which can come to anyone, the grace and direct guidance He offers to the urgent heart.

The two things we have to offer Him, the two broad avenues which open the door, invite His access to us, are love and wisdom. The wisdom might not manifest as what we know, what we expect to know, it might be what we long to know, an amorphous, prayerless state which knows only that it does not know, that it needs to know, that it must know. Without even a conceptual predication of the divine we can still be led to the truth, although this long, difficult route is clearly one to avoid because it entails an endless pursuit of routes marked no exit, empty streets and ruined houses. We have to investigate until we can say it's not philosophy, it's not music and the arts, it's not anodynes like alcohol which do nothing to end the pain, it's not stimulants like drugs which promise what they cannot deliver, and we have to reject it all, come to the end of pleasure and pain, then, only then, if our body is still intact and we still hunger to know, He will look at our folly with His compassion, His mercy, His magnanimity, and open the door.

He will open the door if we have also discovered something about love, not the self or ego centered love of my child, my family, my husband, my wife, a universal love encompassing all human beings, even all living things. A teacher might learn this love by caring for all the children, not any one child, but all of them, absolutely and abstractly; a doctor might learn this love by caring for patients, healing their suffering; any one of us might learn this love by caring for the dispossessed, the homeless, loving not a specific individual but suffering humanity. This ability to love without focusing on something we think belongs to us is important since that is a different kind of love, a love which ushers in the possibility of absolutes, a necessary basic for understanding the divine nature of God, the omnipresent, omniscient, absolute One. If we are open to a single absolute, any one of the ninety-nine, the door swings open wide, but even though the door is now open we do not always know what to do next, we do not know how to cross the threshhold, walk in. Without signposts, a map or a guide we cannot find our way in, not to the center, not back to the beginning.

We might have been floundering endlessly until our state allows the door to open, now our approach to the truth must

168

change, must become more directed, now we need to develop the aspect of faith we can identify as determination, as the point of strength to carry us beyond intention to performance, action, the belief that we believe which will take us to the supreme conviction we need. There are unique, historical moments for each individual, an intersection of the human and the divine that we call revelation which might propel us into the open, waiting space; there are quieter intimations, like studying the presence of God in His creation, or studying the divinely inscribed text of the human heart or sacred writings which extend confirmation. Once we learn how to drive we can't just fall asleep at the wheel and expect to be taken to our destination, this is nothing more than the introduction, everything remains to be done, the practice of driving, learning what to avoid, how to be safe, how to navigate, all this needs to be learned.

This is the point at which the wisdom and experience of a true master, an enlightened master, become indispensable. Why, we might wonder, can't we do this on our own, why do we have to do this in the company of someone else, someone who has gone this way before and knows the road, knows the dangers and traps that might lie in wait for us anywhere ahead, isn't

God alone enough? God is always enough, but there are things He has conveyed to a higher state of consciousness than ours, secrets told and mysteries unbound that such a guide can make available to us at a level accessible to our own wisdom. Without such instruction and guidance we can take every wrong turn, even end up in the wrong place. We must search for such a teacher with dedication and fervor, then God will see our need and send the right person at the right time; never give up, that master will find us.

For our part, we have to be discriminating too, it is up to us to verify the master's credentials. There are several criteria he or she must satisfy: he must appear to be wise and actually be wise, he must act with divine wisdom, he must utter the pure words of God, show no difference between his words and the things he does, he must emanate the presence of the divine and nothing other than the presence of the divine. This means his or her words, thoughts and acts are totally consistent with the ninety-nine beautiful names and the three thousand gracious attributes of God. If the teacher passes this rigorous test it is safe to accept such a being as the master God has sent, then we can start to learn on the inner planes, start our apprenticeship in faith and wisdom. Sometimes He might send a friend, a companion in wisdom who will teach us and keep us on the right path until we are ready for the ultimately true teacher. There are many friends of the divine presence and only a few total masters who can teach us the things that will change our destiny.

Absolute faith in God has been described as consisting of three components, the belief which is the essence of faith; the unswerving conviction that this is belief in the truth, the One, the reality; and third, the determination to persist in the truth, to insist that this is our way, our prescribed pathless path taking us home. The belief which is the first part of faith is not hard to grasp and hold onto, we all have beliefs, we believe the earth is round, we believe the remedy will cure our illness, we believe that good is preferable to bad, right is better than wrong, we believe in democracy, a market economy or trade unions; we believe the sun will rise in the morning; in fact, we can't take a step without believing the earth will hold us up, we are immersed in our beliefs. What we have to put at the very core of all our belief is the existent omnipresence of God, one God, and not only a belief in one God, but also that God is One, a very different proposition, this affirmation of the fundamental nature of reality taking us beyond concepts of heaven and hell to the essence of permanence and totality.

As for the second part of absolute faith, the conviction that this belief is and remains the truth, God is One, this is intimately connected to the wisdom we acquire as we ascend beyond the conventions of ritual practice and reach for the radiant crowning jewel, the fruit of wisdom at the top of the tree. We cannot bypass lower tiers of knowledge, they must be learned or subsumed as we climb and learn, the soil has to be prepared and cultivated, it has to be fertilized and nourished if the tree is to grow and put forth a harvest the soul hungers for. With undeviating conviction we must know that the jewel exists, it can be produced if we are certain and God permits. Determination, the third component, means we are unflagging in our effort, we never give up, we never turn back and go some other way. The mountain is high and difficult to climb, an Everest of deprivation, but that tree grows at the top of the mountain, up there where the air is thin and the ground is ice and snow, and so we put away everything unrelated to the ascent and follow our guide, determined to reach the top no matter the pain, no matter the hardship, the goal to taste the fruit of wisdom and hold the jewel of truth in our heart.

This jewel in the heart is the *la ilaha illallahu,* a radiance that shines, the *nur* within wisdom which has become the guide

172

commanding the recitation of this *kalimah,* this pure utterance of truth. When this *kalimah* is recited to Muhammad, the messenger of light, that purity is the essential Islam, the path of surrender, the inner Qur'an. Every aspect of creation has been brought into existence through the *Nur Muhammad,* nothing would exist in this world or the next without that declaration of Islam within the inner heart. The soul of everything in creation, whether we think of it as living or not, depends for its existence on that essential Islam; everything, in its own way, is in constant devotion to God, praying to Him with the purity of absolute faith, everything worships Him, praises Him and offers the vigil of total gratitude and surrender.

We have to see that messenger of light, we have to see that Muhammad as the face of gnosis, of divine wisdom at the level of *ma'rifat* to know what Islam is, what true Islam means. We have to know it was the *Nur Muhammad,* the light that emerged from the essence of God, who was sent to earth as Muhammad, the prophet, the messenger of that light. The *kalimah* we recite announcing the oneness of God, in the presence of His prophet, the light of the *Nur Muhammad,* is the purification of wisdom which rids us of our imperfections and draws us into that state of oneness with Him. As we recite, with the out-breath, the *la ilaha,* we pull up every impurity from the body and expel it through the left nostril; with the in-breath, the *illallahu* through the right nostril, the self is dissolved in the affirmation of His unique omnipresence. *La ilaha illallahu,* there is no deity but God, nothing exists but God and You are that God.

If we do not grasp the nature of the inner and outer secrets, if we do not understand the outer and inner prescriptions of Islam, the outer called the five precepts which constitute the five pillars of Islam, we cannot find that radiant jewel, the fruit of wisdom, divine knowledge, it will remain beyond our reach. These secrets are to be understood at the heart of any understanding of divine love and divine knowledge, they are not exclusive, they are inclusive. While the vocabulary of faith may change from tradition to tradition, the analysis of the heart, the mind and the conscience is a constant, the urgent hunger for truth and wisdom, for the purification of our baser aspects is a characteristic of the open, melting heart. When we look at these five precepts from a universal stance, we hear the equilibrium of resonance sounding everywhere.

The five precepts are five steps which are also the five daily times of prayer, five steps of ascending divine wisdom and five opportunities for wisdom to analyze ourself and these duties in a state of conscience, love and compassion. The foundation, the root which must be strong and secure, is pure faith, absolute love and worship of God, the supreme, the acknowledged ruler of our lives. And let us be quite clear, this is something we have to choose, it makes no difference to our God whether we praise Him, worship Him or not, He still feeds, protects and sustains us. The difference it makes is to us, the life we have, the peace we have, the wisdom we acquire, the truth we possess.

Love and worship of the supreme deity are at the core of every approach to the divine, even among traditions which honor or pay homage to a favorite lesser deity, a local god, a household god, a revered saint, any of whom are considered to be more sympathetic under specific circumstances; but the knowledge and love of the ultimate authority, the ruler of all the worlds is there as well. Monotheism tends to shudder at the thought of multiple deities because they divert our attention from God, they dissipate our focus when we need to be one-pointed in our remembrance of the creator, protector and sustainer who functions without limits, for all of us in the human family, everywhere, at all times.

This first precept or obligation or duty, however we feel comfortable to think of it, remembering always there is no compulsion to accept the truth, no compulsion to love or serve except as we feel enjoined by our own sense of what we are required to do, this primary thing is total and absolute faith in God. The overwhelming need to express the love we feel in our worship, our praise, our care for others is the luminous faith of the melting heart. Accepting our God who is without limit, without beginning or end, without attachment, preference or prejudice, who is the essence of love, mercy and compassion, who protects and feeds us whether we acknowledge Him or not, this is our initial obligation or duty, our first prayer in the predawn hours of the morning when the world is still quiet and at peace.

When we surrender to God at this first time of prayer, when we sever our connection to the earth and all the properties of earth, the forms and treasures created from the earth, the desire to create forms, the generative urge, when we surrender the images, the concepts, the doctrines of form that have been used as instruments to focus our thoughts and prayers, we are free, we have overcome any kind of fear born of ego and attachment. As we prostrate on the prayer mat of inner inspection, examining the sanctuary where our less attractive thoughts and acts have been stored, we look at our faults and flaws in the emancipating light of conscience, distinguishing right from wrong, good from bad, accepting only the good, the just and true, discarding the rest. This deliberate exclusion of the things about ourself we know to be obstacles which must be removed is the first step of our spiritual journey, recognition of an authority beyond the mind, beyond desire, recognition of the divine authority in matters of right and wrong, accepting the importance of discovering the nature of these divine injunctions then adhering to them scrupulously.

The second precept or obligation is prayer. If we have not given ourself to God completely in that resonating state of totally luminous inner prostration, we have to find our way to that perfected place through our prayer, regular prayer, irregular prayer, praise and worship, reciting His names in *dhikr*, remembering Him in our words and thoughts all day and all night, whatever keeps us in the recognition of His presence. This prayer will emerge according to the rituals, or lack of rituals, in all the different traditions; what is important here is to establish practices which turn us towards God as often as possible. Once we have understood the difference between what is essential and what is useless, when we have resolved to keep the good and throw out the bad with the determination to stay in that place of the good alone, and we have succeeded in this, we comprehend the illusory nature of the world and know the only One who is permanent, who neither begins nor ends.

This prayer, this second possibility of finding the entrance to Him, of being submerged in Him, has inner implications as well as any outer performance the prayer entails. Perceiving our body to be composed of letters which are light, we read our inner scripture as the affirmation of faith, *la ilaha illallahu,* I am not, You alone are the existent reality. We read this, certain of its truth and illuminated by the three letters which are pure light, the soul, the *nur* which is both light and wisdom, and God Himself who is universal light. If we stand firm on this second pillar of purity, this is our second time of prayer, the midday prayer, the midpoint of our life when the fires of strength and maturity burn their hottest. At this time we have to subdue all the inner fires burning at the center of the body, the area around the navel; these are the fires of anger, of

178

jealousy, envy, arrogance and greed, the passion for authority and dominance, these are the fires we extinguish with *la ilaha illallahu*. This is the second obligation, the second prayer and the second level of ascent in the divine progression.

Charity, alms, giving something we have to someone who is in want, whether material or non-material, helping with our hand, our heart, our word, our prayer, giving not just the requisite tithe but all that His generosity and His magnanimity dictate, that is the next route to the melting heart which stands in the grace of His resonance, that is the openly obvious and inwardly secret path dissolving the mystery of communion, One speaking to One. The Islamic ideal is to give everything away by the end of our life, to share so completely what we acquire that we return to God as we arrive, with nothing. We came with nothing, we leave with nothing; if we keep more than our fair share of the material blessings of this world it means that someone else is deprived, we have taken something that is not rightfully ours. Are we not accountable for that?

We have to develop an understanding of charity which begins with the assumption that nothing belongs to us, everything belongs to God who has graciously bestowed all that we have.

If the material things of the world do not actually belong to us we cannot think in terms of mine and yours, it is all His, we can only look after these things as custodians for the time they are in our keeping. Any other attitude is at the very least tinged with acquisitiveness, greed, envy or jealousy. When we couple the understanding that nothing truly belongs to us with the knowledge that God is the only possession worth having, He is our wealth, our richness, that He alone is valid and precious because He alone will never leave us, then we can know the significance of charity, then we can grasp the inner work of non-attachment to material things. We came from Him in the world of souls, He is the only thing of value here in this world, and if He decrees, we return to Him there in the hereafter.

By late afternoon, the third time of prayer, the afternoon of our life, we know that nothing in the world is ours, we are detached in our attachment to parents and children, to family, friend, country, position or status, job, money, home, to all the things of mind and desire which tie us to the world of mind and desire and its inherent suffering. By the late afternoon prayer, at the level of the heart where we find the light and the dark, where we find angels, spirits and the formless animals who are more than mere symbols for our qualities, we are at the third step or stage of proximity in the ascent to our exalted Lord who is God. When we have harnessed all these potent forces which assemble to keep us from the unswerving route, we can rise up to that place where direct conversation begins with God, where He speaks to us and we speak to Him; presence, access, communion, this is our *mi'raj,* ascension.

There is a painting, a pictorial representation of the *mi'raj,* the night journey of the prophet Muhammad, which Bawa Muhaiyaddeen painted many years ago in the middle of the twentieth century, that gives a visual display of what this ascent, this journey to proximity entails. In the middle ground we see some structures which might be houses, and the Ka'bah, the sacred mosque of Mecca, the beginning of his transforming journey; and then behind, in the background is the sacred ground in Jerusalem where he was taken next, Quds, this holy city represented by a mosque not yet in existence which was to house the rock where all the prophets have prayed. When Muhammad was transported to this immense and extraordinary rock, tradition has it that he went straight up through it to the heavens and beyond, and there is today a large, smooth circular hole towards one outer edge of this flattened, pie-shaped rock which marks his passage through it, transcending the elemental stuff of this world without question.

What commands our attention immediately when we look at the painting however, is the upper right foreground dominated by a beautiful, mysterious winged creature, the *buraq* on which Muhammad in the company of the angel Gabriel rode up to heaven. Neither the rock, the angel nor the prophet himself appears in the painting except implicitly: we know what's inside the Dome of the Rock, the angel is suggested by the exquisitely jewelled wings of the *buraq* in its improbable flight through space, and it is not within the tradition to attempt a visual portrayal of the prophet's physical presence. Bawa Muhaiyaddeen's description of the remarkable creature which became a vehicle for the prophet's ascension tells much about the forces which must be mastered to enable us to rise up in the presence of God. This *buraq* has the jewel studded wings of the five colored peacock which represents the five elements, earth, fire, air, water and ether, that is, outer space.

The human being is composed of the material, these five elements which Bawa Muhaiyaddeen often refers to as five kinds of life. There is a sixth as well, the non-material light

182

life. It is the five that have to be controlled to release and free the sixth for the flight beyond this world. What are the other characteristics of the *buraq?* It has the back of a donkey to carry all the burdens the world heaps on it, the legs of an elephant which trample the world in arrogance, the tail of a horse which flies faster than the mind, the heart and chest of a ferocious tiger, and finally, the face of a beautiful woman who is not a woman at all, but maya, illusion, the deceptions of mind and desire, the deceptions of duality. All this is to be brought into submission by this third time of prayer, the *haqiqat* level of wisdom which is charity, the third precept or duty of Islam.

Fasting is the fourth obligation: denying the food and water the body clamors for makes God very accessible as the world and its demands subside, falling into place behind the driving imperative to stand in His presence, to merge with Him, be one with Him. Outwardly we fast during Ramadan to observe an injunction that comes from the Qur'an, God's own word, outwardly we fast to know the hunger and suffering of those for whom fasting is not optional. Inwardly we fast to dissolve the barricades of the body standing between God and ourself, inwardly we know our only hunger is separation from God. We know that God feeds all the appetites that thrive in the world, He feeds our hunger for a companion with a wife or a husband, He feeds our hunger for activity with meaningful work, He feeds our hunger for substance, for money, with a job, He feeds our sensual appetites with the aesthetic pleasures of the arts.

This fourth duty is the fourth time of prayer, the evening prayer immediately after the sun sets, the evening of life when our physical strength has peaked, has begun to decline, and consequently the arrogant presumptions of immortality have also dwindled as the sun disappears. The wisdom of this time of prayer is the gnostic wisdom, spiritual ascent at the fourth level, intimate knowledge of the divine, merging with the divine. This is *ma'rifat* associated with the head, the face of a human being which identifies who we are, and with this exalted wisdom we move from the outer obligations to the inner. Instead of seeing with the outer eyes which perceive all the scenes of the world, we see with the inner eye that looks only at light; we hear with the inner ear that hears only the sound of God; we detect the fragrance of God alone with the inner nostril; we have His taste, not the taste of any worldly thing on our tongue; we rejoice in the silence which is merging with Him, but if we speak we say only His words; and we

184

recognize His light in the open, melting heart as our nourishment, our food which ends the fast. In this state we are merged with Him, our thoughts, our words, our acts are His; we are not, only He exists in this obliteration of selfhood, of ego.

If none of these avenues have opened the door to our absolute faith, the presence of Allah as the only reality, there is the fifth possibility, the obligation of *hajj* or pilgrimage once in our life if we can afford to go. This is the outer understanding, we go as pilgrims to the Ka'bah, the center of Islam for the world, in Mecca where Muhammad was born, and to Medina where he was forced into exile and buried later on. There is a third place of pilgrimage according to the traditions of the prophet, we can also go as pilgrims to Jerusalem, a holy city for the three major monotheist religions. When we go to Mecca we have finished with the world, have concluded all our worldly business, distributed all we possess as if our time here had ended, we go wearing nothing but a shroud to cover the body, we go announcing our presence to God.

The inner understanding emerging at this final time of prayer, the night prayer which marks our closing period of life in the world, is the wisdom of *sufiyyat*, the fifth level of spiritual ascent. This pilgrimage is the death before death for the Sufi, a total subsistence in God; we are gone, He alone is here in a place, in a time of absolute light where there is neither place nor time, neither birth nor death. There is no day or night because there is only light, we do not age, we persist in the perpetual beauty of an ageless youth performing acts which are God's alone, thinking His thoughts, uttering His words, being nothing but a manifestation of His grace and wisdom. The light from Him which pours through us illuminates everything, everywhere, we have become that transforming example, the perfected human being whose goodness and wisdom can save whole planets from extinction.

REMEMBRANCE OF GOD

The remembrance of God takes many different forms or no form at all—what happens on the outside, what we see being done is no indication of what happens inside where God alone can assess what has been absorbed, what has been lost or gained. Not everyone will aspire to the remembrance of God in purity with every breath, although His devotees and servants long to be in that state of perpetual prayer which defines both their connection to Him and the understanding they have of this connection. Most of the people in the world do not have the need to express more than routine observances, minimal ritual practices, some even less than that; however there is a tiny minority who are so obssessed, so lost in love, they want nothing other than the Beloved, to be reunited in the paradise of the present moment at each breath.

It may be that God requires no more than simple customs from the majority, that outer practices or no observances at all are

187

enough if the heart has not opened to more, but it may also be that more will be required later on, at the final investigation and judgment of our words, our thoughts, our acts, when each letter of the body will have to recite the things it has done or failed to do, then it may not be enough. With the remembrance of God an active, functioning part of our breath and life, the faults, sins and errors of daily experience are wiped away, erased. If we have been forgiven for every mistake while we are here, there will not be anything left to inquire about at the time of our questioning, we will be admitted at once to the state beyond the reckoning, no further demands. Still, it may not be fear of the final consequences which opens us to the longing for a constant posture of prayer, for most that is too remote, too indefinite, even uncertain.

This inner compulsion to know and to pray because of what we have learned comes from the positive insistence of love, not the negative prompting of fear, although I used to be acquainted with a person who insisted it was only his fear which made him do anything right. Remember that we say *bismillahir-rahmanir-rahim* before we do anything, eat, walk, drive, work, whatever it is, just as every *surat*, every chapter but one of the Qur'an begins with these words, the *bismin* invoking His mercy, His compassion, words reminding us of the fundamental nature of the divine power, words to reduce fear to a respectable minimum. The sense of awe when we contemplate the immensity of the distance between our imperfection and His perfection never leaves us, and we experience a similar, altogether humbling awe in the company of a perfected master who emanates nothing except God's presence, but while fear invalidates and incapacitates, love is a key which turns in the lock, opening the door wide and admitting those who hold this key. If we are afraid to sit in front of such a master, knowing that he knows our intimate depths, we lose the opportunity to learn what we have to learn, an opportunity offered to us by God Himself.

When we contemplate the qualities of God, focusing on the terrifying rather than the merciful, compassionate, loving, protecting, nourishing, sustaining, we place limits on His ability to forgive, we equate our own incapacity with Him, something not acceptable to Him or to us. Trying to understand God by projecting an image of ourself onto Him is backwards, we have to penetrate the great mystery of His depths so that we can come to grips with who we are, know what it means to be His servant, even His slave. Only by plunging into the expanse of His love for us can we recognize our own capacity to love. Fear comes spontaneously on its own from time to time, why plunge into an ocean of fear, why expand something which will diminish us when there are oceans of love and compassion to fill our aching lives? Why choose a tyrant when a magnanimous, loving master holds out His hand saying come, come?

Since we need to remember God with every breath, we need to know who it is we are remembering, what is He like, what does He want from us, what do we want from Him? If we want to know God, if we want to have that precious, intoxicating intimacy with Him, it is imperative to know ourself. He has already given us everything, He has already imprinted His light upon us, He has already placed the *Nur Muhammad* within each human life and endowed us with the divine attributes, what can we ask Him for that has not already been given? It is said God prepared our food and water seventy thousand years before He created each being, how then can we ask for what has already been given? He has foreseen our need, He presides over our effort, He watches us write the script yet He knows how the story ends.

God is a formless power who can be known through the attributes He dispenses in all of us, most specifically through the beings He chooses to be His messengers, His prophets and *qutbs,* those who offer the divine explanation. Although the time of the prophets is over because the message was made complete with the revelations to Muhammad, there is never a time without *qutbs,* saints and people of wisdom. Because so much was remembered and subsequently recorded about the life and words of the prophet Muhammad, we can learn something about the life of an exemplary human being from these accounts. No matter how imperfect the recollections eventually written down might be, and we have to acknowledge that when the oral tradition was an essential mode of transmission memories were probably trained to be more accurate, we still have the most complete version describing the life of any prophet available to us, and from this we can read, in outline, what a person God chose to be His messenger was like.

He was known for his integrity, his justice and fairness even before the revelations began; his surrender to God, his absolute trust in the most impossible circumstances, his patience, tolerance and compassion were equally evident once the

191

messages began to arrive in the years of his prophethood. The reverence for this prophet, shared I think, by Sufis of every disposition and not only those who find their roots in the Islamic tradition, does not preclude a strong interest in the other prophets from the fragments preserved about them in often scant scriptural sources. Certainly the plentiful documentation on Muhammad's life, in addition to what we know and can deduce about him from the Qur'an, makes him an ideal starting point to study the life of a man invested with the qualities of God, a man whose actions were dictated to him by God, whose words were brought to him by God.

There are more direct routes open to those who know how to navigate inner channels of communication. Bawa Muhaiyaddeen, who was the *qutb* of all the *qutbs* for this era, said more than once that if he wanted to know what a certain prophet thought or said about something, he would consult that prophet directly, and he did, conversations which he sometimes reported to us. What is remarkable, aside from the fact of such an amazing gift, is that much of what he told us was recorded during the later period of his life, especially in America, literally thousands of hours on audio tape and hundreds on video as well. This means we have the explanations which

192

poured through him like a river running down to the sea, intact, exactly as he said the things given to him to say, accompanied by simultaneous translation of course, but we have all these unedited versions of the things he said. Never has the message coming from God been preserved in quite this way. The difference between a prophet and a *qutb,* according to Bawa Muhaiyaddeen who never himself claimed to be the *qutb,* is that a prophet can say only the words given to him by God, while the *qutb* can give an explanation of its meaning.

If we want to know God we have to know ourself, if we want to know ourself we need the right mirror to examine our likeness, if we have a perfected being as our instructor or guide, that person can hold up the pure, polished surface in which we look at ourself without flinching, see what needs to be seen, correct what needs to be changed. At the same time, the other side of the mirror reflects the light of that being already submerged in the divine, we see the qualities and attributes we aspire to, we bathe in the wisdom we are searching for, take joy in the love poured out upon us, recognizing these things as emanations of the divine we long for. Seeing ourself on the one hand, and seeing the formal representation of the formless on the other, is at the heart of the

193

need for a teacher with the ability, the knowledge and the love to convey what must be transmitted, passed along. This is an essential outer understanding of the way Sufism is handed down from master to disciple, although it makes no reference to the inner channels, those remote and utterly mysterious levels of recognition and communication available to the enlightened master.

Also at the heart of Sufism, and to a certain extent Islam in general, is the concept of perfectability. We are born, not in a state of original sin which must be expiated, but in a state of immaculate purity which is clouded over by the things the world heaps on us, first the parents teach the separations of race, language, religion, class, status, politics, then the schools reinforce all this adding to it the prejudices of their education and finally, the professional prejudices of the work we choose complete the obscuring of our original purity. These are only layers however, like outer gaments which can be removed they can be peeled off one by one, possibly even all at once in rare cases, but for most of us it's a slow process. First we have to accept the need for change, for some this first step is the hardest because we are so blinded by habit, the way we think, the way we perceive, by expectation and false goals, by an unexploded sense of destiny, all these corrupting the view of ourself, the baby emerging from God fresh and pure. Who has not recognized the undistracted innocence of a newborn child?

We have to taste the world, we have to learn the experience of the world, have the knowing of knowing and say yes, this is good but not good enough. We have come here for knowledge, for wisdom, innocence alone is not enough; we must choose it knowing what we know and return to it, an arrow flying to a target with determination, no faltering, no hesitation. If we choose to change, to accept the limits of the world and understand the strictures of mind and desire, if we accept the need to take off the garments of this world and put on the robes of the next, the wisdom, the love, the truth, the purity, then the grace of the all-Powerful will clothe us with His compassion, His patience, tolerance, justice, gratitude and clarity, then we can begin to manifest the divine actions and qualities which define the essential character of the truly human, God within us, ourself within God. This ecstatic reclamation of the divine within the human is the manifestation of the formlessness which can only be known in the evidence we provide, and the evidence is who we are, who we become.

The mere decision to return to a pure state with trust in God, the pursuit of wisdom and love of all created beings is not enough by itself; it is necessary but not sufficient without props and guidance for our intention because a good idea is just a good idea we will have to leave at the grave unless God Himself shows us how to sustain it, nourish it with thoughts, prayers and practices. At this point we are urgently in need of the decisive intervention which must come from God in the hands of a wise person already established in sanctity, we have to realize there is too much work, too much wisdom to acquire on our own, we cannot do all this alone. We must search for this person as though our life depended on it, and it does, but when we are ready, when the time is right according to our own inner calendar, we will be found, mysteriously the teacher will be present in a place where we never expected to find ourself, yet we will be there in the presence of the only person who can save our life and validate it too.

In addition to the ability to show us what we ought to see about ourself, to demonstrate and unfailingly display the characteristcs we yearn to see in ourself, there is another duty for such a sanctified being who lives merged in the presence of God. We have a simple equation to analyze, an available route to the oneness with God; if this wise being is merged with God and we merge in total surrender to him, losing our sense of individuation as we allow him to occupy our being and we move into his, then we too may merge with God. This is a primary Sufi tenet, to merge with God we merge with the master, the teacher, the guru, the sheikh who is already merged with God. In doing so, we become part of an unbroken interconnectedness with the light of God, that is with the light of *Nur Muhammad*, the consciousness emerging from God at the beginning of the beginning, subsequently impressed upon the forehead of Adam, our primal father, and passed from one perfected being to the next in an unending chain.

What then are the practices which such an enlightened being might enjoin, offer instruction in? Obviously, much of this can only be described verbally to a certain extent since it clearly depends on an intimate transaction between master and disciple, this is not something to be learned from a book. I do remember once, years ago, teaching myself a mantra from a book, a word I did not know the meaning of except implicitly, a practice I did not grasp except vaguely, with the fortunate consequence that nothing much happened one way or another, and just as well, it could have been the road to disaster. To begin with the initial practices however, which entail no possible misunderstanding or potentially destructive results, quite simply we begin with good behavior, something we used to get marked on in public school, our conduct, our actions in relations to others. We begin with a remembrance and practice of courtesy, respect, tolerance, compassion, friendliness and sincerity.

We learn to help each other, to be polite with each other especially if we have different opinions, ideas, attitudes, doctrines, religions. We dress in the robes and attitudes of diversity which we have to be comfortable in, both for ourself and whoever else we find in our company because it is only possible to come to that place of loving unity when we accept the irrelevant costumes we all wear. This is easy to say, not so easy to do except if we remember that point of God in ourself and in everyone we meet, if we remember that wisdom looks only at the light not the dark. This first step, the first practice, right action, courtesy, *adab,* whichever word suits the understanding we bring with us, is perfectly conveyed in the traditional Hindu greeting which brings one palm together with the other, head slightly bowed. The two hands coming together, flat against each other, signify you and I are one; we say this in our greeting to God or to each other.

The importance of this practice of love, the practice of respect, the practice of politeness and good manners cannot be exaggerated and must not be ignored. It might make us nod and groan, isn't that what our mother said, isn't it there in all the religions, but if we are sincerely dedicated to the path of truth, this is the first step, the *shari'at* of wisdom, of the enlightenment which rises in a direct line above that solid foundation. This also brings us to the value of community, a diverse group of seekers who have come with good intentions and shaky practices. We are not invited to meditate in seclusion, the anchorite's cell or the cave up the mountainside, instead we are to spend time in the company of good people, others who are doing what we are doing. This is the crucible held to the fires of diversity, behavior, disposition, race, language, religion, education, class, food, dress, whatever we choose as identification, the tags of separation, the flags of otherness which we choose to fly as a way of asserting the self. There is no escape, not from our own bad qualities which surface from time to time, not from someone else's bad qualities which also surface from time to time. Working out the difficulties in a forgiving way provides an excellent opportunity for change at the deepest level we can take it to.

If we can learn to be tolerant at first, then compassionate and loving, we can discover the nature of the refuge to be sought in these exquisite qualities. Eventually, with God's help and always remembering it is only with His grace, His guidance, that change is possible, we might learn to stay there, to be in that state of unconditional surrender, unconditional love available and offered without hesitation, a supreme gift. When we have the example of a truly wise person leading such a community, his or her love and wisdom ignite the longing for these qualities so intensely it becomes unbearable to fall short, and so whenever we make a mistake in our relations with each other we make amends, try to make amends and carry on. The actual process of learning not to yell, not to give way to anger, envy, jealousy or all the petty irritations we can devise for ourself might take years, more years than we are ready to predict, yet the necessary improvements do come. The trouble with living in a cave or in the solitude of self-imposed isolation is that at the end of twenty-five years when we come back down the mountain, we are in danger of losing it all with the first difficult encounter.

Sufis stay in the world, doing the work of the world; for most of us the difficulty is trying to be inconspicuous, invisible, doing the things required of us by the world while at the same time remembering God. We function in two worlds simultaneously, only giving the appearance of accepting the world, of believing in its conditions and demands because what we are really doing, is living under God's dominion in His kingdom, fulfilling His conditions so that we may take up permanent residence there when we have learned what we need to learn, experienced what we need to experience. If we behave with the qualities and actions of God without making a show of being righteous or other, we can do what we need to do and slip through the world; if we are in a state of constant prayer, a prayer that courses through the breath and beats with the pulse, we can be alive in the reality of His dominion.

The reclamation of the soil for mystical ascent, this spiritual weeding of the garden, pulling out the things we do not want to make room for the things we must let grow will continue for years, while we simultaneously build the structure which will rise on this fertile soil. This structure is built by our prayers, prayers that form an essential part of the weeding process as we build the platforms to ascend. There is a sense of progress, of moving along on this path of no path, we can look back to see where we have been and what we have learned, things we can verify experientially that seem to be tied, on the one hand, to the wisdom transmitted by the master guiding us, leading us forward, and on the other, to the effort we make with our attempts to be better and do better. For this a primary instrument is prayer, the inner struggle to know, to be, and this struggle can be mapped by endlessly different approaches.

There is a formless, wordless prayer of surrender when the soul merely contemplates, aligning itself with the faith of absolute trust: my God, beloved master of my life, my soul, You who see and know everything before I am even able to recognize my situation, I do not beg, I do not need to tell You, it is all Your decision. This not asking is a pure assumption of knowledge and intimacy, knowing that He knows is enough, but it is a specific act of prayer. The formal equivalent is the regular performance of daily prayers at prescribed intervals, again not asking, not demanding, merely affirming worship, acknowledging His presence, the immediacy of our connection to Him, using words spoken by others for generations which have become our own.

Then between these two are versions of asking for protection, asking for special favors, pleading that events turn out according to our own imperfect assessment of good and bad, right and wrong. Such prayers include reciting a certain name of God or set prayers which are said to produce results, like a guarantee on a purchase. There are also spontaneous prayers of thanks and praise which pour without premeditation from the grateful, groping heart. My God, we say, the splendor of Your grace, the beauty of Your creation is so immense, how can I thank You, how can I praise You with words, here is my heart, take my heart, my praise, my trust. In addition to all these, are the millions and millions of different prayers of pure remembrance, chanting, singing, dancing, moving, reciting in remembrance of God, His angels and prophets, His saints.

The prayer which is the ultimate prayer of remembrance is the *dhikr,* the *la ilaha illallahu* recited silently in conjunction with the in-breath and the out-breath. It is the prayer which heals the body, controls the mind and attaches the soul firmly to that wisdom manifesting the presence of God, the prayer which builds the most exalted ladders for our ascent. Clearly the following brief outer description is not intended as instruction, merely as reference because this *dhikr* is a complex and delicate inner prayer, ideally learned from an enlightened master and practised, at least for a time, under that watchful scrutiny. It begins with the out-breath, the *la ilaha* gathering everything from the lower part of the body, channeling it up through the left side and expelling it out the left nostril. The hands do not touch the nose, but remain lightly cupped or open on the lap. Certain slight movements of the eye and thumb may accompany this extraction of all that is not God from the body, as well as the consciousness and affirmation that nothing exists but God, He is the reality, the totality and the permanence. Then we have the inhalation, the in-breath through the right nostril which may also be accompanied by small movements of the eye and thumb, asserting that God alone is God. The breath travels to the gnostic eye at the center of the forehead, then to the throne of God on the crown of the head, back down the throat to the heart which distributes the light to all parts of the body.

The up and down movement of the breath works somewhat like a pump, movements changing the breath to light, passing through the heart where the light beats into and with the blood. We pray this prayer like a baby, an embryo in the arms of God transformed by light, the self, the ego, dispersed in His existence. This prayer is the most profound instrument, the deepest exercise we have been given to bring mind and desire to that surrender, that submission to His unicity. With this *dhikr* we rid our body of illness and our mind of discomfort; with the practice of this *dhikr* we study non-existence, our own, and learn the totality of His, the true remembrance of God.

Sufi

THE BELOVED

To love God, to be in love with God is not the same as loving, being in love with a person because this love is a different kind of love, hard to describe since it is both familiar and unknown. This love is more demanding, more consuming as it gives us peace and steals our peace forever, or so it seems, at least until we come to that point of communion which heralds the merging, that union of one with One. It has nothing to do with the body except in the ways that love commands us to offer our body in service to Him and to those who experience love as we do, love as worship, love as an offering of duty, a connection through love for God to each other. Wisdom looks at God within each melting heart and sees itself, a luminous presence radiating His love back to us, and so we are continually with Him, continually reminded of Him even though we are never able to see Him or touch Him materially, physically.

The relations between the devotee and the Beloved are summed up in the word love which has been used, in every tradition, as the emblem or symbol of that mystical longing of the soul for its return to the source, the origin of its existence. Although human love and divine love are not interchangeable they have certain things in common. If we love someone because we expect something in return, that love is not disinterested, not pure; and if we love God because we expect favors in return from Him, that love is neither disinterested nor pure. If we love another concerned only for that person's sanctity and joy, filled with the love that requires nothing, that love is pure; and if we love God filled with worship for the creator of our human existence, asking for nothing, offering only service, that love is pure. If we fall in love with someone and become so obsessed with this love that nothing else matters any more, nothing else except being with this person makes sense to us any longer, that is like falling in love with God. We give up everything for this love, we surrender to this love, we are a slave to this love.

We are subject to obsessions of every kind as human beings, work, success, family, position, titles, money, office, and as long as these obsessions allow us to function with a reasonable appearance of something resembling normal, we are not labelled psychotic. The obsession for God, if we cannot manage to keep it under wraps, deliberately conceal or obscure it, will have us labelled faster than any of these other obsessions will. There is a very fine line between determination and obsession, between love and obsession, a line easily crossed in pursuit of the invisible unknown. The *majnun*, the obsessed to the point of apparent madness, while not common is occasionally encountered, and sometimes it's hard to tell whether they are the only ones who really get it, understand what this love is about, or if they have merely crossed the line into genuine insanity. Our consolation, or theirs, is that we must assume a cure will be forthcoming because there is no unrequited love for God, this love is always fulfilled, although not necessarily in ways we can all see or recognize.

Since love is the most intimate basis for relations among us, and love of God lives at the deepest place in our being, parallels between human love and love of the divine are not hard to find. Initially, we might think that unattainable love, the love that is placed on a pedestal and never really known is similar to our love of God. After all, we cannot approach Him, we cannot see Him or know what He looks like, sounds like, but in fact, we do know Him if we know ourself, we can speak to Him and experience an unmistakable vibratory response; sometimes we catch His fragrance, His taste. Then it's not that, not really that, it has more to do with a willingness to put our own apparent interests to one side while doing something to help someone else, offering our appetites and desires, our attachments and preferences as sacrifices on the altars we build to love. The similarity lies in our ability and capacity to submerge the self, the ego, in someone else's requirements.

Getting rid of the ego, what I want or need, what I think or believe, what I identify or prop myself up with, these are the sacrifices we make for love, and to the extent we are successful in this, the love survives. When we marry, a sacred symbol for the union of the lover with the Beloved, we are so intoxicated we are persuaded nothing will change the way we feel about each other. Then as time passes and that haze of passion begins to subside, we discover a range of annoying imperfections, a laugh, a turn of phrase, bad taste, a bad quality like anger, jealousy, a lack of restraint, frugality or its opposite, extravagance, and love begins to die, it fades like a flower past its day and we call it a day. If love is founded on spasms of passion and not much else, it cannot survive the death of passion, it is not love and has no common ground with that pure love which is love for God. Nevertheless, if we can examine our own flaws with the same hard scrutiny, correct our own shortcomings with care, the example we set might inspire the other to correct his or hers, then we can join our hands together in respect, understanding, and come to the reality of genuine love for one another.

Marriage, the emblem of God's divine love for us and ours for Him has produced exquisite literature in all the traditions, both monotheist and other, the image of the bride and the Beloved occurs again and again. Marriage implies the same union on the spiritual plane that it assumes on the physical level for human love, this most intimate union of one with One more than an interpenetration of soul with soul, it signifies the disappearance of one in the other so that what was once two becomes One. This is like a drop of water falling into the ocean, who can say where that drop is now, who can identify this drop or that drop, yet it is there, part of the whole, the surging sea of totality.

Whether we take the meaning of our relations with God to this exalted level or not, the most important, the most meaningful

211

thing for our lives is to recognize the significance of love as a divine quality, let our heart be completely open to it and make love a part of our regular experience with each other; we need to be loving, exemplify love and teach everyone to love. Each one of us must learn to love every living being as if it were our own life, and once we have that love firmly planted in ourself, we will be able to find it everywhere, we will see it on the faces around us. But this will happen only if we have that quality in our heart, since we cannot recognize something out there if it is not first in here. This is true for all the qualities, good or bad, what we have is what we know. How can we recognize it unless we already know it?

We have to contemplate everything in a state of love to spread that love, this is what we have to give each other, the love that confers peace, the love that causes happiness, the love that is an emblem of God's love for us. Sadness, sorrow, distress, even hunger can be dissipated by love because love is the reflection of Him, of the grace, the love and compassion He comforts us with. The things we learn from pure love are the treasures we have to dispense because these are the gifts of Allah, these are intimations of His love which He offers in His limitless capacity whether we are interested or not, whether we love

Him or not. Because He exists as the form of love, simultaneously everywhere, His love is necessarily without limit, it falls equally on everything like the light of the sun or the moisture of the rain, and because the soul which has no fault or flaws is a reflection of His light, it must fill the world with that love.

There is a profound connection between love and the duty or service we offer to God and to each other. Unless we carry out our duties or obligations with love, they cannot really be described as duty which is an exalted concept. We should not confuse duty with the things we do because someone is forcing us to do it, and consequently we do in a state of discomfort, dislike, even anger. We need to see duty as an opportunity to do something, no matter how inconsequential, with the energy of pure love, we need to crave such opportunities, search for them with wisdom and be eager to do it, finding happiness in the performance of any such task, otherwise it is not duty at all. This does not mean indiscriminate plunging into everything lying across our path without the careful circumspection of wisdom, that is not necessarily duty either. We have to learn what to accept and what to reject or we might just end up running around foolishly, avoiding the need to sit still, contemplating the Beloved.

One of the hardest things is to help someone, offer love and service when it is clearly dangerous to do so. Our *qutb,* Bawa Muhaiyaddeen, used to say if you go to help a snake take a very long stick, do what you have to and then make your escape. The snake can't help that its fangs are filled with poison, it is only natural for a snake to bite if it feels threatened or in danger. When we are filled with that protective, loving concern for our fellow human beings we might feel obliged to help in situations which offer no avenue of escape, then wisdom counsels not to do it, this is for someone else to manage. Don't get caught up in the drama, love does not invite love into inevitable disaster, love that is pure, God's love, is never blind. Wisdom says if there should be a conflict between love and wisdom, the love is not pure, follow wisdom; love without wisdom is not that quality. Meanwhile of course, the love that is imperfect shouts the opposite, let everything yield to love, never mind the danger, this is what God commands.

There is another perspective on love and duty to look at, we should not for a moment expect to be thanked for what we do, we should not look for gratitude or to be given something in return. Duty that is done in a state of love is like God's duty, the Beloved doing some little thing without a thought or the expectation, ah now at last that person will know Me and love Me. None of this should come up, quite simply because the person we help can only offer us what he or she happens to possess, and it could very well be the poison we used a long stick to avoid. Selfless duty with no thought of return rises automatically in that state of pure love. Sometimes we can see this to a certain extent within the frame of merely human love, even the shadow of that purest love is such a compelling condition it can become the counterfoil, at least for a time, for many less desirable qualities. Human love will often bring out the best in us for awhile because we want something in return, we want the person we love to love us in return; God's love is different, it gives, it offers, it provides freely with no expectations, His love is a treasure for us to keep.

The difference between the love of the Beloved for His creation and the fragile, changeable human love we sometimes have for each other is unfathomable because His love is eternal, undivided, seamless, complete. His love emanates from the essence of the *Nur Muhammad,* the light of creation, the reason for His creation and its cause. If we want to know pure love, if we want to be pure love, we must have the wisdom to understand that the One who gives this love is the One who receives it, otherwise the love is something else, not the unchanging perfection, the unity and totality found in the completion which alone is the Beloved. It is His love that is the source of unity, it is His love that creates unity. The unity based on commonality of opinion or idea disappears when opinions and ideas change; they have no permanence, they are not even shadows of wisdom because they are products of the mind with no origin in truth and faith. A good idea is clearly not enough when we know that all our ideas, good and bad, are left at the grave. If we find that point of unity in the love that flows from the Beloved and connect with each other through this love, the unity, the oneness is genuine, it surrounds both worlds, now and hereafter.

We have to search for peace, that most elusive gift, through unity in our relations to each other and love for the Beloved. The human condition is a catalogue of woe, the sorrows of sickness, hunger, poverty, death and those miseries we invent for ourself, fear, boredom, anxiety, neurosis, all converge in a symphony of distress with dissonance the dominant note. Even when we go in search of the Beloved it is not always peaceful, sometimes we are in bliss, sometimes discouraged; we are still subject to the moods and tremors we have not yet discarded, still subject to the attachments which blind us, the qualities of anger, intolerance and impatience which impede our ability to move on. The peace that is more than balance or mere equilibrium, both hard enough to establish and maintain, comes from a fundamental contentment and gratitude rooted in the purest love and selfless compassion for everything in creation, for all living things. This alone brings true peace to the heart and freedom to the soul.

As wisdom emerges from the deepest faith, as qualities that interfere with our pursuit of the Beloved dissolve in the metamorphosis of determined change and we become more loving, we begin to see love in places we could never see it before. We need to be loving ourself to see love in others, and once we see that love our compassion and forgiveness are quickly aroused as well. When we look at each other with the wisdom of pure love we understand each other, it becomes easy to forgive what we understand. Someone who is wise, looking with love at the things others do, realizes their actions are appropriate for the wisdom they have, for the level of understanding they have at the time. Compassion says if I had been in that person's situation I might have done the same thing, I would probably have behaved in the same way. How much more magnanimous is the Beloved; when we can find the way to forgiveness within our limits, know how ready are His mercy and His compassion, which are limitless, to veil our faults.

Our precarious human love with all its flaws and longings has to be examined, we have to change our selfish love into selfless love, a love that is pure, so pure that it becomes essentially indistinguishable from the love flowing in a constant stream from the heart of the Beloved Himself. Love is the opener, possibly the most accesssible of His qualities; and since each quality, pursued absolutely, pursued beyond the ends of limit converges with all the others at the source, this becomes the most easily defined way, the approach to Him which is open and available.

TO BE FORGIVEN

What does it take to be forgiven, what is it that has to be forgiven, who forgives and who is forgiven, why do we need to be forgiven, what is forgiveness? Questions like these roll, sometime unanswered, through the endless immensity of the gap between His perfection, His radiant totality and our imperfect human condition marked by disaster, sorrow and the incomplete scripts of longing, of stories with unhappy endings. We do not need to propose concepts of original sin to account for the haunting sense that we are less than perfect when we realize perfection exists and can be known, we do not require the terrible rigors of self-flagellation to remove the blots and stains of our existence, but we do have to acknowledge the succession of petty indiscretions, errors in judgment, pain caused either accidentally or deliberately which we are responsible for, not to mention the catalogue of greater mistakes, the lies, theft, lust, murder, deception, treachery, betrayal range of flaws.

When we produce this list of major mistakes we might not find ourself guilty of all that, still, the shadow of something falls at least marginally across our natural innocence, a state of original purity we must find our way back to if we are to unite with the origin of all purity. We might think, well I've certainly never stolen anything, but if we have taken more than our share of anything, food, clothing, water, while somone else went hungry, naked or thirsty, that is a kind of theft too. Or we might say, I've never murdered anyone, yet we have eaten everything without compunction, without the thought we have taken a life to sustain ours, without a moment of regret for the slaughter of insects or wildlife to sustain our own comfort.

Only when we look at the lesser sins which are more likely to have composed a routine part of our daily experience do we begin to face the implications of consequence. We are answerable for every malicious word, thought or act, every gesture of unkindness, the careless actions of our hands, feet and tongue; in fact, at the time of our death and the questioning which comes with our death, every part of our body, every nerve, bone and muscle will testify, proclaiming what it has done, both the good and the bad. We are responsible for the harm we have caused and blessed for the good we have done. These two, the good and the bad, are the only things we take with us to the grave, the only things that matter about our life at the end. Everything else, whether we have built empires or destroyed them, whether we have written books or given great performances, whether we were challenged every inch of the way or sailed easily through it all, whether we suffered or escaped without a blow, without injury to the body, the ego or the heart, the only things that matter when we die are the good and the bad we've been responsible for.

With this understanding we have to realize how urgent it is to come to some reckoning, some admission of culpability before we reach the grave, because if we look for forgiveness in this life and make amends, if we are forgiven in this lifetime for all the mistakes and errors, things we did unwittingly before we understood the difference between right and wrong, as well as the things we did when that darkness had been lifted, then there will be nothing left to ask us about, we will return in a state of innocent purity, the state we arrived in. Forgiveness is about the purification that begins with a minute examination of all that we have intended and done, all that we have seen, heard, smelled, tasted, said, all that we have experienced or known at the level of the heart. This point by point examination of who we have become in terms of what we have actually accumulated, all the dust in clouds of expanding karma, this does not mean adopting a life of endless howling and remorse, a Sufi does not wallow in it. We look at what we have done or failed to do, make amends and with a pure, open, melting heart we ask God, the source of everything, both good and bad, we ask Him to pardon us, to remove the guilt we feel for the things we did that were wrong.

If we go to a therapist we might linger over the things we did, the things that were done to us, yet with the wisdom that comes from faith we can cut, quickly and for good, the burdens we might have been carrying around for years. We do not lock ourself in the past, we believe without question that what's past is past, no need to stay there or keep going back, we want to engage the present moment with the remembrance of God, the *kalimah,* the *la ilaha illallahu* which expels all that is not God in the out-breath and affirms His omnipresent reality with the in-breath. We understand that God created everything, everything in existence, which means that He introduced good and evil too, not to distract us, not to punish us, but to give us the opportunity to study, learn to see and choose. We are supposed to eliminate the darkness, as He did during the period before time and creation, we are expected to learn how to choose the good, the light, and be rid of the wrong, the darkness, by purifying ourself with prayer and asking for the forgiveness that obliterates the karmic disasters we have inherited and acquired.

The first thing we have to admit is accountability, acknowledging responsibility; we do inherit, now and hereafter, what we construct for ourself, there is a questioning to come which nothing can divert. While we are still here we have every opportunity however, to cancel the wrong things, the bad things we accept, we take upon ourself, and if we clear the account absolutely by asking forgiveness for all our faults, all our poor intentions, reckless actions and the devastating consequences of what we have done, if we can find that total forgiveness from God which wipes the slate clean, when death comes and we have to leave this world nothing will remain to be asked, the account is balanced, nothing is owed, there are no debts to be paid. This is not an easy matter, not something we can be glib about or pretend to have finished with, He sees our most carefully preserved secrets, everything stored in the hidden places of every level in our consciousness, our Augean stables which must be cleaned.

How then do we start once we have accepted the importance of beginning? First we ransack the closet, pull out everything we can see and assess what needs the most urgent attention, what are the qualities which have generated the worst things we find, then initiate an assault on two fronts, digging out the bad quality and begging forgiveness for specific events or actions, rooting out those things in ourself which are opposed to God, His qualities and actions. Sincerity of regret at the most profound level we can reach is critical here, we have to be convinced that what we did was wrong and feel appalled, as horrified as we feel about the worst atrocities we have ever heard described, wounded in our convictions about justice, about right and wrong. Yet we must be ready to accept that God's timetable is not the same as ours, we cannot expect instant absolution for everything all at once, it will take time to eliminate the things we spent years acquiring and reinforcing. At the same time we must maintain the conviction that it can happen this way, all at once, if that is God's will.

For the things which just won't go away, do not seem to yield to our prayers, we must persist with determination, knowing that God will observe our continuing effort and intervene by unlocking closed gates from His side, He can dissolve the karmic obstacles littering our path. We use the times of prayer to engage the inner struggle, we use moments of reflection and meditation to examine our past actions, we recite the names of God for purification, we use the *kalimah* to wipe away the flaws and failures, with every out-breath begging for forgiveness, with every in-breath confirming His oneness, and we never give up. We never think we are beyond repair, beyond the reach of His grace and mercy, we know forgiveness is possible and available. Then just as eagerly as we search for this forgiveness for ourself we must extend it to others, be ready to see the difficulties inflicted upon us as the natural consequence of another's level of understanding, lack of wisdom.

If God does not punish us for the things we did in our time of darkness, when we unwittingly courted ignorance, should we not learn from His generosity and pardon those who deliberately or accidentally hurt or offend us, should we not be compassionate enough to forgive them completely, no little tags of remembrance, this person did this to me, that person hurt my feelings? We have a story, alluded to in the Qur'an, from the life of the prophet Muhammad, one that our *qutb* told more than once, which illustrates the nature of true forgiveness at the human level. It seems that during the years of the prophet's enormous difficulties in the city of Mecca before the *hijra* to Medina, when he and his struggling little community endured so much abuse from the other Meccans, one angry, small group inspired an elderly woman to spread thorns on the route he took from his home to the Ka'bah where he went to pray. Every day he would pick up the thorns along the way so that no one else would be injured, every day new thorns would be spread on his path, and he said nothing, routinely clearing the obstacles.

This went on for some time until one day he noticed with surprise the path was clear, no thorns spread to injure his feet; this continued a few days until he was finally compelled to ask why, what happened to the woman who had deliberately created so many problems for him and his followers. No one could tell him anything about her, and so without hesitation he went to the old lady's house, found her ill with a high fever, alone, parched with thirst and not a person there to help. How carefully the prophet brought water to her mouth, how tenderly he made her comfortable again with soothing words and compassionate gestures. Finally, when she was able to speak, she had to say how extraordinary it was that the people

226

who had put her up to all that mischief gave no thought to her
once she was no longer useful to them, that it was the victim of
her attacks who came to help in her illness. The prophet
explained the true nature of Islam, something she was now
ready to hear, taught her the *kalimah* and accepted her into
Islam.

If this is an example of human forgiveness, how much greater
must the forgiveness of God be, if this is an example of human
compassion, how much greater must God's be. When difficulties
present themselves we must not think that God is angry, that God
is testing us—if He were to test us, think of His power, could we
survive any such test? We have our whole life to examine and
express who we are; God does not place limits on how or what
we choose, He does not require an account from us until the last
breath. Until then we are free to construct the good and the bad,
units of the residence He will give us one day, meanwhile we
build that place, brick by brick, stone by stone with our words,
our thoughts and acts. Our destiny is not prescribed or written in
advance, we write our own, we change our own each day with
the things we do or fail to do. God has placed this in our hands,
it is entirely up to us how we manage what we are given, how we
use the gifts bestowed upon us so freely, so lavishly.

Once we understand that God has made everything available to us, the good and the bad, and that we are free to choose how to deal with what is given, we have to reassess our approach to the things we tend to look upon as problems, the things we worry about, situations which cause distress, anxiety, fear. If everything comes from God, it does seem appropriate to reperceive the things we are not ready or eager to accept as a different kind of gift, something given as a way to study patience, tolerance, forbearance, forgiveness, something to strengthen the qualities we need and help us erase the things we do not need. The difficulties may be the best opportunity to invest in the purity we long for; it's one thing to be gracious and loving when things are going well, when we have what we want and think we have what we need, it's a rather different consideration when we are under stress or pressure, when there is distress for whatever reason. These are the moments when it is possible to extend our limits; as in weight lifting, we have to increase our capacity by practising regularly, often. Only when we build up the load do we gain strength, and this is not something which can be done theoretically, we have to engage the muscles.

There are many avenues to purification, through *dhikr* and prayer, reciting the names of God, through changing our idea of ourself, who we are, who we can become, digging out what we must get rid of, nourishing the qualities we want to improve. If we long for truth we must be truthful; if we are eager for love we must be loving; if we want humility we must be humble; and if we want to be forgiven we must be forgiving, recognize the failings we see spread out before us as a map of our own imperfection. When events unfold in a way that we conceive to be contrary to our happiness, our interests, we are not to think of this as retribution, a punishment from God, we get what we get because we create what we get. If God wanted to stamp out all evil once and for all He could, then how would we learn, how would we acquire His divine wisdom? It's up to us to determine how to use what we receive. When we construe something to be a disaster it is, but if we reperceive our situation we can undo every apparent misfortune by taking it as an exercise in building our divine attributes, a divine instruction course offered in patience, tolerance, forgiveness, humility or whatever else we choose to major in.

If we take each one of the ninety-nine names of God as a step we have to climb, an attribute whose acquisition is imperative for the freedom of our soul, we can choose to focus for a time on one quality, recite its name, meditate, contemplate the implications, look for occasions to practise it when we might not in the past have done so. While we concentrate on one quality, we do not ignore all the others, we merely work harder on this one subject we might be weaker in, or stronger for that matter, if we think we can make better progress in it, understanding that each attribute converges in all the others as we climb higher and higher. And so with the question of forgiveness, we can recite His name, the forgiver, and learn forgiveness by searching for that seedling in ourself, nourish it, water it and let it grow, watch it bear fruit. We meditate on the inner implications and practise the outer manifestation, allowing the beauty of that quality to become a functioning part of our own available truth. If we keep going, if we persist we notice the stench of our own imperfection less frequently and catch the scent of His fragrance from time to time.

When we have reflected on the history of our actions for some time, searched earnestly to be forgiven for specific mistakes and errors we have committed in the past, we might begin to wonder how to know when we have been forgiven. We pray, we meditate, we ask forgiveness, and as our capacity for purity increases we begin to shudder at the thought of the things we have actually done, we feel the enormous weight of the mistakes we have made, either inadvertently or deliberately. But we are not to bind ourself in chains of guilt, we are not to suppose that forgiveness is not forthcoming from our God whose mercy and compassion are the attributes most frequently mentioned in the Qur'an, words which He dictated. As the days and years build around us, we gradually realize we no longer make a certain mistake, we no longer even feel inclined to commit that fault, that error of judgment and conduct. Once we have passed through the gauntlet of years, secure in the wisdom which no longer commits that mistake, we know we are forgiven. No longer commiting the fault is the sign, the indication we have been forgiven, we can forget about it, what's past is past.

Asking God to forgive our mistakes, the unhappiness we cause, the sin and mischief we are responsible for, is often called repentance; the one who is begging for His forgiveness is called the penitent and the place where we lock up those who are supposed to be asking for forgiveness is the penitentiary. The burden of grief and guilt implied by these words seems excessive, the image of a fire breathing preacher demanding repentance is too vivid, too critical for a loving, compassionate, merciful God who observes our faults like any indulgent parent. Of course He wants us to improve, to get it right, be correct in our thoughts and acts, as any parent does, but He does not have pain and punishment in His heart, He has no vengeance or retribution in all His might, His power and authority, and it is inappropriate for us to attribute them to Him.

Although there are rigorous images of self-flagellation in all the major traditions, this heavy conception of forgiveness rings out specifically from certain Christian religions—it could be they are just more familiar—and it seems odd that any religious group which has love as its identifying characteristic should also project such strong barricades around the idea of forgiveness, if for no other reason than love is so implicitly forgiving. The idea of a savior who has died for our sins, without whose intervention forgiveness is impossible, implies that it is just not available at the merely human level, it also implies an exclusivity which denies His oneness, His totality. But God has given everything to us all, and not just one community or one religion; in any case, why should He withhold this? He has kept only creation, sustaining and nourishment for Himself, the rest, including forgiveness, has been made available to us; it is a concept bathed in light, not in darkness. This is not meant to diminish the effort, the dedication and sincerity required for true forgiveness, nor does it imply that anyone except each one of us, individually, for ourself and ourself alone, is able to bring about forgiveness.

The depth of the forgiveness we extend to each other, our capacity to forgive the insults and injuries the world inevitably delivers, teach us more about the nature of forgiveness than any description or discussion, it is a purely private and inner matter on the personal scale. Yet it does have significance on the national scale as well, country to country, state to state, our international ability to forgive reflects the collective ability, the community of forgiveness which evolves as individuals mature in their personal capacity. The reformation of society depends upon the extent of individual reclamation, goodness is a light which spreads from heart to heart, from house to house, an irresistible contagion. The purification arising from true prayer, the prayers we offer in the mosque or church of the inner heart where the treasure we store cannot be affected by the winds of time and the world, this is the forgiving gift we offer back to the human community.

Sufi

GOOD AND EVIL

The conflict between good and evil represents the ultimate drama, the endless battle of our human experience, a battle fought individually at the inner level and collectively at the national and international levels, a battle which identifies clearly, more than any other characteristic of our lives, who we are. It is a drama in the classic sense, this is a struggle involving one or more people, it has a plot with a beginning, middle, a resolution and an end, and style reflecting the qualities of the protagonist. So many of the great dramas in literature are considered great, at least in part, because they engage the soul resonating between the dark and the light. In Milton's *Paradise Lost* the epic war for Adam, for the human soul, is defined explicitly by Satan's proclamation, "Evil be thou my good," with this invocation inverting our divine affinity. On one side we have God and His attributes of perfect purity, on the other we have Satan who has permission from God to lure us away from the truth, from the goodness which is His nature.

This is a battle each one of us is required to deal with, to fight and win. Shakespeare's tragedies, perhaps more than any other dramas in western art present the awful polarities, the decisions demanded of us when we wrestle with the forces distracting and blinding us, the evils which deliberately rob us of the qualities we have been given as our birthright. Shakespeare's heros exemplify the devastating consequences of having one bad quality that dominates the good, the ambition of Macbeth, the jealousy of Othello, the petty vanity of Lear, the doubt, the uncertainty of Hamlet, one overmastering propensity and the life of a hero is in ruins. The rest of us who are not heros, who live in circumstances which might be less dramatic, still live the story we write with our thoughts and acts, still have to face that pull of our darker side while the light beckons irresistibly. What we see in the large, clear letters of their heroic struggles are the no less heroic but smaller struggles each one of us must endure, and with God's help, bring to a less disastrous conclusion.

All these dramas, in terms of our spiritual ascent, are merely describing scuffles at the foothills of the mountain we have decided to climb; this combat for the life of the soul, which is a struggle between good and evil, right and wrong, is nothing more than the *shari'at,* the first step on the pathless path. That the immensity of the Shakespearean dramas gives us nothing more than the first step of the arduous flight which the soul undertakes, provides an enlightening perspective for the journey that lies ahead. Mind and desire, the instruments of illusion, routinely and automatically profer difficulties all along the route because the illusion that this world exists and that the things of the world are valid is what distracts us from the life of the soul, our only ultimate good. God has provided certain disjunctions for us to examine, opposites to stimulate understanding, to compare and choose, and so we have good and bad, heaven and hell, illusion and reality, the light and the dark, truth and falsehood, form and formless, hidden and revealed. What we experience directly, or through observation and inference, is the instruction course which makes the whole world a necessary school for our education in truth and what is inherently ours.

We have been given good and evil to engage and defeat the destiny implicit in our genetic confluence and the socio-economic deal that goes with it, a package sometimes called karma, sometimes called destiny. We are not bound by karma, we are not bound by destiny once we start to investigate the secrets that lie in the formlessness hidden within form, once we determine to identify ourself with the good and reject the bad. This is the first step, the obstacle Shakespeare's heros could not overcome, with the tragic outcome that failure entails. Was Shakespeare offering the *shari'at?* Some might think so, persuaded by the hidden message of his name, although it seems more likely that he had grasped a universal truth from the school of understanding available to everyone, and conveyed it with all the artistry he could bring to the service of truth. What is required of us is to acknowledge and accept this unquestioned identification with the good, then move on from there. When we penetrate the outer form, the body, we begin to perceive the secrets of the hidden, inner form, then the secrets of the formless life within that form open up revealing a hidden, inner light which houses the *nur,* the radiant light of God's plenitude.

We learn that heaven and hell do not exist as separate conditions or places, they are fully functioning states within each of us, elaborate structures we build for ourself here and inherit there, later on, distinct pathways carved as we chart a course through the experiences we receive. These experiences are of every kind, apparently good and apparently bad, all of which we receive as a curse or a blessing depending on our ability to transform what we perceive with the inner sight, inner ear and inner heart which accept the reality of God and discount the illusions of the world. Most of us know both sorrow and joy without recognizing they are extremes of the same polarity, an axis of experience we can allow or disallow because they are emotional states connected to the ego, to the mind and our desires. From that perspective there is not much to choose between them, an excess of either is distracting, unbalancing; we need to detach our attachments to avoid the chronic ups and downs that percolate through the grounds of our daily experience. It's not always possible to understand the nature of a specific event, we do not always have the ability to interpret what happens along the way, and yet we persist in the drama which courts disaster, predicts misfortune.

When we have the inner muscle to assess the strengthening grace of things that look like disaster outwardly but resemble blessings inwardly, we recognize the distinction between purity and impurity, accepting that purity is heaven and impurity is hell. The only hell is separation from God and the imperfections which keep us from Him; the only heaven is proximity and the purification which draws us near. By extracting the good from the bad privately, and presenting the good publicly as an example of God's beauty from which others can be inspired to this purification, we demonstrate a method for the world of handling the evils we find everywhere; we know that as good approaches it is the source of happiness, we also know that as evil retreats it is the source of happiness. Then when we hear the tremulous inquiry, why would a loving God let this happen, and we hear their faith crumbling around this point of inquiry, we can show that it is not God who precipitated the wars, the slaughter, the divisiveness rampant everywhere.

If we can offer our soul the nourishment that comes from God alone, we have less and less problem satisfying the elusive demands of the elements which compose the body, our illusion of form. There is an analysis of the apparent dualism shrouding our perceptions which clarifies the relations between inner and outer, form and formless, an analysis which has nothing to do with the methods of science or their requirements, and everything to do with an understanding of God and His requirements. The human entity consists of six basic components, five of which belong to the elements, one of which belongs to God. What belongs to the elements in our human configuration, to earth, fire, water, air and space is transitory. We use all this for a time, we feed it for a time, offering the food of the elements to the elements, then when we're done with it, all this is to be returned to the elements; the elements have no permanence, our body comes and it goes.

Science might not accept this analysis as either useful or valid, but science is hardly ever relevant to divine knowledge, something that annoys the mind which has to be left on one side for this pursuit and become the servant, willing or unwilling, to an enlightened master. The sixth basic component has nothing to do with the elements, it is the soul which comes as a ray of light from God and returns to Him; it is permanent, connected to the reality which has no beginning or end. Just as we feed the body with food appropriate for the elements, we have to feed the hunger of the soul with food appropriate for the soul, and that food is the grace and beauty emanating from our good qualities, good actions and good thoughts. We starve the soul by feeding it bad qualities, evil actions and bad thoughts. What is permanent is invisible, inaccessible to science which has not yet figured out a way to find the soul, but this is our reality, the truth that must struggle to find expression through the barriers of the impermanent and unreal. God has the ultimate responsibility for both the grace which is His essence and the form bestowed upon us, yet it is up to us to discover that He alone is the gift of our existence, the treasure nothing can corrupt or change.

We have to be able to assess our qualities, thoughts and actions to know if they are right or wrong, good or bad, we have to do this to destroy the hell we live in and replace it with the purity which alone is peace, living in the oneness, the unity which transforms the world of form, transforms the elements bringing them into the divine realm we can choose to live in here. We do not need to wait for the kingdom of God, it is here, we can create it here; those who choose purity, who examine each particle of their existence to eliminate everything that does not belong to Him and His dominion live there now. When we cut off every separation generated by our attachments, when we remove the acquisitiveness of selfhood and ego, that sense of me, mine and what belongs to me, we shine with the luminous beauty of His grace, His essence, and this light illuminates the whole human family as we discover that everyone, all the people in the world are members of this family.

His grace is the seat of justice which exists in each of us, hidden within the inner heart, an imperishable place filled with the worship of God. Our eyes perceive light, our ears hear sound, our tongue tastes or gives shape to words and this tiny place in the heart worships God, it looks at Him, it listens to Him and offers prayers to Him. Because it is the seat of His justice, this is what distinguishes right from wrong, good actions from bad actions, this is what knows which of our thoughts are good, which of our intentions are wrong, and although it is concealed in our body composed of the elements, it never dies, it cannot be destroyed by the elements. This conscience, awake after our death as well, will declare our fallibility when we are questioned in the grave. It is the radiant wisdom of the *nur* which identifies and locates this seat of justice in the heart that functions like a scale weighing the good and the bad. If we use the *kalimah,* the *la ilaha illallahu* as our scale and put everything that is rejected on the left, the *la ilaha* which discards all that is not God, and put all that is God on the right, the *illallahu,* our scale will balance in perfect faith as we eliminate the bad and accept the good alone. That unshakable adherence to the good is our second step, our *tariqat.*

243

We reject the body and the world as evil, impermanent, counting instead on the permanent, the formless light of truth which hears the voice of conscience while we observe the suffering around us everywhere, and hold out God's gracious qualities as a lamp in the darkness. If the suffering touches us directly, we come closer and closer to Him, knowing that He is our protection and our only comfort because He has the ultimate responsibility for all the good and evil, although their manifestation is determined by the choices we make. Instead of rushing back into the arms of the world when we are confronted with distress, a typical gesture of blind frustration, we learn new depths of surrender, new trust in Allah, using the grace of the *kalimah* to purify ourself further, to acknowledge and remove the blemishes we find there. Then we radiate His beauty, His qualities, and spread peace all around us no matter the difficulties we endure; because we are focused entirely on the light, the darkness disappears.

We are responsible only for the good and the bad emanating from our own actions, it is not relevant to our purpose on this path to judge anyone but ourself. We can't really know someone else's heart, know if that person is actually good or bad, this is God's jurisdiction, not ours. "Judgment is mine," saith the Lord. We find this scriptural admonition in all the monotheist traditions, but it is the purity of Islam, the surrender to light, which obliges us to look at ourself, to use that seat of justice lodged in the inner heart for personal reformation, discover our own shortcomings while we try to obscure someone else's faults instead of advertising them. It's easy enough to stop the verbal flow, the judgment all too ready to pour from the lips, what's harder is to silence the inner commentary which comes in many disguises, simple observation, character analysis, even a sympathetic nod. There's no room for this kind of action as long as we focus on our own inner landscape and bathe in the attributes of God with each purifying breath of prayer.

The Sufi injunction to die before death means the death of the world within us, the death of the pleasure and pain the world has to offer, and all the evil we house in this body of the elements we take as binding or real, even though it is quite clear to us, one day we have to give it up. This injunction means we are not dead to the world, the world is dead to us, we still function in it as a manifestation of grace, love and wisdom, we still exist but in a perfected state, embodying all that is good, all that is just and true. This is a truly exalted state, this

245

fourth step, *ma'rifat*, gnosis, divine wisdom in which we display nothing except His qualities and His wisdom. In that state there is no day or night and therefore no aging, there is neither birth nor death, the temporal no longer functions, only the eternal. Such rare beings do exist, and for those of us who have had the grace to spend time with someone like this, there is agreement about the happiness which spreads around them. They have a presence compelling the understanding of God, in part from the wisdom pouring through them, wisdom which can come only from the source of all knowledge, and in part from the luminous radiance of the divine, an unquestionable revelation of His existence and our proximity. The joy in this sense of being close to God is unlike pleasure, unlike the mere satisfactions of other experience, it is a transcendent bliss incomparable to anything else.

What is eternal is the good that comes from God, what perishes is the created evil that dies, the body which shrouds the tiny place in the heart that is the seat of prayer and worship. What belongs to the world dies, what does not die belongs to the divine kingdom in existence now and hereafter. All created things have a form which dies and a connection within it to God's grace, to His essence, the good, the eternal that has no

246

death. The good qualities we use to serve others here will become our servants there, but if we fail to bring them to life through our prayers of purification, through our good actions here, they will not be available there; if we fail to build our heaven with His loving qualities here, we will not have this place to live in there. When we discriminate between good and evil here, choose the good, stay in it with unflinching determination, without any reservation and eliminate the evil, when we have divine knowledge, perfect faith and purity, we stay in that place which comes from God and returns to Him.

In addition to the testimony of each part of our body at the time of death, two recording angels, one on the left shoulder who has noted down the wrongs we committed and one on the right who took note of the good we did, they will give their report while we are being questioned. The body will be in the ground; so what is it that faces this questioning? An inner body, a construct of thoughts, emotions, desires and the shadow forms of those entities which haunted us in life will rise up to be questioned, then face the consequences of the actions it led the outer body through while we lived. The evil qualities, all the bad things, the wrong thoughts and acts must suffer and be judged in the hell of separation from God, while the good qualities, if we have lived with goodness, will know bliss in the presence of God, His angels and all the heavenly beings, we will be in His kingdom, we will know this.

We must find that seat of justice within our own heart, use the powerfully purifying instrument of *la ilaha illallahu* to distinguish the good, all that belongs to God, from the bad, all that belongs to the elements; we must know the difference between the essence and the created then return to each what belongs to each. The beginning, the first step, our *shari'at* which is the knowledge of good and evil, pursued with unswerving diligence in the company of that wisdom and the divine attributes which grow in absolute faith, this can take us to our goal, the presence of God.

THE *QUTBIYYAT*

The *qutbiyyat* is the state of divine wisdom that knows God, understands His mysteries and can explain them. The *qutb* is the manifestation, the embodiment of this wisdom in human form, but the literal translation of *qutb* means axis, the pole around which the whole universe turns, and when some of these mysteries are revealed to us we comprehend the staggering extent of the literal implications too. If we are to have a truly meaningful idea of the *qutbiyyat,* we have to look at some of God's mysteries which have been revealed by a perfected human being, by a *qutb,* a being who exists in the world although the world no longer exists for him or for her. This person, and it might not even be correct to use the word person, has transcended the temporal and lives in the eternal, inseparable from God, displaying only His qualities and attributes, uttering only His words, doing only His duty.

The mystery of creation and the era before that, before time was inserted into our universal consciousness, before human consciousness was initiated, is something we have to look at again for the context to grasp the significance of this level of wisdom, this divine level which knows, which stood at the gates of creation, observed, understood and was given both permission and the capacity to explain what it was that happened, what it means for our understanding of the source, the origin, how all life began. These are mysteries which have nothing to do with science or with the methods of science, these explanations that come from revelation are acceptable to faith and the trust which is founded on that faith, but there is nothing to compel reason to acknowledge any of this, unless reason becomes the dedicated servant of an enlightened master. Fully realized human beings are rare enough; to have the grace which brings us to the *qutb* who is the leader of all such saints and illuminated beings is also rare, but only such a being has this divine knowledge and the authority to dispense it as God directs.

Bawa Muhaiyaddeen was the *qutb* whose presence in my life gave me access to the things he knew, to the grace which flowed from God through his sanctified existence; he is my source and my verification of the truth he offered, the truth he lived. Because he was unquestionably the exalted being he never claimed to be, because he spoke about things he could not have known if he was not that exalted being, we have been given knowledge and a perspective on three worlds containing countless universes whose secrets and mysteries do not approximate the least one of His. In our human consciousness, the wisdom this *qutb* proliferated on every imaginable subject concerning this and other worlds, that is the sixth level of wisdom or consciousness, the divine wisdom which analyzes, understands and explains. It is a level we are all endowed with although we do not all have access to.

This very high state represents a coalescence of grace, purity and capacity which we can slipstream in the presence of a truly enlightened teacher, another critically important reason to find the right master; there are secrets which can only be revealed by someone who knows them. We do have intimations, from time to time, of this wisdom's existence within our own experience that are both useful and engaging, we know what it is, we are committed to it, we want it yet it remains elusive, we do not have the ability to stay at this divine level of functioning wisdom as the *qutb* himself does. While we aspire to climb the levels of spiritual ascent, the *shari'at, tariqat, haqiqat* and *ma'rifat* steps to enlightenment, we are simultaneously moving through levels of wisdom, rising from the fourth level of discernment, discrimination or correct assessment, to pure wisdom as our faith deepens and our qualities change.

When an undesirable quality surfaces again, as it does, take anger, jealousy, vengeance or envy for example, we fall below the grace inspired level of pure wisdom and apparently below the level of discernment since we have already chosen to eliminate such wrongs. Nevertheless, the imperfectly controlled mind and the appetites of desire will sometimes resurrect things we no longer accept, and we move down instead of up. The work of prayer, the purification we have undertaken in our search for wisdom and truth will scrape away at the unacceptable until our own consciousness restores the purity eclipsed by these clouds. Progress is not necessarily defined by a straight line, it might waver for awhile, and this is the point at which the aspect of our faith called determination becomes specifically important. We must keep going, we must never abandon our pursuit merely because we make a mistake, because our wisdom falters, we must know that God will never let go of us, and so it is also up to us to hold on too.

There are many Sufi stories about the lives of certain *qutbs,* some quite transferable from one historical person to another, most of them illuminating the amazing wisdom and character of these remarkable beings. There are two stories I heard quite early in my discipleship which seem relevant here as an indication of their more human side: *qutbs* also need instruction and guidance, they do not merely emerge as a completed package, they begin as people like us, or so they say, they have extended periods of prayer, study and purification to undergo as well. The first story I heard was about Khwaja Mu'inuddin Chisti, a great Sufi who was responsible for the spread of Islam in India during the later twelfth and earlier thirteeth century. The name Mu'inuddin, which is a variant of Muhaiyaddeen, suggests the continuity of the wisdom embedded in Muhaiyaddeen, the reviver of pure faith. Although the physical embodiment might change, the light of God's transcendent wisdom from the beginning, from that period before the beginning, is an uninterrupted flame of truth.

Now it seems that God sent Khwaja Mu'inuddin to the north of India to revive the faith of the people there at a time when magic and sorcery dominated the hearts of many. As he went through through Delhi, he passed close to the king's gardens which included a magnificent orchard filled with exotic fruit. There was a pomegranate tree whose fruit was so ripe, so delicious and fragrant he was drawn irresistibly to it, and he crept in to take one piece of the fruit, but the king's guard saw him and chased him away. When the guard's back was turned Khwaja tried again, and again the guard caught sight of him, scolded him and sent him away. Three times Khwaja tried to pick a pomegranate for himself until, at last, he gave up and continued on his way to Ayothi in the north, a place where his path led through a dense forest up to the top of a tall mountain.

The dark, congested trail finally took him to a narrow passage through rocky boulders and towering cliffs where his way was blocked by an old man sitting astride the path, deep in meditation. Khwaja waited for some time, staring in wonder, watching as a huge wasp repeatedly stung the toe of this ascetic lost in his prayers. Finally unnerved, Khwaja addressed the old man, "Please, if you don't mind, could you just move a little so that I can continue my journey?"

"No," replied the old man, "Why should I move, this is my place."

"Well then, why can't you at least chase away the wasp that keeps stinging your big toe?"

"Why should you say anything to me, Khwaja, about one little wasp stinging my toe when the whole world is still stinging you?"

Khwaja was amazed, "How do you know my name?"

"I know who you are, Khwaja Mu'inuddin, and why you have come. How can you do God's work if you still have the whole world inside you? Three time you went back for a pomegranate that does not belong to you, yet God is sending you to teach the people pure faith. Don't you know you have to face a great sorcerer with enormous abilities who holds the people in his power, inspires them to blood sacrifices and actual murder to win the favor of their deities? This sorcerer already knows about your desire for the pomegranate; he won't hesitate to create the illusion of one that will appear to be even more delicious, but it will be poisoned fruit that will kill you."

Now Khwaja fell at the feet of the sanctified being blocking his way, begged his forgiveness and asked, "What am I supposed to do now?"

"Stay in this place for twelve years praying to Allah, then you will be rid of the world that still stings you." Khwaja Mu'inuddin Chisti prostrated at his feet, and when he looked up the old man had disappeared. So Khwaja took his place in the narrow passage among the rocky boulders and towering cliffs where he stayed for twelve years praying to God, until all traces of the world, ego and self had been obliterated.

This story was one of the first indications I had been given that the way was long, that I would have to stay with my guru, my teacher, for twelve years, initially not quite grasping that this twelve-year period was introductory, the time it would take to be rid of some of the darker qualities before the real work could begin. It was also told, I believe, to remind us that the *qutb* is a human being with strengths and weaknesses, with flaws like anyone else that must be overcome in a process involving minute self-inspection and prayer. This reminder serves to keep awake the idea that the sixth level of wisdom, divine wisdom is there and available if we are prepared to do the work. The other story about the training and instruction period the *qutb* must undergo is the same as the one I told earlier about the eternal prophet, Khidhr. I learned it first as a story focusing on the *qutb*, his initiation into wisdom and mystery.

The extraordinary being of unknown origin encountered in the Sufi world from time to time, Khidhr, who comes to instruct prophets, *qutbs* and all of us in the ways of God is now himself the teacher in this version of the story, one among the many traditional accounts told of his miraculous appearance and intervention in mortal affairs, one which sheds defining light on the earlier version. His role as a teacher during the life of a certain *qutb* Muhaiyaddeen in this story illustrates the revelatory work of a true guide who demonstrates God's truths experientially. He doesn't preach or punish, he describes, he shows, he lets us see what we need to see to be persuaded of the truth. Khidhr manifests in the life of this *qutb* to show him that God alone knows the meaning of a person's condition, that it is a mistake, it is wrong to suppose He doesn't know what He's doing, and it is also wrong of us to blame Him for things we are not in a position to understand.

In this version, one day Khidhr allowed the *qutb* to accompany him on his travels through the world, reminding him at the outset he might see things he would not understand, but he should hold his peace until the meaning became clear. Later in the morning they came to a beautiful little lake where some girls and boys were swimming and playing together happily, laughing and enjoying themselves, except for one boy, ten or twelve years old, who was sitting by himself, alone on the shore. The *qutb* looked hard at the boy, noticing with all his compassion that the child was blind, "Why is this poor boy blind, why should he be deprived of sight and prevented from playing like the others? O God it is not right, please give him eyes, restore his sight."

Khidhr listened to what the *qutb* said and observed, as Gabriel had once admonished him, "Didn't I say there would be things you might not understand, didn't you promise to say nothing until the meaning was clear?"

"Yes I promised, but now I see how the life of this child has been ruined by his blindness. God should grant him sight and let him look at the world." Because it was the *qutb* who made the request, the boy's sight was restored, and before they left to continue on their journey the *qutb* saw the child's delight and wonder as he splashed the water everywhere, playing with the other children. They continued on their way for about twenty minutes when Khidr suggested they should retrace their steps and go back the way they had come. "Why return there? Let's go another way," the *qutb* answered.

But Khidhr was firm, "No, no, we have to go back the way we came." They came to the lake where the children had been playing, where the boy who had been blind was still throwing water all around. Four of the eleven children were floating, dead, on the surface of the lake while the boy kept calling to the others, asking them to come and play.

"Now do you see?" Khidhr asked the *qutb* who stared at the scene in horror, "Now do you understand why this child was blind? In twenty minutes he has taken four lives, how many more will he take during his lifetime? If he continues to see he will cause the death of thousands and thousands in his life."

Appalled by the destruction the boy had already caused, the *qutb* pleaded with God to take away the sight he had so recently begged for. "O God," he prayed, "I was wrong to ask You for eyes for this boy, please take them away so that he can do no more harm to any living thing. Please forgive me, I was wrong, what I asked for was wrong because I did not know, I did not understand." In response to this, God not only took away the child's sight, he brought the dead children back to life.

The explanation of the story is that, in a previous life, the blind child had been a priest belonging to a satanic temple where he served a swami who lost an eye. The priest was sent out on a murderous round collecting replacement eyes wherever he could, until he came one day to one of God's saints who warned him not to take his eyes. "If you take my eyes you will have to come back blind in birth after birth," but the priest paid no attention to the warning and took the saint's eyes. The priest was reborn as the blind child, while the swami came back as the mother who had to look after him.

From the details of the story itself, and the explanation, we are to recognize several things. We do not understand our own inability to assess what we see in the world around us and mistakenly think that individual affliction or suffering is arbitrary, that God is at fault. We blame God for the suffering we heap upon ourself through our own actions, our own misconduct. God does not produce the horrors and atrocities abounding in the world, we do, we create the climate and conditions of our existence with our thoughts, our words and acts. God knows not only the end of the history but the beginning as well, yet we are deeply preoccupied with the middle alone, quietly oblivious to the whole story. Like the *qutb,* we have to learn how to climb the mountain of wisdom to see more and more as we get higher and higher, closer to the top where everything can be seen all at once. Like the *qutb,* if we undertake the journey we will find that wisdom because the truth is accessible.

These two stories are to show us something of the living embodiment of the *qutbiyyat,* the human manifestations who come to point out the untravelled path to God. The prophets came to give us God's commandments, say how we are to behave outwardly, what we need to do or avoid doing to fulfill our obligations to Him in the world. Messages came privately, in a mysterious and secret way from Him to the prophets who reported what God said to the rest of us, spreading this information as extensively as possible, making it as public as possible, but telling us only what God said, nothing more. The *qutbs* also receive secrets from God, their duty however, is a little different, they go beyond reporting because their messages are directed to higher levels of consciousness, the levels beyond intellect. As our wisdom matures, the *qutbs* give explanations which become deeper and deeper as we move from subtle wisdom to divine wisdom, and from there to the luminous wisdom of the *nur.* It is actually the *qutb* who becomes the divine wisdom offering explanations, then becomes the luminous wisdom which is the *nur,* the radiant light of His plenitude proclaiming His names and powers.

There are maps, directions, routes to follow for any worldly goal or destination, yet if we want to go to God we have to make our way alone, along a path we have to create ourself with the wisdom of perfect faith and absolute determination. We must go in a state which is our surrender to Him, which is the dedication of one-pointed concentration with complete balance and wisdom. If we make the decision to travel this path where we can have no arrogance, where we have to leave our karma and all illusion behind, where we have to leave our religion behind, we need to see the disembodied wisdom, the *qutbiyyat* which exists within each of us, we must have some understanding of what it is, how it works and how to use it.

We have both heaven and hell here within us now; the seven hells, our baser instincts come from the earth, fire, water, air, ether, mind and desire which compose the body of illusion that functions in the world, a body we have to control and transcend. Each of the seven hells is a deep chasm of fire ready to consume us, to reduce us to ash, and the only way across

262

these chasms is the bridge we build with the seven levels of consciousness, a wavering, fluctuating bridge which is as narrow as the seventh part of the seventh part of a hair. With wisdom we have to analyze, assess and understand everything until we discover the sixth level, the *qutbiyyat,* then with the wisdom of the *qutb* we enter the state of *la ilaha illallahu* in which we throw away everything but God, we are secure and established in the truth that nothing exists but God. From here we have to continue to the seventh level using the luminous wisdom, the light of the *nur* which is Allah, in complete, annihilating surrender to Him. Now we can cross that bridge which is able to transport the total surrender of one alone and nothing more, the other six levels have to be left behind or the bridge will not hold, we will fall in.

At the beginning, at the time of creation, each of the five elements witnessed the oneness of Allah in a state of purity. When the wisdom of the *qutbiyyat* restores the purity of their life, their essential nature, these five are transformed, they become five heavens instead of five hells. These five together with another three make eight heavens in the pure human form, the other three being the *anma* which is the essence of the elements, the *avi,* the pure spirit which functions with the soul, and the *ruh,* the soul which functions through light. It is only the conjunction of the *qutbiyyat* with the *nur* who is identified with the *Muhammad* of creation, two lights igniting each other, the luminous radiance of divine wisdom which can know the power of God because God Himself pulls these two lights into each other. This means we, as purified human beings, have to find the *qutb* within ourself, let that exquisite wisdom grow until we find the *nur* within the *qutb* and let that incomparable radiance flower, then we will know God, God will know God.

To be that purified human being in whom the *qutb* and the *nur* will grow, we have to transform ten of the twelve openings of the body which are two eyes, two ears, the nostrils, the mouth, the navel which has been sealed and two openings below. These are the ten in need of transformation along with the other two, the *'arsh,* the opening at the crown of the head and the *kursi,* the gnostic eye at the center of the forehead, both remaining in their state of original purity. We need to stay in a state of surrender with a teacher, an illuminated master, learning the meaning and transformation of these twelve that constitute twelve worlds within us.

The two lower openings are the openings of birth and of karma and arrogance; the poisons of jealousy, pride and envy which come through the navel are brought to life by anger, desire, hunger and passion; the master teaches us the qualities of patience, contentment and trust in God to overcome or transform what must be changed or eliminated, the wrong associated with each opening. He also teaches us to how to transcend the outer data of the eyes and ears so that we distinguish between what comes from God and what comes from mind and desire, we learn to see with His eyes and hear His sound, we use the breath flowing through the nostils to establish the *la ilaha illallahu,* throwing away all that is not God, affirming that He alone exists. The master teaches us how to use our mouth and tongue, how to taste His taste, use words which are good that cause no harm, words which are His, promoting the happiness of proximity, removing the sorrow of distance and separation.

When the ten worlds housed in our body are brought under control, the master can show us how to open the *kursi,* the gnostic eye God placed on our forehead, the *qutbiyyat* or light of wisdom which shines irresistibly as the *nur,* explaining everything we need to know, where we came from, who we are, why we are here, where we must go from here, how to reach that destination, everything, everything. Each one of these eleven openings in the body is a place where the *qutb* takes birth in us as the wisdom that clarifies, showing us how to be rid of the deadly characteristics where they exist, revealing the meaning and function of the *qutbiyyat* to be the purity and wisdom that point to the destination. The ultimate instruction from our enlightened master teaches us the connection between the gnostic eye and the *'arsh* at the crown of the head, our twelfth opening called the throne of God. Here God and the *qutb* as the *nur* shine together, one light illuminating both the crown and the eye of wisdom. It is the soul within the wisdom of the *qutb* which provides the explanations, and it is the *qutb* which is the mechanism that allows the *nur,* the light of God, to exist and be radiant in the purified human being.

STATES OF CONSCIOUSNESS

The world is a dream and we are the dreamers—we think we are awake, we think the world is substantial and real, that it exists as indubitably as Dr. Johnson believed when he kicked the stone to prove its solid reality. In fact, when we contemplate the totality, the mystery of God and His creation, we recognize that the unique characteristic of the reality which is the truth, the unwavering, unchanging truth, is permanence. Any created thing has a beginning and an end, it is only the uncreated which has neither structure nor content in time, it is only the uncreated which has no beginning or end; we may take this as a primary clue in our effort to solve the riddles of illusion. Illusion is suffering, reality does not cause any pain. For the most part, we carry on unthinkingly in the duality of the world, in the separations which constitute the sense of self and other, and for the most part, we are consequently subject to the spasms of unhappiness and even misery which accompany the dream.

267

How do we wake up from the dream, how do we begin to perceive what is true, what is actually real? Conventional descriptions of consciousness define four states of awareness, conscious and awake, asleep, unconscious and semi-conscious or comatose, that is, each one measuring a response to external stimuli, to the data of sensory perception which originate in the dream, in the illusion of the world. From the perspective of that wisdom which knows what is true, unless the 'I' has surrendered, has been effaced in the totality, we are asleep and dreaming we are awake, it makes no difference whether we describe it as waking, sleeping, conscious or unconscious, it has disengaged itself from the truth that is reality. To be awake we have to engage the inner planes of consciousness which are defined in terms of wisdom, the wisdom which has its origin in faith, in the reality of God within the heart and the heart within God.

We begin to be conscious, we begin to wake up when we start to question who we are and why we are here; only then do the curtains of sleep part slightly as we peer from the threshhold of the dream into the open space, move from the *la ilaha* to the *illallahu* where we affirm the reality as God and nothing but God. The trigger for this wakeup is different for each of us, a specific experience, an evolving process, a dream, a longing, a dissatisfaction, the unfulfilled conviction there must be an answer to the questions we scarcely know how to ask. Whatever the trigger, once we start to wonder if the earth will really be there again if we lift our foot off the ground, we can either be paralyzed by indecision or keep going until we discover what must be known. It is dangerous to turn back, useless to stand still, the only way is to keep trying, keep moving. The company of someone who has mastered steps beyond ours is essential, we need a guide, we need signposts, validation, direction, the experience of the experience.

The trigger is not necessarily a question, it could be a towering revelation of God's presence, so overwhelming, so persuasive, the need to hang onto it, to stay in this presence becomes an imperative dictating the search. Once the necessity of searching for the truth is established we proceed on our own as best as we can, we might study and read, we might entertain some of the practices we hear about or read about, we might consult individual sources which seem promising, we might march off in several wrong directions, going backwards instead of forwards, but no matter what we do or which way we go, if our heart is pure and our intention is strong God will not let us wander in darkness forever, He will send a guide and guidance. If our purpose here is to know Him and He sees us struggling to do that very thing, why should He deny us, why would He?

These progressive, ascending states of consciousness are like some post-Darwinian evolution of pure choice, states we choose to search for because we are dissatisfied with our own imperfection and the disappointing illusions of the world where the promises it dangles before us are found to be hollow, one after another, no matter how much we succeed or even fail. But these steps or states are not discrete at any of the levels, they tend to overlap somewhat, and sometimes we function at one level, sometimes at another, depending on the qualities and the depth of faith we bring to a specific situation. We can identify the unfolding layers of wisdom as states of being which change who we are—we change in every conceivable way, even physically, our face changes, our body changes. People who have known us a long time will look at us and ask what we have done to ourself, why do we look so different, and they will resent the change they see. As we move closer and closer to God, the world we used to know and live in will conspire to tug at us, try to pull us back and pull us down, expressing its inborn antagonism to God and the truth.

We aspire to these higher states because the soul which contains the light and the wisdom teaching us at the sixth level, the *qutbiyyat,* the soul knows that hunger for God which will never end except in the return to Him. It is the light which knows and directs the successive transformations because without this ultimate evolution, which is more than a revolution of consciousness, we cannot even rise to the place which is able to speak to Him, be in direct communication with Him. The *haqiqat* level of communion, the *mi'raj* or ascension so perfectly manifested in the mystical night journey of the prophet Muhammad, acknowledged by everyone as a genuine experience of God, is at least what we can know. If we can control the forces of mind and desire, the bonds attaching us to the world, we rise beyond the world, past all the distractions, the illusions, misconceptions and errors which manipulate capacity and harness our intention. During this experience we pass through stages and states which are those very exalted states except for the fact we cannot remain there, they are temporary, still attached to time, we have to come back. We hear the rocketing crash of planets and worlds as we go past them, the voices of this world calling us, teasing us, tempting us, but they cannot touch us for this brief excursion into that permanent timelessness which will not elude us forever.

271

States of consciousness have been classified or defined to help us analyze our position on the larger scale in relation to three worlds, where we have been before, where we are now and where we will be afterwards. On a smaller scale the analysis defines our movement on the pathless path, sometimes up, sometimes down. We have to know how to assess what we are doing, what we have done, so that we can modify what we will do; we have to correct our mistakes and eliminate our flaws, the weeds, to make room for the flowers of good thoughts, words and acts which are the true indicators of our qualities, our truth and divine knowledge. God so completely loves our truth that in a sense we can say He needs our truth just as we need His. The only meaningful things we have to offer Him are those qualities which are His, ignited by the wisdom which is His, the qualities of love, patience, mercy, justice, peace, contentment, truth, forgiveness, tolerance, compassion, goodness, the first, the last, the manifest, the hidden.

We need a guide who has gone on ahead of us and knows the way, we need to hear that wisdom and take the blessing pouring from the wisdom compressed in this experience; nevertheless, eventually we have to teach ourself, we have to learn how to change, how to acquire the qualities which will

272

waken His in us, and this must come from our own effort, this is the work we all have to do. It doesn't much matter where we are born, what we have been raised in, what we accept as the true description of who we are in relation to God, we all have the same work to do. If we love God with an open, melting heart, if we long to be one with Him, this heart must be ransacked and purified. There is no monopoly on bad qualities in the east or west: the qualities of anger, greed, jealousy, envy, fear, arrogance, cruelty all find an opportunity to flourish anywhere. These are the opponents we must engage until the world and our karma stop manufacturing them, until we are free of the bondage they require, the walls they erect between the truth and ourself.

In the mid to later years of the twentieth century it was common to hear descriptions of altered states of consciousness, states which were frequently although not invariably induced by psychotropic interventions like drugs, sensory deprivation, diet, yoga, mantras and other forms of self-hypnosis or persuasion. Whether the source of the changes discussed came from drugs or therapeutic spiritual practices, it should be clear by now that this is a different use of the word consciousness from the one we have been using here, a use

273

which refers primarily to the projection and reception of sensory data, more closely connected to illusion than to the wisdom that is connected to faith and truth. The so-called altered states do fall within the range of feeling, awareness and intellect, the lower three of the seven states whose analysis is most familiar from the frequent descriptions given by Bawa Muhaiyaddeen. The three lower states are certainly relevant to sense perception, recognition and the handling of perceptual data, although not to the specifically human characteristics which begin at the fourth level, the ability to assess or put some ethical value on the information.

There was an eagerness during these years to explore the techniques which might bring us, if not closer to God, at least closer to that mysteriously elusive peace we clamor for. At the same time as the expression altered states of consciousness was much in use, the words mind altering were also used more or less synonymously, and this seems quite accurate because the changes brought about by drugs or all the yogas or sensory deprivation affect the mind, which is in and of itself a primary source of illusion, and not a pathway either to God or to peace. Still, if the mind has a lock on the understanding, asserting a supremacy it cannot rightly claim even though it does, and that mind's grip is relaxed or changed, if sensory data are experienced in variable forms, it is possible that these changes can open up or illuminate the essentially human discernment which can say this is right, this is wrong. Then when that recognition becomes available we can initiate the first step of wisdom, the beginning of the spiritual journey, the consciousness which gives us access to the capacity to discern and distinguish right from wrong.

Before this, in the first three steps or stages of a consciousness that might become wisdom in the progression or development which, with the right guidance, will build on them, in these first three steps, feeling, awareness and intellect, we are merely gathering and manipulating data. Feeling here does not refer to a state of mind or an emotion, I feel happy, I feel sad, it refers instead to the sensation we feel when something touches our skin, whether it's only a hair or the blow of a hammer, we feel something, that feeling. The consciousness that is cognizant of this feeling, the mechanism which transfers the information to and translates it for the brain is awareness. Now we know that something has touched our arm. The third level of consciousness, intellect, decides what happens next; it is intellect which handles the information and determines what

275

follows, if it's just a hair the hand will brush it away, if it should be the blow of a hammer it might be necessary to develop a complex plan of action.

In the west at least, there is a traditional insistence upon an intellectual ascendance which this systematic understanding of consciousness does not subscribe to. Here intellect is considered to be a rather debased level no different from the problem solving ability of nest building birds and shelter seeking or foraging animals. Intellect deals with cause and effect, plan and mobilization in much the same way that a map lays out terrain without indicating the route—put to the right use, intellect is a useful servant but never the master. This is not to be confused with the anti-intellectual bias of the uninformed, it is quite different; in fact, there is also another tradition, especially among the romantics and neo-romantics, which tends to make intellect the villain of the piece, as Hawthorne does in *The Scarlet Letter,* for example. In the understanding we are dealing with in this method of classifying seven levels of consciousness, intellect is not so much a villain as the corruptible servant of mind and desire. When it is used as an adjunct of wisdom however, it becomes a valuable instrument to help in the search for truth. Bawa

Muhaiyaddeen used to tell us there is a certain swan in the east which is so subtle, if you give it a dish of milk mixed with water it will pick out the milk and leave the water. This is the proper use of intellect which is not to be thrown away, not to be despised, merely controlled.

At the fourth level we have the level that practises ethical discernment, that looks at the reckless propositions of intellect and accepts or rejects them with the wisdom which distinguishes right from wrong, true from false. This ethical concern is uniquely human, there is no right or wrong in the animals' world because they have no choice, no input in who and what they are. We anthropomorphize their characteristics because we recognize some of our own baser instincts in their behavior, we see arrogance in the elephant, rapacity in the tiger, cunning in the monkey, savagery in the lion, sometimes even offering respect for the very qualities we dare not admire in ourself. But the truth is, they do what they do and they are what they are without any sense of right and wrong because there is no such thing for them, without choice there is no ethical component. All the animals pray to God, each one worships God in its own way, but God has given Adam and his progeny certain gifts he has withheld from the rest of creation,

He has given us the freedom to accept or reject Him, to know or disregard Him, to be good or bad, pure or impure, to love or to hate.

God has given us sets of opposites to learn the truth, learn the secrets, to immerse ourself in the mysteries no other living creature has the capacity to understand. This capacity begins with the ethical assessment which constitutes the fourth level of wisdom or consciousness. The good we choose and the bad we fail to eliminate are not remote considerations of some life in the hereafter we are not ready to contemplate, we have to use the wisdom we possess to choose correctly here, understand the difference between right and wrong here so that we can pass judgment on ourself before we die, so that we can identify ourself exclusively with the good and come to that place of death before death where the world has already died within us. With the understanding of right and wrong we begin to know something about the life of the soul, where it came from, what it came from, where it will go; as we begin to know ourself we begin to know God.

But this fourth level of wisdom which functions on the basis of perceived external phenomena is limited by the illusory nature

278

of the things it has to assess, the earth, fire, water, air and ether or outer space which it takes to be both substantial and real. This is not the wisdom of faith, the wisdom which knows with absolute conviction that there is something permanent, there is one God; it is not the wisdom which can discover that God is One. For this we have to proceed to the fifth level, subtle wisdom, the wisdom which can extract the essence of the things the previous level can only examine outwardly, from here we begin the inner examination, moving into a world which is as different as quantum physics is from Newtonian physics. Here we plunge into the mystery of the unknown, the heart is turned upside down as the point which once faced the earth is now directed up towards God. The journey on the pathless path has begun—subtle wisdom takes the discernment of the fourth level into an examination of essence, recognizing and understanding permanence, discarding illusion.

The ascent to this fifth level of being represents the wisdom called *tariqat*, the path which corresponds to the second major step in the spiritual progression to the One. At this level we have found a teacher, a guide who knows how to point the way and illuminate what lies ahead. Generally in Sufism, an aspirant has a succession of teachers, learning from one and

279

then passing along to the next who explores a deeper aspect of the consciousness to be established, and the process might go on for years, possibly continuing for the lifetime of the disciple. My own experience has been slightly different however, Bawa Muhaiyaddeen has been the only teacher I've had on this journey, although I do see that many of the experiences which apparently preceded my connection to him were teachers in a different sense, as they are for us all. I have to say apparently because it is still unclear to me at what point in the stream of my life the connection was formed on some other plane.

If we have the grace of a teacher who can give us everything there is no need for more than one, but we have to know that to know that. Subtle wisdom guided by the right teacher means a change in personal qualities, the slow, deliberate uprooting of anger, arrogance, envy, intolerance, and an understanding of our life and the karma embedded in it. We have already committed ourself to choosing the good, the just, the loving, the compassionate, now we engage in the scrupulous adherence to the good and the absolute avoidance of the bad. When we fail in this intention, if we lose our temper, get angry or jealous, behave with less than compassion, we drop below wisdom until we establish ourself in the good, the loving once more. Our karma and our less than perfect qualities are like an illness, recovery is not always in a straight line, we have good days and bad days, but the important thing is to keep going and never give up. We are supposed to learn from our mistakes, not repeat them, yet inevitably we do for a time. If our intention remains firm and our commitment to God and the truth do not falter, we will act wisely again, if for no other reason than this subtle wisdom is so irresistible.

A characteristic of this level, this state, is that things we once accepted as self-evident and true now seem false, especially along the ethical/aesthetic axis. What we once found appropriate in terms of the world and its values will now seem false as we learn the values of God and His kingdom, and as this wisdom begins to shed its luminous grace on our experience, the darkness of our karma, our inappropriate thoughts will dissipate in its light because the light always dominates the dark, the *illallahu* obliterates the *la ilaha*. This is the wisdom which takes us to inner patience, absolute contentment and gratitude, to complete trust in God, surrender to Him and the unconditional praise of pure worship, this is the wisdom we use to dig for the truth, to release the waters of revelation lying deep within us which alone satisfy the thirst of the soul and carry us beyond the currents of illusion.

For most of us who are seekers on the pathless path, sometimes we fall below this fifth level and sometimes we rise above it, most of the time however, this is the level on which we do our work, this is the level on which we cut our attachments, subdue our mind and control desire. Subtle wisdom is the platform we use to launch our qualities, to investigate the inner pathways leading us to God and His truth, first by moving through the five outer senses, the outer obligations, into the six inner senses, the inner obligations which teach us to see with His eyes, hear with His ears, speak with His words, taste with His tongue, detect fragrance with His nostrils and know truth with the inner heart. When we search for this truth in a state of wisdom, with the consciousness which knows where the truth is to be found, an inner beauty of stunning light appears on the face, a visible light.

The truth does not reveal itself on its own, we have to use this wisdom to keep examining words, acts and thoughts until we discover the strength of the inner meaning, until the power is known which gives meaning to meaning and light to light.

282

Wisdom and its acquisition are not a burden, on the contrary, this is the only way to relieve ourself of the weight of the world we carry around with us wherever we go. The world we have invested in, the whole world we keep inside us, the dramas, attachments, the illusions and desires, these are the burdens that weigh us down, but once wisdom begins to function we can look at this heaviness, see it for what it is and throw it all away. Wisdom is characteristically weightless, like light, and until we are in that state of light, until we examine the inner dimension of each thing, each word and act, we do not know that weightless joy.

There is a secret hidden within the manifest, the outer form, which only wisdom can penetrate, and the secret within our human form is this divine, subtle wisdom which contains its own secret, and that secret contains another secret which in turn contains more secrets within secrets that we must unfold, we must investigate one by one until we come to the ultimate hidden truth, the radiant light which is the power of God, until our wisdom merges with His and our light merges with His. When wisdom which is the key unlocking all these hidden secrets emerges, then we see God in everything, wherever we look He is there, we are lost in the pure wonder of His presence and our only happiness is expressed as gratitude to Him, as worship of Him. When the light of our wisdom becomes bright, it is a radiance which attracts God's light and pulls it in, then we can understand His words, His power, then we can understand the mysteries within the secrets.

The *qutbiyyat* was described first, in the last chapter, because it is the *qutb* functioning as subtle wisdom which takes us to the place which can see, which can understand, and then the *qutb* emerges as the *qutbiyyat,* the sixth level of wisdom, the analytic wisdom which unravels these mysteries. Beyond this sixth state of consciousness the *qutb* emerges as the *nur,* the radiant light of God's plenitude, the seventh level of consciousness which is to be found in that ultimate surrender alone, complete annihilation in God, when day and night, birth and death are transcended, and nothing exists but God. It is only in this state of total surrender, existing in the *nur,* the light of absolute divine perfection that we can merge with God; we exist as a ray of light, and this means the previous six states of consciousness have been given up. This is *ma'rifat* in terms of spiritual ascent, when we are engaged with Him as the *nur,* and beyond this is *sufiyyat* when we merge with God in the form of light and disappear in Him altogether.

When the *nur* within the *qutb* emerges within us, God shows us everything, the light of the *nur* which is the *Nur Muhammad* Allah placed on the forehead of Adam and the children of Adam, God shows us all the worlds compressed within the twelve openings of the body and the five elements. He shows us the totality of our being, our history and our non-history in the timelessness before and after, everything we want to know, everything we need to know. If this light, this *nur* which came from God, if this state of consciousness or wisdom is made luminous within us, it will go back to God and lose itself within Him, light merging indistinguishably with light.

Sufi

SURRENDER AND THE *ALHAMD*

The *alhamd* is the heart of all praise formed by five Arabic letters, *alif, lam, mim, ha'* and *dal* in a state of absolute surrender to God. We say *al-hamdu lillah,* we offer all our praise to God alone, and that is the praise of the purified heart in a state of surrender. What is the meaning of surrender, how are we to approach this perfect instrument of submission to God in duty, intention, expectation, fulfillment, the completion of experience, the totality of who we are inwardly and outwardly, how are we to understand it? It's not a military kind of surrender when we hold up our hands because we've run out of options for the moment, we are defeated in battle but determined to continue the war, it's clearly not that kind of temporary acquiescence to the inevitable, it's an unconditional surrender which not only ends the war, it turns over every implication of futurity in any sense to the One we surrender to. We do not plan, we submit to His plan; we do not think, we allow only His thought to flow through us; we do not pray, we are the praise in Him and He is the praise in us.

How do we arrive at that state which takes us to Your will my God, not ours, a state which is neither defeated nor supine — on the contrary, it is vigorous, active and filled with an energy that must express itself in service to Him, duty in word, act and thought. From the description of the highest states of consciousness, we know that deepening levels of surrender take us to higher levels of wisdom, yet we also know that God alone can take us there. We have to strip the ego bare of all the garments it has chosen to wear, the I am a poet, I am a scholar, I am a Sufi, even the I am a lover of God; anything which separates or individuates must be thrown away.

Then there are the desires and attachments which the ego or the self uses to identify itself to itself, I am attached to my children, to my family, my country, my job; we don't have to abandon our responsiblities, we have to detach the attachment so that we fulfill our obligations without expecting anything back. I have raised my child with such love and care, now he must be devoted to me; I have done my job with with such excellence, now I must be given a raise; I have served my country with such diligence, now I must be honored. All these presumptions are built into our unthinking assessment of who and what we are at the level of the mind which has nothing to do with wisdom or surrender. We have to reperceive our relations to each other, to the world and to God, subtracting the demands of selfhood so that we do what we do without expectation, without conditional reservation, we simply do it.

The desires which clutter the landscape like a jungle have also to be dealt with, but we can't just turn them off as if they were water flowing from a tap, we have to be careful and subtle. We can't say to the mind, sorry, you won't have this anymore or it will howl like a two-year old, what we have to do is promise to give it what it wants a little later, not refusing outright, merely deferring for awhile, extending the time frame of the possible. Eventually, the things we have clamored for do subside, although it usually takes longer than we think it will. No matter how enlightened we are, no matter the spiritual gifts we are granted, even if we smell the sweetest roses in midwinter, we are required to do this long-term work of changing our qualities, getting rid of mood, disposition and the inclinations which stand between God and ourself. Without bringing about these changes we remain someone who has had interesting experiences, but we do not illuminate anyone or anything, and we do not penetrate the mysteries of surrender. It really doesn't matter what religion we are born to, what spiritual capacity we begin with, we are all required to undertake the same reclamation, the same reformation of thought, attitude, emotion and action. No one is born with it all, no one has earned a free passage, although admittedly, a few very rare beings have less work to do than others.

It's not so hard to map the character flaws in those we know, much harder to have that perspective on ourself; nevertheless, we can use the information we acquire from looking at others to study ourself. If we see a tall man strutting with unrestrained ego and arrogance, learn something, don't find fault with him, turn that spotlight inward because we will find inside what we were only able to recognize outside. Learning to identify the areas of our persona we have to labor with is only the beginning, an important beginning, however nothing more than the first step of what is sometimes a long journey. Here that aspect of absolute faith which is described as determination is crucial, we must keep going in the right direction, we must proceed even if progress is so slow it seems invisible. And this is the work of the prayer mat, this is what our prayers are about before we can know the depths of surrender and the heights of wisdom. What complicates the process sometimes is that our very strength can be a double-edged sword, it can be our weakness too; there is only a fine line between determination and stubbornness, between innocence and ignorance.

To purify the heart so that it will resonate as the *alhamd,* the heart which has nothing, holds nothing but truth and the resonance of His praise, this is the true nature of prayer. This purification entails the surrender of everything the ego who is the representative, the spokesperson of mind and desire, would like to keep; and so the battle lines are drawn, a battle which is the great battle, the only battle of true Islam, fought and lost or won in our prayers, not with each other. When we look at the five outer obligations of Islam, the ritual duties known as the five pillars, with the need to understand what this surrender means, we can see them as steps or phases in the surrender of every cherished obstacle we encourage and permit to block our way.

If we do not exist in the oneness, the perfected surrender in Allah, the absolute faith that is the first obligation, then we must use the prayers of the second obligation to bring us there, relinquishing the responsibility for every step in our life to Him; and if this does not induce a total depth of surrender, we have to give away everything, charity to those who are in need or those who have less than we do, we have to give away the world and the things of the world, acknowledging that God is our only wealth, existing in the prostration of absolute faith; then if we are still not successful we have fasting, knowing the hunger and suffering of the poor as the next instrument to take us over the obstacles we refuse to surrender; and finally we have pilgrimage, the journey to the heart, the death before death when we go in a shroud as if to the grave, we have this fifth prescribed duty to take us to absolute surrender, absolute faith, oneness with God.

We ask God to forgive us for the mistakes we have made in the past, we praise, we exalt Him now at this moment, this breath in time, and we surrender the next breath to Him because it is up to Him whether we will live to breathe it or not. This surrender means that we have unconditional trust in Him, then even the desire for Him is extinguished and we can truly know what the death before death is, we can contemplate our physical death knowing there is nothing we are still accountable for. If we do not surrender we do not have the wisdom which alone can acquire divine knowledge, knowledge of ourself and of Him. If we do not lift up our hands and say there is nothing we can do, everything that happens occurs only with His consent and permission, we will not be able to relinquish the things thrust upon us by family, society, religion, culture, karma, illusion, preference and desire, we will not be able to free ourself of the hidden and visible networks constructed by the ego for preservation of the self.

It is possible to surrender everything all at once, it is posssible to give it all away at any one moment and know that complete liberation of the soul, it is possible until the very last moment of our life on earth, and if we are successful God will receive us. It is however, more usual to give up one thing at a time, perhaps over a period covering many years, as we discover what we once thought we needed is actually a burden, as we discover the weight of the props and ornaments suspended from our ego and learn the weightlessness of pure wisdom. Quite often things simply fall away on their own, no special effort required, we just realize we are done with a thing and it slips away. Each thing we discard like layers of clothing on a day which is suddenly hot brings us closer and closer to contentment and gratitude; they are the signs of trust in God

293

and the surrender which is the pathway to divine knowledge, to the merging with His light, the highest state we can know, illuminating everything.

The twenty-eight letters of the Arabic alphabet mystically, that is to say actually, compose the letters of an inner Qur'an which is the human body, an inner body, a book of truth we must learn to read so that we can comprehend our essential nature as it remains inseparable from God, His truth and His light. Some years ago, at the request of his disciples, Bawa Muhaiyaddeen made a drawing indicating the arrangement of these letters making up the human form, a drawing we affectionately refer to as the alphabet man. The letters we need to look at more closely are the *alif, lam, mim, ha'* and *dal* which form the *alhamd*, the inner heart, the purified heart resonating His praise. There is an equivalent to this in the Hindu tradition, the *na, ma, si, va, ya* which is recited as the *namasivaya* we recite in our unperfected state and as the *sivayanama* in our perfected or purified state, the prayer, like the heart, inverted so that the point looks up to God. The literal understanding of the *namasivaya* prayer is that it is the foundation of both religion and divine wisdom, it is the way to secure release from future births and union with the supreme deity, the One.

294

The *alhamd* in its purified state is known as the *aham,* the inner heart, from which the names Ahamed and Ahmed are derived, names which mean the beauty of the heart. To investigate the meanings compressed in the *alhamd* entails diving into its components, the individual letters taken one by one. But first, there are six letters in its English transcription, (although in the Arabic itself, which we are primarily concerned with, there are only five) collectively representing the six constants of our human existence, the five elements, earth, fire, water, air and ether or space from which our body is formed, and the most important sixth aspect, the light which is our soul, our life itself. The *alhamd* is body and the soul, in an unpurified state initially, then purified through the labor of prayer, the labor of surrender, the labor of transforming our imperfect qualities.

The opening chapter of the Qur'an, the *Suratul-Fatihah* is also called the *Suratul-Hamd,* that is, the *surat* or chapter of *alhamd,* the praise. When we open the chapter of *alhamd,* the praise, read the letters which make up the words composing the *surat,* our body or form, and when we understand the meaning of offering all our praise to Him, this is the opening, the beginning of understanding ourself and knowing Him. The *Fatihah* also refers to a set of prayers frequently recited which consists of this *surat* or chapter and the three short, final chapters of the Qur'an, four chapters corresponding to four areas in the human form, to earth, fire, water and air and to the four steps, the *shari'at, tariqat, haqiqat* and *ma'rifat* of spiritual ascent. The *Suratul-Hamd* is a key unlocking mysteries within mysteries if we can recognize it as the doorway to our form and all that is concealed there. The *alhamd* is the inner heart of the twenty-eight letters which make up the inner human form.

The *al-hamdu lillah* which offers all praise to Allah, to God alone, follows the total submission and surrender of our open heart to the One whose responsibilty we recognize for every aspect of our existence, our life which is filled with the things we consider good and the things we want to push away from ourself because they seem too difficult to bear, too hard to handle. We say *al-hamdu lillah* for the good and the bad in our life because the failure to do so is a failure in gratitude, a failure to understand the totality. He alone knows the outcome of every situation, He alone knows whether a thing is actually good or bad for us, He alone will reveal everything as His gift, He alone will show us the strength we can learn in disaster. *Al-hamdu lillah* is the strongest ship to take us through the roughest seas, it is the hand of His grace steering that ship.

This affirmation of faith in Him is the pure recognition of His responsibility for everything, it is the only way to have nothing and be nothing, to reach that exalted state of *la ilaha illallahu* where there is no 'I,' no ego, it is gone, submerged, because everything belongs to God, we have no thoughts, no words, no intentions or actions which are not His. Since we are subject to change, and all that exists in the world around us is subject to change, we need that *al-hamdu lillah* which has put absolute certainty in His management of our affairs, which will bring us to a changeless place of permanence and gratitude, of complete contentment with whatever comes, whatever happens. It is entirely possible for the *al-hamdu lillah* to come as a direct transmission from an enlightened master to his disciple, an opening or awakening to grace which inexperience and inability might otherwise blind the student to; it is not a thought or an emotion, it is a revelatory state, a condition which arises through specific transformation.

The *alif, lam* and *mim* of the *alhamd* form a group of their own unconnected to earth, they are instead the body of light within a truly human being. These three are not in any way a trinity in the Christian sense, more like a triptych or a three-part harmony in which each voice resonates distinctively yet is subsumed in a unitary sound as they emerge from and return to the One. The *alif* is Allah; *lam* is the light of the *nur* and the *qutb,* the wisdom emerging from the *nur;* and the *mim* is the *Nur Muhammad* of creation, the *Muhammad* about whom God has said He would not have created anything without this, without him. To know who we really are and to know God, and to understand the importance of the right teacher, we must understand these letters. We are *Muhammad,* the *mim;* the *lam,* the light is inside us; and the *alif,* Allah, is within that light. When we have as our sheikh, our teacher, an enlightened master who has merged with God, the letters represent God, the sheikh merged with God and the disciple merged with the sheikh, three distinct lights shining, only one visible: God, wisdom and the soul are one.

In Arabic, the *alif* is represented by a single stroke, a line, the letter *l* which corresponds to the English letter *a,* the beginning, the first letter of the alphabet, and it is also the number one, the One. When we say God is One we mean more than there is only one God, we mean that there is only one reality, one permanence which is the totality containing everything, everything that exists. This character, this letter *l* in Arabic is mute, unvoiced without a diacritical mark above or below it to show us how to pronounce it, just as God Himself is unvoiced unless we function as the notation to give Him sound, to do His work. The seven diacritical marks of the Arabic alphabet are the seven states of consciousness within each of us, the resonance of wisdom, the instruments of God.

The *lam* is the light, the radiant plenitude that emerged from Allah at the time of creation, the essence from which the light of wisdom emerged, both impressed as the *Nur Muhammad* on the forehead of Adam, the gnostic eye. From the plenitude compressed in the *Nur Muhammad,* He brought all creation forth, His attributes made manifest. The *lam* is the light which is the divine explanation called the *qutb,* successive phases of inner wisdom revealing the secrets, the mysteries within this light. If we leave the body and go into the heart of wisdom, we exist in this light as His light. The *mim* itself is the inner heart, the *Muhammad* who took form; he appeared again and again on earth in two hundred and one successive manifestations it is said. The *mim* is creation, the created, the pure light form filled with the longing to return to its source, the origin which is the totality of One.

299

The *ha'* and the *dal* of the *alhamd*, the *h* and the *d* in this transcription are related to the physical, the material of the human form. The *ha'* of the *husna*, His beauty, makes a protective repository in the crown of the head, the throne of God, for the *asma' ul-husna*, the ninety-nine beautiful names of Allah. The ninety-nine names of God are alive with His essence, His attributes, His secrets and His praise, all resonating in this letter of the *alhamd*. When we who have our source in His essence learn these names and recite them as praise, in worship of Him, realizing their significance, our praise of Him becomes the ultimate divine name, the one hundredth name, Allah, God, the truth and the reality shining with His grace, with His *nur*. In this way the *ha'* protects the *alif, lam* and *mim* within His ninety-nine names.

The fifth letter which is the *dal* is the world, the *dunya*, the human body, the illusion forming a part of creation. Although it comes from God, it is everything rejected by God, filtered out in the purifying process that produced the emerging light. This fifth letter, the world, illusion, the forms taken by desires, by the lesser deities projected in our thoughts and emotions all manifest as the separations, prejudice, bigotry and pride of the ego which cannot conceive of anything greater than itself.

Even though the five elements from which the substantial world was created began by affirming their oneness with God, they cause havoc and ruin because they fight against each other. Nevertheless, the *alif, lam* and *mim* protected in the *alhamd,* the heart of all praise, exist forever.

Sufi

THREE WORLDS
AND THE SEARCH FOR TRUTH

If we habitually perceive ourself in relation to the world of the senses, what we see with our outer eye, hear with our ear, taste with our tongue, feel with our hands, then we fail to perceive ourself except in relation to the world of illusion, a world of deliberate deception. The deception occurs because the evidence is so persuasive, Dr. Johnson kicking the stone, it occurs because we have been taught to accept it as the reality we ought to engage, because we have lost any consciousness of the divine kingdom where we began in the world of souls and have little faith in the world to come, the hereafter which sweeps down from beyond surrounding the here and now in the eternal.

Yet we all have small scale recognition of the illusory nature embedded in the sensory information we take for granted, we have seen the railway tracks converging as they curve away down the road, the ship diminishing in size as it moves closer to the horizon, we recognize color blindness and acknowledge the individual nature of taste in food, some repelled and some attracted by the same thing, or auditory cognition, bliss for me but hell for you, we have this small scale recognition that we are deceived, that what we take to be true may be false or only true for me and not for you, but we brush it away large scale. How can the whole world be nothing more than misconception, how can we be deluded when the evidence for this world is so overwhelming and the evidence for that world is so elusive? The fact is we are using the wrong instruments to look, to hear, to taste, to smell, the fact is we do possess instruments of immense subtlety which function in bliss when the senses, ego and intellect are controlled and subdued.

The outer senses work with and for the elements, the earth, air, fire, water and ether or space components of our material form, the physical we take for the total when the opposite is true, it is less than partial, the shadow cast in the presence of light, the dream of the sleeper who never wakes. This is the secret we have to be told, this is the mystery we have to penetrate before the light form of the soul becomes a persistent reality in our experience. We are composed of the material and the non-material, the human and the divine, the left and the right; to impose the exclusivity of the one upon the other is to deny who we are, to deny the life of God within us and our life within Him. To reach beyond the physical we need first to accept the intimations which have haunted us offstage, signs of the unseen we questioned and rejected as too improbable to accept, those immortal whispers we look upon as coincidence, as accident, as synchronicity or whatever words we choose to disguise the information reaching out to us from another realm, another level of wisdom or consciousness.

Sometimes, it is true, we find it hard to distinguish what is genuine input rising through the intimacy with an impeccable source from the imaginary speculation inspired in the hotbed of mind and desire, and if we accept these prophetic murmurs as valid, if we act upon distant warnings and go another way, cancel a plan or change a decision because of these forebodings, we never know if they were right or wrong, true and accurate or false and misleading. If we ignore them however, we'll know with certainty when it's too late, when we cannot undo what once was future and now is past. On the whole, better to act upon these admonitions than to ignore them, until we are competent to tell them apart. If we choose to accept these signs from a level of consciousness which is higher up the mountain and therefore sees farther along the path we're travelling, once we understand that successive levels of wisdom do exist, then the elements that function as the physical form and servants of intellect interfere less and less with our perception of the light form which houses our connection to God. Only when we enter the light and the worlds of light do we leave behind the relativity of outer sensory perception and encounter absolutes.

In the search for truth we have to differentiate between knowledge and wisdom. Knowledge is an accumulation of information about things, objects which exist in God's creation that are known, measured or grasped through the admittedly fragile sensory data of this world, a world which constitutes nothing more than deception; wisdom is our access to the divine and our understanding of the divine that comes from faith, that deepens as we purify ourself, as we eliminate obstacles to absolute faith. Our wisdom and faith together must fall in love with God, be so persuaded of His omniscient totality, His unique omnipresence that we live in the truth of *la ilaha illallahu,* only God exists, You are God, You are Allah. Then we hear, we understand the resonance of One, the sound which comes from Him, which responds and vibrates sympathetically with the tuning fork of truth in our own heart. The truth is one and God alone is One; what we hear coming from the world is the resonance of deception, the multiplicity of disturbances coming from the master of deception, the dark satanic force ruling this world, a world which belongs exclusively to mind and desire. What comes from God and ends in God is the truth known to wisdom alone.

When we think of who we are and how we live, persuaded by the lies we take for truth, how is it possible to disconnect ourself from the illusions propagated by the senses, how do we engage the reality of where we were and where we will be? First, our faith must be made strong, so strong it sees through the sensory limits of the things in the world to the beating heart of truth, God's presence in His creation, in every atom of His creation, in everything that breathes and does not breathe, in everything that moves and does not move, in everything that speaks and does not speak. The trees, the grass and the mountains worship God because their life exists in the certainty of Him, the animals everywhere, each in its own way, worship His immanence in them; we alone, the human creature endowed with the gift of wisdom, of knowledge unavailable even to the angels, we alone are free to discredit and disbelieve. There is no compulsion in Islam, if we choose not to know, not to worship, God still protects and feeds us until our final breath when we become accountable, when our strengths and our weaknesses are assessed, because we are given until the final in-breath and out-breath to acknowledge the reality, to discard the illusion.

Along with the perfecting of our faith must come a profound purification of the self, including our intentions, words, thoughts and especially the acts. Prayer, which begins in the meditative struggle to know our own flaws and failures, a purposeful examination of each dark shadow, is a primary instrument to move us from the world of the senses into the realms of light. Prayer and the ascent to higher and higher levels of wisdom, for which God alone is responsible, take us from the outer understanding of the obligations described as the five pillars of Islam, the faith, ritual prayer, charity, fasting and pilgrimage, to the inner understanding at the level of gnosis, divine wisdom. Here we learn the perception of the inner senses that look only at God, long only for God, recognize God alone; here we find the inner eye which sees what He sees, the inner ear which hears His sound, the subtle tongue which savors His taste and utters His words, the inner nostril breathing His fragrance and the melting inner heart of His compassion.

The true companion of this prayer, this *dhikr,* the remembrance of God, is the deliberate change in the way we act, the way we are, because if we do not make these necessary changes we can pray until the dissolution of time without changing a thing, we can pray for ninety-nine years and still be arrogant, still be the toy of desire. Without this necessary reclamation of the inner landscape the body of light cannot manifest and emerge, without the fine cultivation of God's qualities by nourishing those pure seeds within ourself and cultivating the soil which fosters their growth, we are lost in the elements and the illusory propositions they espouse. It's not at all difficult to be disengaged from the world, not at all difficult to disavow the ephemeral, the material, to choose the permanent and perfected once we taste the ashy flavor of the world, once we recognize the restlessness and recurring dissatisfaction surrounding the sweetest moments of worldly pleasure, worldly triumph, that unfulfilled sense of now what, what's next?

Some dispositions find it easier than others, if we have ever been in love with the arts, with music or painting and poetry, we know that we never placed so high a value on the things of the world, but the attachment to the delight of the outer senses, or to an aesthetic which has little to do with God and everything to do with gratifying these senses, that is an equivalent difficulty. We are here to taste the world, to learn from the world, recognize the sweetness it has to offer and say yes, this is good, this is very good, but it's not good enough; like Abraham, we want the sun that never sets. The difficulty of leaving the world behind is made more difficult by the demands and attachments of parents, family and friends who want us to want the world, want the things they want so that we look like them, talk like them, act like them, and when we don't, when we turn our face away from the world and begin the search for God, the whole world rises up in protest to attack our choice, our evident disavowal of them, our preference for the divine over the human.

When they try to pull us back, turn us from our intention by offering something they think we have always wanted, and perhaps we have, perhaps we did, we feel that tug of the world once more, we remember the longing and the sense of loss that went with it, then we have to have a steadfast affirmation that the pathless path is there, the guides are there, the light is there, our light which may be only a candle in the dark or a floodlight is waiting to become one with the source of all light. It is true that a good, loving human being is rare, that a wise human being is rarer still and a perfected individual is infinitely rarer, yet they exist and the capacity to become such a purified being is alive in each of us. If we want to know ourself, if we want to know God and offer service as He does, it is essential to persist in the possible, we have to be alive in the possible, vibrate with the reality of continuity and never give up, never turn back or turn away.

It doesn't really seem to matter whether we find ourself on this Sufi journey through our residence in time in the Christian, Hindu, Muslim or Judaic context because the truth is one and God is One. There are certain patterns to contemplate: paradigms of selflessness; paradigms of recovery from illusions rampant in the world and this world itself, illusion propagated by our outer senses working in tandem with mind and desire; paradigms of the earnest examination of ourself and our karma without judging anyone else, without finding fault with anyone else; paradigms of duty or service to all living things; of unity and merging, the convergence of one with the One; of purity and transformation; of accountability, right action or correct *adab;* of the ascendant annihilation of ego. In all this the vocabulary might vary from tradition to tradition, yet they are conceptual constants. What we might find is different clothing, the ritual presentation of interface with the world, but it's all the same to the melting heart in love with truth, in love with the meaning of truth, it's all the same to the wisdom high enough up the mountain and the perspective to see it as the same.

The Hindu *namastay,* a greeting of peace with its characteristic gesture, one hand pressed flat against the other at the level of the heart, head slightly inclined or bowed, means I worship the divine in you, or you and I are one. This is essentially no different from the Islamic *salams,* the Hebrew *shaloms,* greetings of peace offered and returned, looking into each other's eyes conveying the blessings of the divine, recognizing the divine in each other's heart. The reality of God's existence in every living thing is the vibration of continuity we must be alive to and keep alive for others to see. Awake in the world of souls before we came here, awake in the kingdom of God, the eternal hereafter which awaits our return, we pass through this era in time as a sleeper who has forgotten what it means to be awake, and in this dream filled sleep of ours we have forgotten that it's all the same whether we chant *namasiviya* or *alhamd* because we are the children of Adam and God is One. The kingdom of God which is Brahman's world is available to purity but not to deception, it is available to wisdom but not to knowledge, it is available to the light of truth but not to lies, to goodness but not to evil; it does not matter where this purity, this wisdom, this truth and goodness come from or what they wear, what language they use, what skin they walk around in, it does not matter because we are the progeny of a single set of parents and the family of God.

It is only through indifference to this world of deception, this world of dream filled sleep, that we can know all three worlds, be alive in the continuity of the three which owe their existence to God alone, to the grace and power of His existence. And it is only through the endless contemplation of His duty to us, His creation, His protection and His nourishment that we begin to comprehend the nature of His duty, the totality of His dedication to us, and consequently our responsive duty to Him, to all that He has created. We begin everything with the words which evoke His duty to us, the *bismillahir-rahmanir-rahim* which translates outwardly as in the name of God, the most

313

compassionate, the most merciful, and inwardly as in the name of God, the creator, sustainer and nourisher. By repeating these words which evoke the immensity of His power to unimaginable depths, we invite His protection and at the same time remind ourself of the focus on Him. Then as we proceed each day through the tasks which compose our existence in Him and our experience of Him, the *la ilaha illallahu* resonates on our breath and in our blood, left and right, keeping us in the remembrance of the divine kingdom while we walk wide awake through the world of dreams.

To remember Him with every breath is the clear passage to an understanding of the three worlds, worlds we are already embedded in even though we might not have the immediacy of their experience. After all, for most of us the nine months of prenatal existence have no reality whatsoever, but that does not mean it did not happen, and we have to recognize that our knowledge of other realms in existence might be equally shrouded, although not in the same way. The soul came into the world of souls in a shower of light particles which had always existed within Allah in the timelessness before the beginning. They came after the light which is the *nur* had emerged from God, explaining its own existence, offering all praise to the totality of His existence, while pointing to the lives that clamored within Him, clamored for the wisdom and knowledge to know and to praise. We came from this purity, this immensity, and it is our destined place of return, but this is not a separate reality, it is part of the continuum of light which wraps itself around and through the deceptive world of illusion. We came here because we hungered to know, and in recognition of this hunger, to satisfy this hunger, God sent us here, He created a world in which we could become students of His divine kingdom, where we could learn the truth about who we are, who He is, and then go home.

To live in the persistent reality of these two worlds of light, where we first affirmed the oneness of God and where we will make that affirmation again, it is essential to make the affirmation here as well, in this world, the world of the senses, of desire and illusion. If we want to know that purity and live that praise, if we want to merge with God, be one with God again, we have to surrender our life of the senses to a life of absolute faith, we have to learn the nature of this faith at the level of gnostic wisdom and give everything up, surrender everything, ego, mind, desire, any limiting concept of self, even wisdom itself so that nothing exists but God. What

315

breathes in is God, what breathes out is God, what affirms God is God alone.

A CHOICE OF DESTINY

In what sense is there ever an accident? What is karma, what is destiny, is there a connection between them? How are we supposed to think about accident, karma and destiny in relation to the will of God? These are questions which come up again and again because it is so difficult to be satisfied with an answer to any one which excludes an answer to the others. If there is a destiny then nothing is accidental, if there are accidents there is no such thing as destiny. If the karma we are born with is our destiny, is the karma we accumulate irrelevant to that destiny? The karma of our birth is a genetic code which dates back to our original parents, an inflexible stream of what has already come and gone, which cannot be altered because it is past, ancient history whose mark and imprint we bear. In addition to that impervious stream there are the conditions, thoughts, desires and actions of our immediate parents at the time of our conception; can we eradicate the stains of history with the purity we acquire, can we destroy the blessings of a

317

pious ancestry with appalling acts of our own? Then suppose it were all up to us, how are we to think of God who is the master of our destiny, who created it all, the good and the bad, how then do we acknowledge His supremacy in human affairs?

The transcendent answer of wisdom, which stirs these questions but does not plough them up or dig them under, is the stance of inner patience and contentment with whatever situation we find ourself in, understanding that everything which happens occurs with His permission, everything which happens comes from Him, and so we surrender the responsibility to Him, knowing that He knows, the outcome is His, He alone knows the end of the story. For this we offer our praise, all praise to God because everything is a gift, an opportunity to learn strength and wisdom, everything is His grace if we have the wisdom to perceive it as such. When we have absolute faith, when we live in the unshakable conviction that God alone exists there is no karma, there is neither accident nor destiny; however, as long as we function in ignorance that very ignorance which makes us choose incorrectly will cause consequences that we label accidents, accidents that we then think of as our destiny because we don't know any better, we can't find another answer.

In fact, we do manufacture our own destiny, we create our situation with the choices we make, good or bad. Yes, God has created both the good and the bad, but this doesn't mean He dictates how we behave, what we do, what we choose to do because, unlike animals and angels, we have options. The concept of predestination is as repugnant as it is unwise. What would be the point of our existence here on earth if it had all been prescribed in advance, why would we be here if it had all been concluded without our having any say in what we became, what we did with the opportunities God placed at our disposal? If we didn't have any choice, why have all the prophets, saints and *qutbs* been sent to admonish, advise and inform us, to show us who God is and who we are? Wouldn't it be an inconceivable irony if they all came to show us the radiant light of the possible, only to slam the door in our face, sorry, not for you, not for you, and certainly not for you?

God has created good and bad, but He has also placed the instruments of choice in our hands; we can select intentions, thoughts and actions to know Him or we can decide the opposite. In other words, there is a destiny, an inevitability which is dependent on the things we do, destiny can be changed, it is not an immutable constant nothing can touch. We

319

touch it, we change it with the life we impose on what we are given. The envelope which resembles the genetic imprint determining our kind, our species, our size and shape can be filled as we like, we can stuff the things of the world into this amorphous bag, overfilling it with the treasures of the senses, the objects worshiped in the arena of worldly experience, or we can inflate it with the joy of His presence, conceding the irrelevance of self and ego in the grace of surrender, in the acquisition of His unique totality, the breathing pulse of *la ilaha illallahu.*

It is true that God created both the good and the bad, He created pairs of opposites to demonstrate truth and falsity, inner and outer, ignorance and wisdom, life and death. This does not entitle us to be supine, to lie down at the intersection and say God will divert the traffic away from us if that is His intention, if not, why bother, we are dead already. It is up to us to move out of the way, we have to do our share, tie up the camel, because absolute faith is active not passive, it is up to us to struggle against the evils and ills of the world. He has given us the capacity for change, and our destiny therefore, is our own construct built upon our intentions, our words and what we do. The only way to discover the secret, the mystery which is also imprinted as an immaculate light of inviolable purity, the soul within each of us, is to do good and be good, to love and be loving, to pursue the divine attributes which are seeds of light already planted in each heart. It is not up to us to look at someone else and say he's bad, she's a terrible person; God alone can assess the good and bad in the hearts of others.

Judgment is not ours, it is His. We might observe the most appalling, the most outrageous acts from someone we rush to condemn without for a moment stopping to think we have no idea of this person's circumstances, without considering we might have behaved in exactly the same way if we had found ourself in a similar situation. If grace and wisdom dawn in the heart of that person, as it might at any moment, everything changes. When the great sheikh, 'Abdul Qadir al-Jilani, was accosted by a band of thieves attacking his caravan, demanding money, everything he had was securely sewn into the lining of his cloak where it would never have been found. Yet they asked if he had any money, and he told them where it was concealed. At first they thought he was making it up, telling them a story, but he repeated the information several times until they looked and found the forty coins hidden in his garments. Astonished, they took him to the leader of the band who asked him why, in such difficult circumstances, he had told the truth. As he explained he had promised his mother he would always tell the truth, he would never lie, the leader broke down and wept, "You only promised your mother you wouldn't lie, but look what I am doing before God." He and the whole band of thieves and robbers begged his forgiveness, asked him to teach them the *kalimah,* the pure words of faith that wash the heart, and became his first followers.

Our destiny can be changed in a single moment. He has given us powerful instruments to change our destiny, regret, repentance, feeling such profound dissatisfaction with the things we have done or with a specific act that we undertake never to do such things again. He has also given us forgiveness, His, He is prepared to wipe the slate clean when we empty ourself of the faults, the mistakes and errors we commit in ignorance, even the mistakes we knowingly commit if we are sincere in our determination to change. This struggle to improve, to change is another powerful weapon which will alter destiny. He has given us the full range of the potential for being truly human as part of the envelope, part of the package which we can access through prayer. As we pray we change who we are, who we will be, who we will become; everything about us changes with the prayer that looks only at Him, begs only Him to transform the frailty and make it strength, to discard ignorance and find the soil where wisdom grows, to let the seeds of light flower in His fragrance.

The genetic code embedded in the elements, the substantial, the earth, fire, water, air and space components, the material body including mind and desire, this envelope of form is so evidently subject to change. Today we can easily alter the color of our hair, our eyes and the contours of our physical outline; we alter the predisposition to disease by altering our diet, our actions; we invite the disease which will end our time on earth with the air we breathe, the water we drink, the food we eat, the thoughts we think and the things we do or fail to do. In this way we cool or heat the fires of the furnace where our destiny is forged, we tear up the pages of our original script and rewrite it with better or worse lines. We can realize that place where nothing exists but God if we turn our thoughts to Him, change our qualities to His and focus on the secret body, the light body which holds the mystery we knew at the beginning and will know again after our end.

Before we can know that death before death our karma must die, before karma can die desire must die, before desire can die the mind must die, before the mind can die illusion must die, and if illusion dies the whole world has died within us. Once the world has died there is nothing left to die, no self, no ego, no family, no country, no word, no thought, no pleasure, no pain, gone, all gone, nothing but the radiant completion of light remains. If we can hold off the Angel of Death and outwit the deposits of negative karma, what we were born with and what we accrued by ourself, we can make the pure body of light dance in His praise, we can make it sing with the bliss of His presence until the Angel of Death has nothing left to say, then we exist in Him and He exists in us, nothing exists for us except the power of God.

What is it that makes us forget God, why do we not automatically, intuitively remember God until that last desperate moment when the words, O God, spontaneously pour from our heart and mouth? Our preoccupation with the world, our dazzling sense vested in the importance of what we see out there, our concern for acceptance out there, the enormous worlds of illusion projected by mind and desire all obscure the inner planes where the supremacy of God is always visisble if we look, if we choose to look. Once we relegate our mind to its correct place, allowing it to function as a competent subordinate rather than expecting it to be in charge, once we learn to ignore the propositions of all the petty and broad desires which litter the landscape with impulse and confusion, we begin to undertand the nature and implications of choice. If we look at the world we see hell, if we look at God we see heaven; this means we must accept the heavy obligation, the burden of change. The obligations Islam prescribes, the five pillars, are prescriptions for a life meant to sustain a new structure, a new body and a new body of experience.

If the body we build is sustained by the qualities of God, by the intention and determination to dislodge the barriers between what we see and the reality of what is to be seen, then we can know the heaven of remembering Him instead of the hell which is forgetting Him, separation from Him. When we understand the obligations of Islam at the level of gnosis, of divine wisdom, we read these duties as a transforming map for our focus, as a guidebook for the maturation of qualities whose light shines with the truth invisible in the darkness of the world, qualities which are instruments of change for the script of our destiny. There is no heaven and there is no hell other

325

than the one we prescribe for ourself, there is no destiny which cannot be changed by God when He sees our absolute faith, when He reads the new text we have prepared, the new house we have built. He has offered us everything, put both good and bad, right and wrong at our disposal, then He watches to see what we choose and how we use the choices we make, ratifying our choice as our destiny, forgiving those who beg His forgiveness, opening the door to those who long for admittance, sealing the unrepentant hearts of stone in their own hell.

If we fail to change our qualities and actions we create the circumstances which make accidents possible, and we need to know that accidents mean a deviation from the possible, from the genetic opportunities we circumvent with the wrong or ill-advised thoughts, words and acts we select instead of the truthful options of integrity, tolerance, compassion, love, justice and patience. Just as we are responsible for the destiny we engage, we are often largely responsible for the accidents we are subject to. A wise human being who has climbed high up the mountain of wisdom can see with clarity in every direction, before, behind, now, after, above and below, a wise person does not create the climate of accident in his or her bodily discourse or action, and in this sense is not subject to accident. If we are genetically disposed to say, a hundred years of life or more, yet we do nothing to foster the health and maintenance of the vehicle which has to carry us for that span of time, there's a good chance we will die of some obnoxious disease, an accident of our own making that cuts short our allotted time. If we drive recklessly, or even cautiously without the complete view of wisdom, we may be subject to accidents which foreshorten the possible, but this is not something heaped upon us by some malevolent or indifferent source, this is our own doing.

When death comes our options are finished, then there is the judgment to be reckoned with, then the script of our life is examined and we are answerable for the good and the bad from which we carved the destiny for now and hereafter. As soon as death shuts us down permanently there is no more relevance for ideas, emotions, possessions, family, friends, property, language, nationality, religion, nothing matters except the good things and the bad things we have been responsible for. As soon as we descend into the grave what difference does it make if we were charming or morose, handsome or plain, what does it matter whether we were rich or poor, it's all the same now as the elements are returned to the elements, earth to earth, water to water, fire to fire, air to air, space to space, it's all the same as we stand before the throne of justice, the throne which restores balance as the good and the bad are measured. We have until our last breath to solve the equation, to make it come out right, and if we don't get around to it in time, if we fail to restore the balance ourself, the thoughts, desires and emotions of this life will continue to torment the subtle body alive to this pain in the life which persists.

God's omniscience does not interfere with His will, His will does not interfere with our creative susceptibility to accident, but accident can interfere with our destiny. When we know that God can change our destiny, that His precognition does not determine the outcome, that we are nevertheless, responsible for mastering the karma of our birth, the karma we absorb, both the good and the bad, we should be able to look at our death with the clarity of understanding, although probably not fearlessly since there is always the gap between His perfection and our accomplishment. Divine wisdom emerging step by step from deep and absolute faith is the method, the technique we must engage to change our destiny—this is what God sees as He watches us alter the script of our birth.

At the first step, the *shari'at,* we learn the difference between right and wrong, what we owe to God, our duty to Him and each other. At the second step, the *tariqat,* the path, we understand that duty and choose it, we have decided on the liberation of our soul, we select the good unflinchingly as we turn our back to the wrong, the bad, the unwise. *Haqiqat,* the third step, finds us so immersed in our prayer we have harnessed the forces of mind and desire using them as the vehicle of ascension, the capacity to be in communion with Him, we speak and hear the vibration of His response. In *ma'rifat,* the gnosis of divine wisdom and understanding we merge with God, we are one with Him in a state which is oblivious to day and night because there is only light. Then if we have merged with Allah, when we come to that *sufiyyat* state of transcendence, the death before death, there is no fear, there is no separation because we exist in that oneness with Him. Here there is neither day nor night, birth nor death as we subsist in God alone, there is no ego, no self, we say only the words of God, think only His thoughts, perform only His duties.

If we cling to the things of the world, the titles, honors, recognition, money, property, ancestry, authority, family, all the things the world values but God Himself has no use for, we will not acquire the liberating wisdom of His truth, we will be stopped by the accumulating karma of possessions which erect themselves, becoming an endless wall between ourself and God. Without wisdom we cannot proceed, and for as long as we perceive the treaures of this world to be sacred articles, the treasures of the next world will remain unavailable. When we surrender everything that is irrelevant to the search for the presence of God, when we let these things fall away one by one under the compassionate scrutiny of maturing wisdom, we allow the gates of truth to open, admitting us to His kingdom, a gathering place for love, justice and peace. Then if we disappear in our prayer, meditation and worship we will know nothing of the world, we will have no thought of karma, destiny or the will of God as we slip into that *fana'*, that annihilation of the self where He alone exists.

THE GREAT EXCHANGE

Anger cannot become patience, haste cannot become wisdom, intolerance cannot become compassion, and since this is so, when we contemplate the mechanism of inner transformation we have to recognize that a bad quality will not slowly ascend into a good one, there is no sliding scale which takes us from the bottom of something intrinsically unacceptable, undesirable, even evil, to something good at the top. The first steps we take on the pathless path therefore, must include the understanding that change is necessary, certain qualities, propensities and attitudes have to be eradicated completely, although it is true their elimination will take time, will require a continuing effort over what might amount to a lifetime of determined effort, but it must be undertaken with confidence and absolute sincerity. One of the differences between a scholar and a student of Sufism is this personal acceptance of the need to change, a scholar will note objectively that Sufis engage in specific practices, but he will not discover the subjective reference as the student does. A student is the subject of his or her own investigations, while the scholar is satisfied to observe, to study an object, something or someone other than himself, from the outside.

When we begin, when we accept this revelation of the *din,* the path of true purity and dedication to God, when our heart melts with the grace of longing to know Him, to return to and be one with Him, we have to know how to jump right in, how and where to start, there is so much in this new realm, His realm, to learn. Our study and our path lie directly within. If we want to know God we have to know ourself, we have to analyze the enormous complexity of the human being we know best, the only being we are uniquely responsible for, the only being whose conduct, whose qualities, whose life and destiny we can actually change. This is not an analysis of the outer body and how it works, although a little of that is useful too since we have to keep the vehicle in good working order, but we have other sources for any relevant information here, this is an analysis from the perspective of faith and wisdom of the worlds within worlds within worlds which lie waiting to be explored.

We start with the most accessible, most readily identifiable layers of the persona, the character, the qualities which offer an outer definition of who we seem to be to others, how we present ourself, the way our family and friends might describe us, O she talks too much, laughs too much, has a short temper, he is kind and generous but unreliable, she's afraid of her own shadow, he's a bit of a bully, that sort of thing. As fearlessly as we can we assemble the data, the evidence and make plans to clean the house, knowing that this is not just spring cleaning, it's a major overhaul. We're going to make a perfect silk robe from a coarse, ill-fitting potato sack. Initially of course, we don't have a complete view of what's there, what's missing, what can be saved and what has to be thrown away; we can't expect to see it all at once, and this is part of the function of a community, the *ummat* in Islam, the *sangha* in Buddhism, to help us see ourself correctly, more fully, the fine print as well as the bold.

The community is our crucible, the place where we are cooked at high temperatures to burn off the dross and rescue the pure. In a community of seekers like the Sufis, unlike the congregation of a church, a mosque, a temple, a synagogue, there is an understanding we are together not just to pray once a week, once a year or five times a day, we are together to learn how to serve each other, to learn how to examine ourself in the mirror we hold up to each other. What we don't easily see in ourself is naked in the person whose company we find it hard to endure in the intimacy of daily association, maintaining at the same time, as well as we can, the love seekers on the path genuinely have for each other. The concept of duty, the path of service to God, the teacher, the community, family, society, in that order, is a communal lesson offering a range of experience which, rightly understood, validates the things we choose to do or are given to do. We discover we can bring the same qualities, even the same joy to washing the dishes that we bring to writing, painting, to our professional responsibility, our job or to any duty, if every task is performed with the remembrance of God and His love.

But first we have to consent to the great exchange, my qualities for Yours my God; my sense of being separate, the selfhood of ego in exchange for Your presence my God; my idea of individuality in exchange for Your totality my God. Each one of God's names represents a specific quality, action or duty of God we are to identify and search for within our own heart, that mysterious place which houses the good, the bad and all the worlds contained within the five elements and twelve openings of the body. We search for the embryo, the seed of His qualities, the patience, love, truth, goodness, mercy, justice, forgiveness, tolerance, generosity, truth, gratitude we have always known, experienced or observed from time to time, even distantly recognized as virtues in and of themselves without much outer prompting or guidance. When Satan says, "Evil be thou my good," he consolidates his perversion of the natural order which recognizes, automatically, intuitively at the minimal level of reason and intellect, the ascendance of the good and all the other qualities flowing from it.

We know at once that Satan's inversion of good and evil is wrong because we have the seeds of His truth alive in our heart, we start with a knowledge of right and wrong which might have been presented, offered to our understanding merely as a good idea, a benefit for the majority, a way of establishing social equity. We can only be persuaded of their validity at the intellectual level because that primary knowledge is already available, in place to verify the good idea. Using wisdom as the instrument, we must care for these seeds of purity while we also work at eliminating the ground cover obscuring their growth, removing things like the disinclination to weed the garden, laziness, confusion about the best method, how to proceed, then we have to clear a place to let the seeds take root and grow, we have to remove the stones and weeds, the anger, fear, jealousy, resentment, arrogance, hostility, worry, frustration, intolerance, bigotry, envy and hatred which want to claim the garden for themselves. We know in that primary knowledge we set out with that these are undesirable, that we must be rid of them before our garden will flower and we can live in its fragrance.

Of course the weeds have a nasty way of growing back, this is something we have to do routinely, pull out the weeds as we see them growing back, each time eliminating them a little sooner, not letting them grow enough to dominate the landscape and dwarf the flowers. This is the *shari'at*, the beginning which we have to learn at the level of gnosis, the highest inner perspective on what it means to understand the difference between right and wrong, a perspective which knows that God has created the human being as His most exalted creation who will understand things even the angels can't comprehend. Because God has planted everything in the heart of this being, in all such beings, this human creation has the capacity unique among all the others to know God. We acquired the capacity from Him when He placed the light of the *nur*, which came from the perfection and plenitude of His grace, when that light was placed at the gnostic eye of Adam and Adam's progeny, and when He placed the two highest levels of consciousness within our wisdom, the analytic ability to understand the divine, and the most complete wisdom, the luminous grace of this *nur*. It is the presence of that light of grace within each heart which draws us back into the source, the permanent light, the omnipresent reality.

The inner heart of man is a secret place holding the treasures of three worlds, the world of souls, where we were before we came here, this world, the world we see, and the divine kingdom, the hereafter we do not see which nevertheless, surrounds us now. What keeps us from seeing the things we do not see are the layers of illusion we manufacture that hide them from view, and among these countless layers are the forms populating them, the forms of the very thoughts and qualities we project to worship, the forms of the idols we create to worship instead of God. When something emerges from our mind it takes up residence in a subtle form within the heart where it is born and born again, a rebirth we can readily

337

understand. The mind creates the qualities, projects them outwardly making them visible, making them idols to worship. We are surrounded by the illusions we make that separate us from God; only by cutting away all these obscuring layers and destroying the idols of the mind will we have access to the light of the inner heart, the light that attracts God and will draw us back to Him.

What we use to sever these layers of illusion and the dark forms occupying the spaces among them is faith and the wisdom which has its source, as well as its verification, in that faith. In Arabic, the word for absolute faith is *iman,* and a metaphor we sometimes hear is the sword of *iman,* but this is to be understood as a metaphor, not a thing to be brandished physically. This sword is the faith necessary to cut through the illusions created by the mind which clutter the world with their darkness; this sword is the fine cutting instrument to separate truth from falsehood, reality from illusion, purity from impurity, light from darkness; this sword never kills, never hurts anyone except the person who wields it against his or her own qualities which must be removed, all at once with a single blow of the sword if possible, or little by little as the consciousness of truth penetrates the layers of illusion, reducing the desires for worldly possessions or sensual gratification to dust.

What was given to us originally is purity and the light of purity—this is the state we had to begin with and this is the state we need to recover, using the fine blade of absolute faith to cut away the acquired darkness and clutter obscuring the grace which is our gift. Some talk of losing their faith, some talk of not being able to find their faith, but Sufis know that faith is a given, it is already there, not something we can lose like an object, a toy, a set of keys, although we have to undertake the task of uncovering it, shining it up so that this faith can recognize the light of our original purity. To make our faith shine, to have it deeply enmeshed in the thoughts and intentions on which our experience is based we need the transforming action of prayer. First we identify the need for change; then we analyze the person we are, determining to eliminate the bad, the undesirable, even the unnecessary, recognizing the absolutes we aspire to so that we make way for the qualities of purity and light; then we embrace the perfection of prayer to deliver us to the truth. The prayer mat on which we prostrate in love and humility before God is the whole world of the experience in which we engage, our prayer is not confined to precisely described ritual acts, yet we include that too, our prayer is the devotion and service we offer to God and each other.

Prayer is not easy, true prayer is not just saying O God help me, I need this, I need that, I want what I don't have, don't want what I do have, prayer is a subtle realignment which is part of the great exchange, it is the transaction which takes us from what we were to what we are; it is saddling the forces of illusion generated by our misconception of who we are so that we can ride in fearless purity up to the level of the heart where we encounter the great open space in which He alone exists. Then we can hear and respond to the vibration which comes before sound, which comes before light as an answer to the matching vibration we travel on. We have to become that single vertical, the straight line which is the *alif* and the number one in Arabic, an unvoiced letter until we bring the notation to it which opens the sound, the *a* of Allah, the opener, the *fatihah* or the *Fatihah,* the verses which are the beginning of our prayer. If we have that sincerity, that *Ikhlas* or purity of intention which we recite after the *Fatihah,* our prayer may also be expressed in our thoughts, our words and actions. Prayer is a struggle, the endless engagement of the exchange, good for bad, right for wrong, pure for impure.

When we make this connection to God in the right way, our heart is luminous with His radiance where we find our soul and His grace, then we understand what *fana'* means, the death within Him, then we know the devotion of service without self, and our body is His, our words are His. As prayer cuts through the layers of our densely impacted wrong qualities, through the karma of our genetic and acquired propensities, through the illusions we once took for the way things are, the separations engendered by race and religion, by language and emotion, by concepts and philosophy, they all disappear in the solitary uniqueness of His power. We change, we change and our thoughts, our words, our remembrance, our actions are fused with the power that is His, we remain who we are, a purified version of who we are while the perfume of His existence fills the air. If we develop those qualities of God, ascend to the highest states of consciousness, His luminous wisdom, if we have an absolute trust in God and know the purity of dedicating all our praise to Him, if we experience the hunger and suffering of everyone else as no different from our own we change at every level of our experience in every world.

Faith, prayer and wisdom are the indispensable instruments we not only have to use, we also have to master. To dominate the undesirable qualities which try so hard to dominate us, we need the wisdom rooted in profound faith—they are specifically interdependent—wisdom alone can direct us on the pathless path, can show us how to eradicate the boulders, thorns and thistles blocking our way, how to dispose of the inclinations coming from our baser persona which encourages and inspires us to commit the gross indecencies violating our innate purity, the deadlier sins like lust, anger, miserliness, envy, falsehood, theft, murder, hatred, arrogance. All these must be dealt with by wisdom to clear the path, and we must have the faith that wisdom can do the job, wisdom that comes to us through the direction of a teacher, an infinitely wise being whose own perfected qualities can address and demolish obstacles as large as those obnoxious impediments. Such a teacher knows how to negotiate with ills as great as these, treating us with love if love is the cure, with compassion if that is the cure, with divine wisdom if that is the cure, with divine intervention if that is the cure.

Until a teacher in a perfected state finds us, (and that is the way it is, no matter how it seems to us, as we keep searching for him, searching for her) there is so much we must do on our own, we must begin to root out the qualities we do not need

342

and do not want on this path, we must begin to dismantle the karmic structures binding us to patterns of behavior before we are too rigid to change, while the suppleness of young energy is still available and we can hear the call to change as a sweet song we can't get out of our head. We proceed slowly at first, sometimes it will feel like one step forward and two steps back, but as our own wisdom begins to mature and we start to correct ourself, see the desires and attachments begin to fade a little at a time, we will have verification of the process when we find that we are reaching out to serve others, that we are eager to find some duty to express the change, that our love for God is becoming obsessive, that we have neither the time for nor the interest in all the things we used to resort to for diversion, that we do not want diversion, we want to keep focused on that one point, we want to know God.

The base desires of the lower self create the hell we live in now and the hell we will know later on, each desire a source of poison in this life and torment in the next when our subtle body will endure the pain and frustration which continue to haunt us there. Whatever deception and treachery we practise here will become the torture we experience there, whatever unkindness or misery we project here will be magnified and turned on us there, whatever evil we practise here will be the evil we encounter there, whatever suffering we cause here we will know there, and this, if for no other reason, should be the goad urging us to be rid of the qualities, thoughts and actions which are not God's. Because we have the unmanifest, the dormant seeds of the good deep within us, we have no peace until they are given scope for expression, whether we recognize the longing for this truth or not.

Peace has nothing to do with race, it has nothing to do with philosophy or language and it certainly has nothing to do with the institutions of religion. Race, religion and philosophy do nothing to satisfy the thirst for truth and the longing for peace, both of which we routinely destroy with our carelessness, our casual neglect of the qualities, thoughts and intentions which make them possible. As long as we fail to throw out the bad, make room for the good, we have no peace. That peace is to be found only in the depthless removal of desire, attachment and illusion, it manifests only in relation to God's qualities even if we don't think of ourselves as seekers on the path or lovers of God, this is true for everyone. All we have to do is ask around, ask anyone if we have any doubts about it, ask the politician, the businessman, the housewife, the teacher, the laborer, the artist, the psychiatrist if they are at peace, and we find that peace emerges directly in proportion to the good qualities, the qualities of God we give expression to in our lives.

What do we take with us when we die, posessions, a child, a husband, our politics, our aesthetic values, national fervor, religious doctrine, ethnicity, do any of these follow us into the ground, do they speak for us from the grave? Will God really be interested in whether we are Christian or Hindu or Muslim, will He care about our enthusiasm for flag and country, for the property we have so carefully amassed or the preference for friends and family, the actions we have undertaken to advance a cause, will He ask us about any of this? He will not want to know about any of the worldly things that engaged us, He will not want to know about any of the preoccupations which seemed so important to us but in fact, only contributed to our death, the food, the thoughts, emotions, the talk, the camaraderie, the entertainments and activities which made us forget Him as they gave us a fleeting sense of pleasure and cleared a path to our end. Everything that enhanced the sense of self, the ego, thinking about mine instead of ours, all this destroyed the clarity in our life, preventing us from seeing the truth about who we are and what our connection to God is.

345

What He will want to know is the good and the bad we have been responsible for, these are the things that accompany us to the grave, the companions of our truth. While we are still here, alive, we have to unload the bad, beg forgiveness for our faults, our errors; we have to make a sincere and wholly determined effort to allow our natural truth, our innate goodness to take root and grow. If we had any accurate idea of how fragile a thread our life is suspended from we would not wait, we would proceed with the urgency of a drowning man gasping for air. God is the essence, the absolute of forgiveness, He always forgives us when we ask for this with integrity. Why should we keep collecting the things that cause misery here and perpetuate misery when we die? If we adopt the qualities of God and make them our own, if we acquire faith, wisdom and His luminous clarity in our life, we will pass beyond this world and return to our original purity.

THE SIGNIFICANCE OF DUTY

Let us resurrect a word which has been clotted with the ambiguities of class, privilege and station, with the repugnance of fulfilling an obligation without enthusiasm, in a joyless state, let us restore it with the primary sense of reverence, the respect we automatically offer to sanctity, to purity and wisdom. The understanding of duty in its highest sense, the original, pure sense, comes from our own purity, a sympathetic response of purity to purity and wisdom to wisdom. Outer duty can of course, be forced, required by an authority, a parent, a teacher, an employer, a govenment, all those who perpetuate the distastefulness adhering to this concept, while true inner duty, offering our service with a melting, overflowing heart is only imposed by the spontaneous longing to manifest the qualities of God in our actions, to be good and do good, to express our love, our compassion.

If we can think of duty as God serving God, disallowing the intrusion of selfhood, I did this, I helped with that, then we begin to understand the structure of a cosmology which has nothing to do with an individual, an ego, and everything to do with the totality of One. This idea of duty comes from the formlessness within ourself, not from any outer thing, it comes from the place of light housing the soul, from the radiance of the inner obligations, eyes which see as He sees, ears which hear as He hears, a mouth filled with His taste and His words, a nose overwhelmed with His fragrance and a heart which resonates His truth, His mercy and justice, His peace, love and compassion. The pathlessness of the One can be described and expressed in His duty, His obligation to create, to sustain and take us back to Him.

The *la ilaha illallahu,* the affirmation that He alone exists, that He is the only reality and everything else is illusion wreathed in impermanence, this can be clarified as the way of the One, the path of *ahad,* the absolute, the unmanifest which becomes manifest in duty. When we illuminate what lies before us, what lies ahead with the qualities, the grace and duty of God, we supply the diacritical notation to that single, mute line which gives it sound, we exemplify the qualities and actions of God in the things we say, the things we do. How do we get out of the way, how do we subtract the limited sense of who we are and replace it with the totality which has no persona, no idea of individual selfhood? To do this we have only to enter the inner worlds waiting for us, abandon the outer and engage the inner, study what lies within in a fearless contemplation of wisdom and God's qualities. And as well, we have to deal with the thousands of worlds opening inwardly from each of the twelve openings of the body and the five elements, the earth, fire, air, water and ether or outer space composing the body.

The twelve openings are the two eyes, two ears, two nostrils, a mouth, the navel which is sealed, two openings below, the eye of wisdom on the forehead and the opening at the crown of the head. The data we accumulate inwardly and outwardly, emotions, thoughts and sensations combine and recombine to form the worlds we construct to inhabit, worlds within worlds within worlds which we travel among freely and frequently, wherever the mind takes us, from illusion to illusion, travelling at a speed resembling the wind. We have to recognize every level and layer of illusion that disguises the light of the gnostic eye and the luminous throne crowning the head, we have to pick our way through the wilderness of all these worlds, discarding the unwanted garments or watching them drop away on their own, then we can live in the kingdom of light, the worlds of grace and wisdom where there is no coming and going, there is only the stillness of being.

The amazingly unknown or at least undiscussed aspect of duty is the joy, the necessary bliss of returning what we have been given. Once we penetrate the illusions and find our way to study the example of a perfected being, then we have some idea of who we are in relation to God and who God is in relation to us, then we begin to grasp the enormous implications of our existence within Him and His existence within us. Now we look around in wonder as we recalibrate experience and understanding to merge with the totality we barely comprehend. When we are conscious at last of the protection surrounding us, the nourishment constantly provided for us, all the attributes and wisdom of God which He has endowed us with, made available to us, we search for an adequate expression of gratitude and discover that only by sharing the wisdom, offering it around as a savory dish, the most exquisite taste imaginable, can we deposit something back into the great treasure house which has poured out so much on us.

350

The realization of this gratitude also takes the form of service to others, the loving duty we perform in whatever situation we find ourself, the service to God coming first and the service to our sheikh or teacher coming next in our priority of obligation. After that is the duty to our community, the lovers of God, preceding the duty to our immediate family which comes next, then to the larger community of nation and world, to the human family. The duty can take any form if it is done without ego, without expectation of reward or thanks; whatever we do without forgetting God for a moment is that duty, whether it's washing the dishes, sweeping the floor or taking corporate decisions. Loving service in remembrance of God is that duty. The ultimate duty of course, is to find the *nur*, the radiant light within our radiant wisdom, our truth and absolute faith, then be guided by that *nur* back to Allah, *nur* merging with *nur*, His beauty, His grace, one merging with One.

When we remove the darkness from ourself as God did at the beginning of everything before the beginning, existing in the purity of light and the grace of luminous wisdom, we live in a state of duty which becomes the expression of our existence, His state of duty, His state of love. This is duty without selfishness, without expectation, it is merely done, and this is the way we are to search for the wisdom holding that light in trust for us; we are to search because it is what has to be done, it is the wisdom we need to open the inner heart where we find God's qualities and His truth. As we open the inner heart we can taste the sweetness of His presence, catch the scent of His perfume and hear the pure music of His sound. When this happens our duty will be like the sun shining equally for everyone, like the rain falling uniformly on everyone or like a tree providing shade, offering comfort for every creature who comes near; when we reach that wisdom which opens the inner heart we treat all human beings equally, not showing preference or prejudice, not acknowledging color, race, language, class, gender or any other arbitrary subdivision of the human condition; when we find the wisdom which melts and opens the heart, our love for every living thing, for all animate and inanimate creatures becomes our duty.

If we scrub something or clean something to restore it to its original state, its original purity, we use different instruments and cleaners, but eventually the cleansing instruments themselves need to be cleaned too, then what, what cleans the cleaner? Conscience, the voice of right and wrong embedded in the light of wisdom is our natural purifier, our natural

352

cleanser, but what keeps conscience clean, what keeps conscience sharp-edged and bright, prevents it from rusting or clotting, what keeps conscience fresh, new and bright? Our prayers and our duty do that for us, our duty polishes conscience and conscience polishes duty keeping it spotless. While we walk this way professing our love with every breath and every step, God looks at us closely, watching our progress, examining our performance with His compassion, yet for those who beg to be close to Him He watches even more carefully, not letting us get away with things the more indifferent manage with impunity. He sees our smallest flaw, the little imperfections we would like to ignore or brush away, He invades our conscience with messages advising us that a certain action or word is unacceptable, not good enough, clean enough, clear enough for those who think of themselves as seekers, as students on the path of His love. This is one of the reasons why progress on this pathless path does not suddenly become easier, on the contrary, it becomes harder, more demanding and more critical as we go.

Our duty and our prayers clean the cleaner, our duty is the instrument cleaning the conscience, and with this in mind we should look at the outer and inner duties or obligations of Islam

353

one more time. If we understand the outer duties at the *shari'at* level, the first step which sees these duties as divine law and therefore not in any sense optional or in response to an inner call, we see how they describe a method of purification ensuring that we live correctly. Satisfying these requirements with this understanding may not be the most exalted life, the most sanctified life, but it is true to God and fulfills the requirements God gave to the prophet Muhammad for his followers, his people. They are to believe, without reservation, in God, the angels, His prophets, His scriptural revelations, in the accountability of Judgment Day and the differentiation of good from bad, right from wrong, adhering to the good.

The outer duties begin with unswerving faith in God, a duty which can be understood at the ordinary, church going, mosque going level, or at the Sufi level remembering God with every breath, cancelling self in the annihilation of ego which lives the truth that God is the only reality. If this faith is unquestioned at the level which accepts the handed down transmission that prescribes ritual prayer as the second duty, the performance of these prayers follows quite naturally, and if we accept the Sufi definition of unswerving faith and realize we are not in this exalted state yet, we might also acknowledge the need for some kind of formal prayer attached to the Islamic, Christian, Jewish, Hindu orthodoxy or some other tradition. This second duty of prayer takes many forms, as well as the recitation of different kinds of *dhikr*, remembering God by invoking His names, His attributes, the hundreds of variables here, either silently or out loud. We might think of any such prayers as fulfilling an obligation or duty to God, in fact we serve ourself when we offer these prayers because this is our arena dedicated to minute introspection, examining and attempting to correct the flaws and failures, studying the imperfections, mastering the ego.

The third duty, the obligation of charity, helping those who are lost, poor, hungry, oppressed, all this contributes to the necessary stripping down of the sense of self we derive from our worldly accumulations, things we think we need to gather for ourself, forgetting that everything actually belongs to God. The real meaning of distributing what we have been given to look after is of course, a duty to relieve distress wherever we encounter it, yet again on another plane it is evident this is a significant purging of ego existence, a literal dematerializing. Charity offered without a feeling of yours and mine is a form of pure love which shows us how to look at the world with the knowledge that everything we see is one of two things, either something we have to learn, part of our private instruction course, or part of our duty. The only other thing that needs to concern us is the merging of our light with His, and if we should have the wisdom to give it all away we can exist in the uncluttered, open space where He alone is. After that, the only thing remaining is our duty.

The fourth duty, fasting, is to deepen our understanding of human suffering by obliging us to experience hunger, no food, no drink for hours and hours, all the daylight hours each day for a month, and then again on other optional days scattered throughout the months and year. We learn this temporary hunger to have some idea of the permanent hunger afflicting those who starve by day and by night. Those who fast voluntarily or those who fast because they believe God requires this of them discover the secret of the fast, it brings us closer to God, it reduces the distractions of the world and helps us to focus on our prayers, prayer becomes the only thing we want to do, revelations come offering wisdom and confirmation. There is a fasting mode so filled with the uncluttered, sweet consciousness of grace it is sometimes hard to relinquish in spite of the physical inconvenience accompanying it.

The obligation of pilgrimage which is the fifth outer duty defined in the traditions of Islam is our death rehearsal, we go dressed in a shroud, and some do die on this journey although the physical difficulties are less now with efficient transportation, hotels and air conditioning, we go having tied up and resolved all worldly matters, we go to be touched by the sanctity of the holy places, the Ka'bah in Mecca, rebuilt by Abraham and Ishmael, which is the inner heart, the prophet Muhammad's tomb in Medina where he lies buried, and finally Jerusalem, the Rock now housed in the matchless Dome where all the prophets prayed. We go announcing to God that we have come to Him in the purity of death itself, the world is finished for us, now we face only Him. In the Sufi understanding this is the death before death to be known and lived wherever we are, not just in a designated spot on the earth, a state existing permanently in the heart, a corpse to the world, alive only in Him. This is *sufiyyat,* the state in which we no longer exist except in Him, saying His words, carrying out His duty in His way.

These five outer obligations recognized and practised by the orthodoxy of Islam are accompanied by six inner duties acknowledged only by those who commit themselves to the

357

mystical path the Sufis profess, the path of union with Allah, with God. They become duties only when we perceive the need to be in this *sufiyyat* state, when we look for ways to detach ourself from the attachments which bind us to the world and the things of the world. The most complex entanglements arise in the places where we have invested most, parents, children, husband and wife, we have invested most because they are closest to us, they affect us and we affect them deeply in ways no others do, they represent our emotional holdings, the stock options of our well-being. To do our duty to God, our sheikh, our community and the whole human community, to do this with justice and equality we have to learn how to detach the attachment which puts my child ahead of yours. The attachment is still there but detached from our thoughts and actions, we function in a way which is neither dependent on nor determined by that attachment.

We have to understand this in conjunction with one or two other important things before we can come to some realization of the six inner duties or obligations. Duty must be carried out in the total absence of any thought that we are doing something, the 'I' must be banished by the remembrance that everything occurs as God chooses and determines, nothing happens without His permission, His will, there is nothing in duty for the 'I' to engage or hang onto. The 'I' must disappear completely in Him to do His duty, and the is that the thanks I get reflex must disappear with the 'I.' To know exactly what God's duty is however, to serve truly and correctly, we have to merge with the teacher, the sheikh, the guru who is already merged with God, then we know what he knows. His knowledge of God will be our source of action. In this state it is possible to see with the inner eye, with the wisdom which sees as He does, which sees only His light and not the darkness of the world. We hear with the ear that hears His sound and not the raucous chorus of the world, we taste His flavor, utter His words, live in the sweetness of His fragrance and in the open space of a melting heart where He alone exists.

There is an overriding duty to know God, the duty to understand God which supercedes all others. We have an outer and an inner, an illusory outer form and our true inner form; we have the choice to dedicate our life to a pursuit of the outer, that is one kind of knowledge, or we can search for the wisdom to know the inner which is something quite different. To know the inner we have to penetrate secrets within secrets within secrets to discover the radiant light of the *nur,* God's grace and plenitude, and then we have to find the light and the power of God, the secrets within those secrets. On the left we take care of our worldly duties, one by one, without attachment, and drop them when we're done instead of carrying them around with us increasing our baggage as we go; on the right we proceed to the destination, we explore our connection to God and the truth, we search for the wisdom to illuminate an inner path to the One. Becoming lighter and lighter, getting rid of everything the world imposes on us, we let nothing stand in our way or interfere with the only duty that has ultimate significance.

THE *NUR*

There was a prophet whose name was Muhammad, may the peace and blessings of Allah be upon him, born in Mecca and buried in Medina, a prophet of God whose mother was Aminah, whose father 'Abdullah died before the birth of his exalted son. This noble prophet is known to us historically, books have been written about his life; his words, thoughts and acts on a great range of ethical, social and practical matters have been remembered, recorded and handed down—we have more actual information about this prophet than any other in the monotheist traditions. And yet this is not really who he was, this historical characterization is only the visible point of a mysterious and infinitely invisible line going back to the place of no beginning, the time of no time. The physical manifestation known as Muhammad was the ultimate embodiment of a light which appeared in all the religions, which appeared two hundred and one times through all the ages of history and prehistory.

And that light, what do we know of that light called the *nur?* We know the light which came from God as His radiance, His grace and His undiminishing, limitless bounty was designated *Nur Muhammad* from the beginning preceding the beginning. It is said that when God existed alone, the silent totality resonating in the darkness before light, the immersion of all that was to be in the solitary, unique One, after a period of timelessness which cannot be described or reckoned, something happened, something changed or shifted and a stunning, luminous presence emerged from all that was contained. In amazement God contemplated this light, radiating His consciousness as perception and awareness, asking it to identify itself, and the *nur* replied to our God that it was a light which had been with Him and had come from Him, a light which was the expression of His grace, His plenitude, His totality. God, who was delighted with the response, gave this extraordinary light the name *Nur Muhammad,* declaring then He would make all that would be created with this *nur,* this *Nur Muhammad.*

It is also said that the *nur* returned then to the totality of Allah, remaining there imponderably before emerging again. Now a shadow separated from the *nur* and spread as another light, the

362

qutb, the conveyor of divine wisdom, the pole, the axis of understanding emanating from that divine radiance. When the worlds were created the *nur* and the *qutb,* glancing off each other, caused the shower of sparks which fell as rays, the souls of every created being in all the worlds, some falling in the divine kingdom, some on earth, some in the waters, some in the sky and outer space, some in the netherworlds. Later, after God had decided to create Adam, to create the human species which would be endowed with knowledge unavailable even to the heavenly beings, he placed the light of *Nur Muhammad* on Adam's forehead as the gnostic eye, the eye of wisdom. This light has been given to all Adam's progeny, this is the light we must use to search for our Father, to search for Him and know Him, to understand that we have our origin in the *nur* and consequently in Him. We came from Him and it is our duty, our destiny to return to Him.

We are born with this essentially human quality, this light which is nothing other than Allah's own light, yet we choose the world instead, we turn our back to or ignore the radiance and choose the darkness of the world as our light. We choose the world because it is easy, seductive, and instead of perceiving His immanence we look at form, the visible, the audible, everything the senses convey. What Allah taught the prophet Muhammad He is willing to teach us, the patience and compassion to illuminate universes and galaxies, to melt the hearts which have forgotten God or turned away from Him in sorrow, in grief or suffering. And we have to understand that since the *nur* is the essence of Allah, the four steps, the *shari'at, tariqat, haqiqat* and *ma'rifat* which also represent four major religious groups, are also fully contained within the *nur*.

From this perspective, the first step, devotion which uses form to focus on God, the *shari'at* is the knowledge and realization of God's qualities, His attributes, the mercy, justice, love, truth, peace, tolerance, patience, forgiveness we are to acquire. The *tariqat* or worship of fire, of the sun, the moon, the stars, means that our intention to know Allah is strong, it is pure; our patience and pursuit of duty are solid, our faith is filled with determination and certitude. In the state of *haqiqat,* the devotion of love in the melting heart, the *nur* has eliminated the darkness of this heart, desire is gone, there is the ecstatic communion with God, and the heart filled with His truth is perfectly pure. At the fourth step, *ma'rifat,* the light of gnosis is the *nur,* the place where Allah and the *nur* become one, and here there is only the form of light, God worships God, the mystery, the essence and manifestation are One. In *ma'rifat* the form of the *nur* is the essence of Allah. In all four steps Muhammad appears as God's messenger, teaching and explaining the truth of God in a way which is relevant to the wisdom of that step.

This light, the *nur* impressed upon our forehead as wisdom, as grace, as divine plenitude, this is the gift we have to return to God unspoiled and undiminished by our passage through the world, and we have come here to do that very thing. For this reason we must engage every aspect of our purification to perfect ourself; in that perfected state of the *qutbiyyat,* of divine wisdom, we become the *Muhammad* and the *nur,* the luminous grace and beauty of His truth embedded in the sanctity of the *qutb.* When all the anger and arrogance, when all the fear and anxiety, the attachments of the ego, the possessiveness of desire, the emotion and speculation of the mind, when they are subdued and harnessed by wisdom, the *nur* does emerge, we exist in the state of pure light, the open space where the totality exists and we do not. When a person becomes a true human being, discarding everything that is not God, and discovers the form of a hidden life within, then

365

discovers the inner light which encloses another light, the *nur,* and then uncovers the essence, the power of God within the *nur,* that person lives indistinguishably within God and God lives indistinguishably within that person.

The power of God flows through the *nur,* but it needs the wisdom of the *qutb,* the divine explanation, to ignite it and bring it to the soul. When the *qutb* becomes the *nur,* the beauty of this grace and wisdom alive in the soul is made visible by the body, and this light of the soul which is connected to God, which is not separate from God, is the imperishable light returning to Him. Human existence consists of seven components, the five elements constantly at war with each other which make up the body, then the light of the *qutbiyyat,* the analytic or understanding aspect of wisdom, and finally the seventh, the *nur,* the radiant light of divine wisdom. This is the light of God's qualities, His wisdom and His limitless, overflowing bounty, the completeness. The *nur* lives in the kingdom of God, and when the qualities and actions of the body make this kingdom available, the total human experience lies within His kingdom. When ten of the twelve openings of the body are closed to the world and only the two at the crown of the head and the gnostic eye remain open, luminous in radiant light, the human experience is the experience of the divine.

The *nur* is the messenger, the prophet who teaches us to know God by showing us His radiant names and the qualities through which they are manifest. Because the *nur* existed within God, inseparable from Him before it emerged, this *nur* knows these names, these qualities, and knows the essence, and since God knew that all this wisdom was acquired, contained and accepted within the *nur,* He made it the messenger, the *Nur Muhammad* with which everything was created, so that everything which emanated from His unique existence would know Him. As God became aware of Himself through the *nur,* we too are destined to know ourself through the *nur.* This secret of the inner heart is conveyed to those whose hearts have melted in the divine, whose love illuminated by the purest wisdom has unlocked the mysteries in prayer, contemplation, meditation, revelation and remembrance. The *kalimah,* the recitation of faith which verifies the existence of the *nur* as His divine messenger, the *la ilaha illallahu Muhammadur-Rasulullah,* rises from the heart of this love, the *kalimah* which asserts that nothing is real, nothing exists but God, He is that One and Muhammad, the *Nur Muhammad,* is His messenger.

The wisdom, grace and light of the *nur* were placed in the human form in a most exalted way, placed there so that we would know God, know the things about God He wanted us to know about the radiance, the exquisite perfection shining from the very heart of His existent being. Before the radiant souls emerged from the *nur* manifesting His qualities of light, His qualities of purity, the explanation of the five letters making up the *alhamd,* the pure heart of praise, the *alif, lam, mim, ha'* and *dal,* was given. We have to know God, we have to know ourself and understand the connection existing between God and ourself. To amplify what was described earlier, the *alif* is God, Allah, the One; the *lam* is the light of wisdom, the *qutb,* the divine explanation, the clarification emerging from the *nur;* the *mim* is the *nur,* the messenger receiving and dispensing the light. These three convergent lights are one, they illuminate as one, they function as one, they exist as one. The *ha'* is a home for the three, a house of radiance and beauty for the ninety-nine names in the hearts of those who were to be born, the *asma' ul-husna* reciting His praise, the hundredth name, Allah. The *dal* of the *alhamd,* the *dunya,* is the world overflowing with secrets, mysteries, delusions, illusions and all the evils to be mixed with the light and purity of the human form.

The soul which longs for the return to Allah must find its way first to the *nur;* the wisdom of the *qutb* has to merge with the light of the *nur* to illuminate the way it must go. The *qutb* functioning at the level of the *nur* analyzes our thoughts, our qualities and actions, distinguishing the good from the bad, the right from the wrong, and with the voice of conscience tells us what is correct, acceptable to God, and what has to be changed or thrown away. It is the voice of the *nur,* acting at the level of the *qutb,* as our conscience correcting the levels of wisdom beneath it, which teaches us how to judge ourself here, before the end, while there is time for reparation and restoration. Since that judgment comes from the *nur,* this means it comes from God, it is His judgment purifying us here, showing us what we need to see so that we can go back to Him, we can come to the place of death before death because there is nothing left to be judged.

The *nur* is the light of God, a light which shines from His essence and from each thing He created, a mystery in this world, in the world of souls and the world of the hereafter. The soul that wants to return to God must learn how to make its way through all the dazzling sensations presented by the world, through the turmoil hatched in the regions where mind and desire rule, through the inner worlds of miracles, revelations and mystery until it encounters the *nur* which comes from God, which was put there by God. Only when the soul merges with the *nur* can it then merge with God, only when the soul recognizes the *nur* can it recognize God, be one with God. We have to rid ourself of everything we have ever taken from the world, of everything the world has either dumped or conferred upon us, the talk, the pleasures and pains, the things we desire, the things we have collected in our karmic bag of tricks, then rid ourself of all the spiritual pleasures and secrets, the bliss, the ecstasy, the inner treasures we find along the way so that the *nur,* the pure, original light of the *nur* can vibrate with His light, His resonance inseparable from Him. It is the *nur* seated in the luminous eye of wisdom that alone can know the totality of God.

There is a state which is imperishable, for which death does not exist, a luminous state of the *nur* and the soul which is knowing ourself and knowing God. We who exist as part of the perishable and impermanent world of form are also connected to the permanent, the eternal, we can exist as lights of grace and wisdom continually offering praise to God. When God created us, when He placed the *nur* on Adam's forehead, his gnostic eye, making the human being the most exalted of all

His creatures, He gave us the capacity to know everything, to know Him, to comprehend the mystery He encloses; and He sent the *Nur Muhammad* as a messenger of wisdom again and again, to show us how to travel the path to His truth. If we realize ourself, if we examine the inner heart we can know this, we can find that place where He is alive forever within our form, our limit, we can stay in the limitless, we can be free of darkness and light the way for everyone else. Then we are luminous, a perfected human being functioning with the three convergent lights, the *alif, lam* and *mim,* God as *alif,* the *qutb* as the *lam,* the light of divine wisdom, and the *nur* as the *mim,* the letter and light of creation, these three lights shining as one in the inner heart of grace, the pure realization of His expectation, His intention for us.

With the *nur* in the gnostic eye, the eye of wisdom, and the *Nur Muhammad* at the crown of our head in a throne of light, we analyze our experience, our thoughts and intentions, assessing everything as right or wrong, identifying the things which belong essentially to the *la ilaha* or the *illallahu,* the things of the world on the left we have to discard or the things of Allah on the right we have to absorb and become one with. This is the Islam, the purity which belongs to us all, it is the unity and understanding of God's creation which is neither the preserve of a religion nor is it an article of dogma or doctrine since it has been available to us from the creation of Adam. This Islam is not subject to barriers or barricades, this Islam is for everyone who comes to it with a profound love of God and an open heart. The gift of the *Nur Muhammad* to the whole human species is the unity of the human species, a unity which is not correctly described as family or anything which implies lateral association, it is an inner unity, the unity of oneness, no distinction between your hunger or mine, your suffering or mine, your happiness or mine, no separation but identity, you and I are one.

When we perform the *dhikr* of *la ilaha illallahu* correctly in the purest state of prayer, with the inner understanding that nothing exists but God, that He alone is God, when we have discarded all the things of the left with the *la ilaha* exhalation, what we inhale with the *illallahu,* only You are God, is the light of the *nur.* As we inhale this light we are taking the ninety-nine powers of God's ninety-nine names into our being, we transform our body with His grace, His light and wisdom, we have the divine sweetness flowing through our breath and beating in our blood. We have the qualities and actions of God inseparable, indistinguishable from our own, His love is ours,

His truth, mercy, compassion, tolerance, forgiveness, truth, patience, forbearance and magnanimity are what we manifest outwardly and inwardly. For us to have access to this consciousness, our own wisdom must be connected to, merged with the wisdom of the soul, the radiant wisdom of the *qutb* who is a perfected being. Only with our connection to such a rare being of wisdom will the light of the *nur* be ignited, a light which can be directly transferred or transmitted if we are one with a being already merged and one with God.

When we are in that transformed state there is an infectious joy which we automatically display and communicate; if we look into our inner heart in this state we see the grace and beauty of His qualities as our own, we see ourself in Him, we see Him in ourself, the mystery of non-duality examined, a secret revealed. The understanding we have from this examination is divine wisdom, the wisdom of the *qutbiyyat.* Ascending from here to the radiant state of the *nur* is *ma'rifat,* gnosis, the luminous wisdom of grace transcending both day and night, birth and death, the divine wisdom which is complete emancipation of the soul. In this state the hunger of the soul, the longing for return to its place of origin, to God, is fully satisfied.

Sufi

THE ENLIGHTENED MASTER

Relations between any enlightened master, who might be called sheikh or teacher or guru, relations between that master and the disciple are unlike any other association we might have because this extraordinary being will fill many different functions in our life simultaneously. The sheikh will be part master of our wisdom, part parent, part instructor and part deity, as well as friend and companion on a very high plane. For the western experience this essential connection is a difficult thing to reckon with, we who are raised on concepts of individualism, independence, even isolation and separation, it is often not an easy leap from this formative structuring into submission to another, surrender of the ego, denial of selfhood, and the urgent, necessary reshaping of our inner landscape that will accommodate the new criteria. In addition, there is the insistent assumption we ought to be able to do this on our own, if we pray, meditate, wrestle our darkness into the light, why can't we find our own way, why should we need a guide to illuminate the path of the soul back to God?

Answers to this question range from because we don't see ourself clearly, accurately, because the way is neither open nor easy, because there is a direct transmission from someone who has gone ahead which alone can show us the path, answers range from there to the deeply subtle understanding that what emerged from God at the beginning is what returns, and that it must return in the same perfect way it emerged. We don't in fact, see ourself clearly, we have an idea, a set of ideas about ourself, often seriously disconnected from the way we are in relation to the *dunya,* the world, and certainly quite often irrelevant to who we are in relation to the divine kingdom and to God. There is a sense in which everything we see, everything we experience is a teacher, but it is experience which must be analyzed, what do we take from this, how is it useful to develop our understanding of the human condition, what do we store in memory as a thing of value and what do we throw away? Is this experience a thing of the moment, something with temporary usefulness but long-term inconsequence, is it a mental phenomenon, a tissue of illusion manufactured by the manipulations of our mind which refuses to acknowledge its lesser state, is it the product of our desire which wants what it wants when it wants what it wants?

When we see the faults in our friends, our family, our associates, we need to see this as the advertising of our own mistakes and shortcomings; what we can't observe in our own qualities and actions shouts to us from someone else. If we learn to read the things we see in the behavior of others as instructive about ourself, people we know even casually can be our teachers too, if we change on the basis of what we see. But this recognition did not come from my own unaided understanding, it only dawned on me when my teacher, a sage of depthless wisdom pointed it out, and although I have no doubt some figure this out on their own, most of us need to have even the obvious clarified when it comes to a correct analysis of our flaws and failures. The teacher, the true teacher holds himself or herself up before us as a reflecting glass in which to examine ourself, see this image of God's qualities and assess where we stand on that scale of perfection. Because the true teacher has the capacity to read our heart, notice our actions up close as well as at a distance, this can be an intimidating, even terrifying event.

For myself in that situation, not so much because I wasn't aware of the disabilites and imperfections I had loaded on during a life of misconception, error and ignorance, but more because from the first time I encountered this towering example of sanctity and grace I accepted him as the master, surrendered everything with the thought, unspoken but certainly conveyed, yes, this is yours now, do with it what you want. I offered him the totality of my existence as a sacrifice to the qualities, the proximity to God I knew in his presence, and so I always assumed he knew the worst about me, was nevertheless, prepared to help with the necessary transformation I begged him for. There were others who could not endure what they feared might be revealed about themselves and avoided his immediate presence, stayed away or left altogether. If the community is the crucible, the enlightened master is the fire which heats it up, makes it burn.

The process of standing before the sheikh is difficult, but running away is even worse because then we live with the knowledge of what we refused, what we chose not to do, and this becomes another ghost haunting us in three worlds, the past, the present and the hereafter. Aside from his ability to see where we are, what we need to get rid of or at least improve, the true teacher with divine wisdom, whose life is the duty imposed by that wisdom, this teacher has been where we are now and knows how he was led beyond, what it took and what it cost, the effort, the skill, the difficulty. These are all vital steps to be taken as the outer practices converge with the inner reclamation, practices guided by the sheikh or guru who also supervises the inner transformation, yet there is something else which transcends inner and outer, and that something is a direct connection to the source, to God. A transmission which cannot be described completely in words but which resembles fire igniting fire or light merging with light is at the heart of the relations between master and student, each searching for the other as eagerly as we search for water in the desert.

When we search for the true teacher, the sage to guide us on the path, there are certain clear signs we can look for, just as he searches for certain clear signs in us. We look for someone who emanates proximity, wisdom, clarity, sanctity, sincerity, ability, we listen for the resonance vibrating sympathetically in tune with the resonance of our own heart, we listen for the words of truth which come without disguise as the truth, words we recognize at once with a tremor, my God this is it, this is really it! Then we catch the fragrance, the actual scent of roses

379

or jasmine or lilies, olfactory confirmation of the divine presence. (I saw roses flowering at the end of November outside the house where my sheikh was visiting when the freeze of winter had settled in permanently at least a month before.) There is a radiant presence surrounding the true teacher, unmistakable when we encounter it, the holiness of purity, the simplicity of grace which reach out to the longing soul in a gesture of recognition.

Nor will there be any question of money or payment, the truth is not for sale, it is dispensed freely, lavishly and without condition. We do not bring gifts to the master, the gifts all flow from him to us, outwardly and inwardly. When we try to present him with something, even a trifle, if we watch carefully we will see it given away, almost at once, because he has nothing of his own, keeps nothing, needs nothing. What he does is no different from what he says, his actions exemplify the things he says and the advice he gives, perfectly and specifically. We will never see anger, impatience or intolerance, we will never see arrogance, lies or deception, he manifests nothing but the qualities of God, and this has nothing to do with some subtle form of hypnotism or illusion, it is the persuasiveness of love, the undecorated core of truth which we are so drawn to, so attracted by.

But it's not all soft and gentle, some warm, unthinking blurr. When we encounter the core of truth which is hard and pure, when our imperfection knocks against the truth there are tough moments as the corrective remedies are applied to the wounds caused by our ignorance and bad qualities. Sometimes it can be more than tough, it can be painful to have the wounds scraped and cleaned, to have the abcess lanced; nevertheless, we have to trust that he knows what he is doing, we have to believe in his competence to administer what we need and be certain he will never insist on more than we can endure, never take us more deeply into our own purification than we are ready for. The relations between the master and each aspirant are both private and public, conducted openly from time to time but always on an inner, non-verbal level which continues without interruption. The instruction course for every disciple is geared to that person's capacity and requirements, while at the same time, as members of a community, they receive the teachings all together in discourse and conversation, in prayer and practice.

Not all the accounts I have read describing the relations between master and pupil make it sound easy or pleasant, on the contrary many read like horror stories, at least on the surface, but based on my own experience and observation I find it to be the most absorbing, most loving and rewarding connection of my life, and my guess is that even those whose experience does not resemble a walk in the park would agree with this assessment because its essential characteristic is divine love, God's love for us and ours for Him expressed emblematically in the love between sheikh and disciple. Probably the disposition of the disciple has much to do with his or her association with the teacher, then again, perhaps some of us are hard enough on ourself, demanding enough of ourself to need no more external pressure from the master, while others might be too fragile to bear as much as some do. Since this traditionally eastern conjunction of teacher and pupil is new to the west, not deeply embedded in our cultural expectations or our understanding, that too might account for the lighter touch I have seen practised on our side of the world.

And what is the sheikh or guru looking for in the student, the disciple? Just as eagerly as we search for the true teacher, that master is also searching for students of truth, students of love and wisdom who have that longing for God in their heart, the need for union, for the search and a meaningful examination of the mystery in the One. We need to be serious about the search, but not humorless, we need to be dedicated and determined, but not fanatic, devoted and loving, but not without restraint. Above all, we need to come as postulants, empty of any idea how things should be, how the teachings should proceed, and we have to abandon everything we thought we knew, begin again with a totally clean slate, write nothing without the master's validation or verification because intellect has only a subordinate role to play, the wisdom born in absolute faith the dominant voice now.

On the one hand, we accept every word of the teacher no matter how imponderable or improbable, on the other hand, we don't stop analyzing the truth in our effort to understand. It is subtle, we have to accept it all, believe it all, yet analyze our comprehension and the things offered to it. If something doesn't make sense to us, if there are points we cannot grasp because our wisdom is insufficiently developed, we are not to discard the information as useless, instead we are to store it away in a safe place from which we can extract it again in the future when the body of our understanding has expanded so that these points now fall into place, comprehensible and necessary. Wisdom is not stationary, it lives and breathes and grows, what we failed to understand yesterday might be open for us tomorrow. In terms of instruction, this complete submission to the teacher is not as unfamiliar as we might think. A music student who goes to a great teacher or a great performer for lessons does not debate the fingering of a passage on the violin, he does not say wait a minute I have a better way, the student accepts the teacher's experience and the results of that experience with the same passionate energy which moves the disciple, the need to learn, the need to get it right, to be perfect.

As the music student accepts the advice, the discipline and practices of a great performer, a disciple follows the teachings of a sheikh or guru, repeating, imitating, adopting the recommended techniques without question, and most importantly, not trying to add or subtract by referring to another system, another source. If we mix anything but the truth with the truth that alloy is no longer the truth, it will be the opposite, something destructive, even deadly. Initially we must empty the bucket of everything we have already taken from the well so that the enlightened master can fill it again, this time with the light of God's wisdom and grace, then we have to be very careful not to drop the bucket back into the poisoned well or the truth will be drowned and our wisdom will dissolve. If we want to pray, if we want to understand God we have to know who He is, directly, without mixing in religion, philosophy, science, without metaphor and simile, without translation from any text but our own experience.

It's not easy, we are not likely to find peace on our own in this difficult life, and that is one motivating, powerful reason to search for an enlightened teacher, because we hunger for peace, we long to have the restless inner chatter finish in the exquisite silence of knowing and being. In the presence of such a teacher we can learn to see ourself, to correct ourself as our conscience is reshaped in the sun of wisdom radiating from the perfected master. False gurus are easy enough to find, they advertise, they invite us with seductive words and irrelevant promises, but they do not know, they do not disseminate the truth, they merely package a product for sale. Sooner or later we see this and have to move on, perhaps to another false guru who promises much he cannot deliver. If we continue to search with an open heart God will not ignore us, He will put us together with a true human being who knows and knows how to dispense what he knows, who has a license from God to say His words, to act for Him.

This is not the end of our work, this is only the beginning, a daunting fact which might well be obscured by the euphoria, the bliss of having come home at last. When the mist clears and we understand where we are and where we still have to go, we realize that although the teacher prepares the food for us, we have to feed ourself, take the food in, swallow it correctly without choking and digest it, assimilate the transforming wisdom at the level of the cell, the nerve, the bone. We change and we are changed. As the love, the compassion and beauty of God begin to grow in our heart, responding to the vibrating love, compassion and beauty in the heart of the master, we see the darkness that needs to be swept away, we see, judge and eliminate every thought and act obscuring His presence, we begin to live the reality of the *kalimah* affirming His existence and annihilating our own. The *la ilaha illallahu* becomes the golden thread from which all experience hangs, from which the soul learns the liberating path to the One.

The enlightened being who is our model, our example, will light up the way for us, the effort is our own however. It is our own faith which must be rooted more and more deeply, more and more firmly, to create the conditions in which wisdom can grow. Like a precious stone our wisdom is buried deep inside us, it takes an experienced miner to dig it up and bring it to the surface where it can be polished and used. As faith deepens, as our qualities change and wisdom grows the sheikh enters our heart in a subtle way, we enter his heart in a subtle way, and that point of convergence is the light on our path, clarifying what is good, what is right, what God loves and what He has no use for. The teacher, the *qutb*, takes us a long way up the path we must travel, teaching us with God's qualities and actions, igniting the light of the *qutbiyyat* within us with his own light of divine wisdom. At a certain point however, he will be obliged to leave and from there we have to proceed on our own, from there we go on alone; when the *qutb* within us becomes the *nur* we are alone.

If we want to merge with God we have to give up the world and the things of the world, not just the things themselves but the idea, the concept of them functioning through mind or desire, and the remembrance of them must also vanish. As we surrender to him, the *qutb* fills us so completely with God's love, with the form of love and His compassionate qualities that slowly, slowly our interests and attachments are disengaged, slowly, slowly we come to the state in which the enlightened master within us becomes the food which satisfies the hunger of all our thoughts and desires, the hunger of every illusion, even the impositions of our karma because he knows, he understands how to treat every sorrow, how to deal with every attachment afflicting the soul, anything that stands between God and ourself. As we become one with the teacher, the guru, as the 'I' with all its props and reinforcements dissolves in the truth and love of the teacher's light, the things of the world become so insignificant the attachments are burned up, they disappear. When the world falls away within us there is nothing left, one thing remains and that thing is what our soul has cried for from the beginning, that one thing is God.

SCRIPTURE AND REVELATION

Orthodoxy is profoundly suspicious of revelation if it is not encoded in a book, scripture, the transcript of revelation, while mystics who are profoundly persuaded by revelation may be suspicious of messages already encoded in a book. Those who find the outer book easier to read will not search for the inner book, those for whom the inner book is accessible cannot always make sense of the outer book, may not believe they have much need for the outer book. If we do not perceive the difference between inner and outer as an illusion we have an apparent dichotomy, a split among the lovers of God we would do well to erase. The trouble with the written book is that it may not address our immediate experience without interpretation which is subject to the fallibility of the interpreter, and the trouble with revelation is the inherent difficulty of validation. What we trust and depend on may not be reliable, may not be the thing we take it to be.

Take the history of the Bible for example, which is without question scripture based on a compilation of history and revelation, yet we also know it has been subject to the fiat of councils which accepted and rejected what was included on the basis of doctrinal or political or personal conviction. There is a truth buried there, but some of it might have been either deliberately or accidentally omitted, some of it might have been corrupted, willingly or unwillingly, some of it might have been lost and some of it might have been incorrectly included. In spite of what is known about the Bible's history, many still accept it entirely as the word of God, trusting that each change or omission was also divinely protected and therefore divinely inspired. That is one kind of faith. On the other hand, we are persuaded that the Qur'an has not been subject to this kind of manipulation, what was revealed to Muhammad was written down then verified by him, what was revealed to him has been so protected from change that not a single word has been altered in its transmission to us today. Nevertheless, it remains a hard document to penetrate because of the depth and range of meanings compressed within it, and the enormous amount of commentary or interpretation.

We can search for the right book or we can search for the truth, then again, until we have the truth and the right to be sure it is the truth, how do we identify the book which is the right book? We can believe that our own revelation comes from God Himself, we can believe this as profoundly as we believe in God and His truth and still be mistaken, we could be anywhere between merely deluded and quite mad. Or it could be the truth. For most people the book, any book, Bible, Qur'an, Torah or *purana* is easier to deal with than the arduous path of inquiry, examination and elimination of the self, a path which might lead us astray or to the truth itself. Why then do we reject the religions and choose the arduous path of revelation, why bother to learn the inner book when the outer book and the establishments which support them are so available, so approved and part of the rituals of the society we are born into? For the most part, the religions stop where we like to begin, the religions are happy to thunder out the *shari'at,* the first step, to expound the right and the wrong with vigor, although today as more and more people express their dissatisfaction with what the church and synagogue have to offer, they are inclined to keep the thunder for a rainy day and present a rather cheerful musical which often relies heavily on entertainment and social services.

For the soul which hungers for God, to know Him, to understand Him, meet Him, return to Him, merge with His totality, the imperfectly expressed rituals of the encoded word are clearly insufficient; doctrine and dogma which close the gates shut when we want them to swing wide open are inadequate. The religions don't pretend to have seen God, they don't expect to, they can't say what He's like, they can't describe Him, they have no remedy for the hunger of proximity and make no attempt to teach us how to find out. We begin alone and we end alone, but in between we search for the guide, a truly wise, enlightened being whose existence validates the revelations about the nature of God, the nature of His prophets, about the pathless path of wisdom where we are led, step by step, to an understanding of the things we need to know for our life in this world, the world we have come from and the world to which we will go.

What the religions omit is not nearly as difficult or dangerous as the things they foster. Each splinter group, each sect, each religion is so persuaded of the unique value of its own understanding, so convinced that God prefers them and chooses them alone, their version of the book, their doctrine, language and race, they exclude everyone and everything else as false and wrong, so unacceptable they are prepared to take up arms to propagate their own perspective and annihilate the others. There is something we can learn from the religions, there is some truth in each one, but obviously not this, God is not punitive, vengeful or exclusive. He created us all as members of the same family, as children of the same parents, he did not divide us into warring factions based on religion, race, politics, ethnicity or any arbitrary separations we improvise. When the religions try to capture the kingdom of God and claim it as their own, they forget that it is not ours to possess, it belongs, along with everything else, to Him.

To understand what the religions have to tell us, we have to work our way back to the revelations now shrouded by an institution, a history of dissension, debate and religious wars. When we read the words revealed to each of the prophets we learn something about them, but then we have to understand the words of God that came through them, understand how the revelations came, understand what the revelations were, learn the meaning of the sound, the vibration and light which came from God through them to us. We have to go beyond the words, beyond the resonance which brought the words. We need to know the grace and mercy of Allah, our faith and wisdom need to know the light that comes from God's incomparable totality, we have to recognize His supremacy in everything, not just for our own life but for all the worlds, all the beings of all the worlds, then with the profound acceptance of His ultimate power and authority we can read the outer and inner books. Whether we follow the practices of a specific religion or not, what matters is to know that we are one, the truth is one, God is One; what matters is *la ilaha,* nothing exists but You, *illallahu,* You are God.

We need to find our own peace, we need to understand the equality of all the souls before God, we need to grasp the nature and importance of our wisdom, our qualities and our actions if we want to know God, to have the intimacy of the lover and the Beloved, something organized religion is not prepared to offer, a mixture of inability and indifference. When the ignition key of wisdom is inserted and turned on correctly, in the right way, the motor which drives our inner sight, inner hearing, taste and smell begins to operate, we smell His fragrance everywhere, see evidence of His existence everywhere and bathe in the joy of His light. Unless we are willing to undertake the transforming changes which make it possible to switch on that key, we are immobilized by incapacity and ignorance, we will not find the peace of companionship, the bliss of intimacy; unless we make a deliberate effort to abandon the self we have identified as ourself and emerge in the qualities of God, we will not know the truth, we will not know God. This is not something apparently known to or acted upon by the religions, this is the reason we choose the private path, the pathless path of revelation.

None of the prophets understood that their mission was to start a new religion, they understood they were sent here to this world to explain who God is, to offer His truth and show us how we must think, feel, behave and believe to know Him, to come close to Him. Their revelations are given to us in words which bring us the resonance, the truth and the meaning of God. The special gift of the prophets is the ability to translate a vibration, a light, a sound into words which are His words; the special gift of the *qutbs* is to give the explanations of God; the special gift of the saints is to manifest the qualities which are His. The special gift we all have is the light of the *nur* within the heart which can attract the light of His words and His power, attract it with the wisdom that understands the resonating meaning of His words.

Wisdom and the qualities of God are the two transforming instruments which unlock the secrets and treasures of His truth.

395

The path to God is not as easy as deciding which church, mosque, temple or synagogue to choose, and if we elect to go this way, if we are called to the esoteric, to mystery, we do have to carve our own path, nothing is laid out for us, prepared like a sermon or a mantra; nevertheless, there are pathways of behavior to follow, signposts which mark ascending levels of wisdom or states of consciousness, there are steps leading to the purification of our faith. Even with the guidance of a good teacher, a wise being who knows the way, who has come back for the sole purpose of illuminating our understanding, helping us find our way, the work, the effort is still our own. No one can do it for us, no one is exempt from the required reclamation, no religion can claim a bypass assuming they have been given it all, trusting that their chosen prophet will stand at their side before God and say O yes, I know this person, he's okay, she's my friend, let them stay with us.

The wisdom we have to follow is not an intellectual prescription that can be learned from a book or a course of study directed to our mind, the wisdom we must acquire is an experiential proposition, a cell by cell transformation affecting every aspect of our being including the mind, the last to know, but ultimately subject to the same reforming process. Since this wisdom is rooted in faith, we should reexamine the steps to deepening faith, and their implications, as well as the levels of wisdom and divine attributes we need to pursue. The first step to absolute faith is the moral distinction between right and wrong, good and evil, a step which the religions comfortably straddle, the de facto script for a good life, sometimes administered with disturbing political fervor, according to the understanding of what God requires us to be and do. This is often the only step religions are prepared to take, composed mostly of the things thou shalt not but mixed with a few divine injunctions to pray, be good, be loving.

The moral base for human experience, occasionally described as divine law, is certainly valid although perhaps a little shallow in dimension since it tends to refer to outer behavior without addressing the inner soil which specifically needs to be ploughed, sifted and redistributed. The scope and range of reference are also limited by the prevailing concept of good and evil, referring only to what I do to you and you do to me when it is the whole scale of consciousness, from sensory perception to divine knowledge, which needs redefinition. If we are trying to divest ourself of the world and all worldly attachments, there is no sense in which the world is good, quite

397

the opposite, the world represents everything we neither want nor need, materially or non-materially, and is therefore to be thought of as bad, wrong or even evil. Since God is the only good, our understanding of what constitutes goodness must be consistent with His uniqueness, His attributes and actions.

At each level rising to the state of absolute faith there is the possibility of ascent two ways, vertically or laterally, because there are four steps within each of the four steps. That is, at the *shari'at* level or first step, there is also a *tariqat,* a *haqiqat* and a *ma'rifat* within the *shari'at* itself. At any of the four levels corresponding to the religions themselves the inner path is available, the grace, the beauty and wisdom of Allah is never denied to anyone. The *ma'rifat* understanding of the *shari'at* then is much more, much higher than the correct distinction of right from wrong, good from bad. This first step begins with understanding ourself and our God, proceeding not with a succession of observations and requirements, the rules of a religion, it moves instead directly to an understanding of that religion at the *haqiqat* level, the loving truth of the heart, or the *ma'rifat* level, the wisdom of divine knowledge. In Islam this means that the five primary obligations, faith, prayer, charity, fasting and pilgrimage are understood as the absolute faith which denies the reality of anything but God; it entails the prayer which affirms this truth with every breath whether asleep or awake, at work or study; the charity which acknowledges the suffering of others as our own; the fasting which accepts the hunger of anyone as ours; and the pilgrimage which is the journey of the heart to the truth

With this understanding the first step means to acquire the qualities and attributes of God, to study the four religions and learn the truth each one possesses, as well as to earn a living honorably and live correctly in a state of purity. It means never to harm anyone outwardly or inwardly with our words, thoughts or acts, to eliminate desires and be certain what this body, this form which houses the light of God involves, to help anyone in need appropriately and speak with clarity about the truth, to learn the inner obligations which awaken the inner levels of perception. It means to live with conscience, justice and wisdom. In my own experience, taking the first step was instant *sufiyyat,* being flung into the deep end of the pool and learning to swim or else merely drowning, which would have meant leaving it, leaving it all and going away, unthinkable when I was in the presence of the truth at last, no matter the strange, exotic garments it wore.

And everything fell into place without difficulty, there was nothing to memorize, no lessons to be learned by rote, there was only the unfolding of experience which led to the truth I had hungered for with such passionate insistence. This was a different kind of school, no books except the book of the heart to be read and examined under the master's guidance, yet the lessons were not always easy. For some they were occasionally painful; for us all every once in awhile, the way was long, tough and exhausting but filled with joy and increasing light, increasing gratitude as wisdom and grace coincided with deeper, stronger faith. Prompted by the admonishments of an enlightened teacher, we discovered the process was largely one of self-examination and self-correction, we measured our ability against the divine example manifested flawlessly by a perfected human being who alternately coaxed, praised, criticized, reprimanded and urged us on, constantly reminding us we had the capacity to succeed, we were never to give up or turn back. Many did.

The paths of study may be steep mountain slopes, yet there are ropes and guidelines to help us climb and keep us from falling off as the way becomes more perilous at the next levels. The *tariqat* level which is unswerving adherence to the good is characterized by pure faith and duty, by unfailing intention and determination, by the certitude of our love for God and true inner patience. No matter what happens or fails to happen we accept whatever comes as God's will, as something to be managed first with inner patience, the pure serenity born of undeviating faith; then with unquestioning, total gratitude in the certainty that everything is a gift from Him; then in more difficult circumstances we surrender absolutely, throwing away the suffering self so that nothing remains to be in pain; ultimately we offer all our praise to Him no matter what occurs, no matter the pleasure or pain, the joy or sorrow—we allow neither praise nor blame for ourself because He alone exists. Each of these four states is progressively deeper in submission, more actively vigorous in profound surrender. This is a *haqiqat* understanding of *tariqat,* the path, the way to God and the truth as we purify ourself, as we are rid of the fires generated by anger, by hunger, by desire.

Reexamining *haqiqat,* the third step corresponding to Christianity, the religion located at the level of the heart in the human body, we find the realization of divine truth and the initiation of communion with the divine, God speaks to us and we speak directly to Him. In this state, at this level, we are a radiant presence helping all humankind understand God's attributes and His mystery, we show others how to purge the darkness of the heart, how to control the restlessness of the body, the desires and emotions of the mind, we give love, we instill love, compassion, mercy and tolerance as the very form of the formless in the hearts of human beings. The actual bliss of this ecstatic state is offering it, offering this blissful contemplation of God as an available treasure we all have access to. The wisdom of this state is the ability to know God and His qualities, to know His wisdom; in this state we can see and use the *nur,* the light of His wisdom which emerged from Him, worshiping, glorifying, understanding; in this state, using the *nur,* the soul knows itself, His grace and the meaning of His creation.

When we look again at *ma'rifat,* the fourth step, gnosis, the divine wisdom corresponding to the head in our human form and to the religion of Islam, the purity of the true, original Islam, we see the state which knows all the hidden secrets of all the worlds. These worlds are only a tiny dot altogether from this perspective, the state of merging with God, with Allah, the wisdom which knows Him as One, the divine luminous presence in every aspect of His creation. The *nur,* the essence of God, is *ma'rifat,* the state of no day and no night, the state in which we commune with Him and the totality, everything is revealed. Each of the four steps, four levels of true faith, *shari'at, tariqat, haqiqat* and *ma'rifat,* each exists within the *nur,* four steps with different characteristics which make up the totality of the *nur.* In *ma'rifat* we are perfected, there is no sin, there is no attachment, there is no time, no karma, no illusion, we are one with Him, we are His sound, His voice. At the fifth level, *sufiyyat,* we disappear into Him.

If we examine the seven levels of consciousness or wisdom again from the perspective of revelation, we see the seven merged into a single function, just one, these seven which correspond to seven worlds above the heart and form the impossibly fine, impossibly delicate bridge to carry us high above the perils and fires of the world. Using this subtle instrument of wisdom we analyze the totality of experience, disallowing everything until we reach the sixth level, the *qutbiyyat* which teaches us to throw away everything but God. Then with the light of the *nur,* the divine and luminous wisdom of God, at the seventh level we cross over that bridge in total surrender to Allah. But only God and everything that is His can cross this bridge; if our surrender is imperfect, if it is not complete, the bridge will not sustain us and we fall back into the flames.

Instruction from the religions, the words of the prophets encoded, written down and transmitted institutionally come to us outwardly, addressing only the lower, the first three levels of consciousness, perception, awareness and intellect. We begin to address the exclusively human level with judgment, the ability to distinguish right from wrong, good from bad and to act upon that distinction. If this fourth level is developed, if we acquire the atttitudes and actions which lead to the understanding of God's qualities and we are transformed by the need to change ourself, change our life so that the garden blooms with His flowers instead of our weeds, at the fifth level, at the level of subtle wisdom we realize the hunger and suffering of others to be our own. In the sense of the religions, it is at this point we are said to be reborn; when we divest ourself of the qualities rising from our elemental composition, from the arrogance, the inheritance and illusions of mind and desire, the physical shroud begins to dissolve, the gift of the soul emerges and in that sense, we do find ourself reborn. This transition requires the active intervention of a divinely wise being to stabilize and guide the process of change, to show us what needs to be changed and to place the transforming instruments in our hand.

When the teacher who might be called a sheikh, who might be called a guru, a saint or a *qutb* gives us the blessing of his or her instruction, he will take us as far as we can go together, but eventually we have to make the last part of the journey on our own, eventually there is only room for one and we have to rely, with God's help, on the pure effort we make ourself in conjunction with the guidelines laid out before us. This perfected being can take us to the sixth level, the sixth heaven where the elemental deceptions are finally dispersed and God's own truth which already exists within us is revealed, then we travel alone through all the difficulties and mysteries that lie beyond. At the seventh level of divine wisdom, the seventh heaven illuminated by the *nur* in a state of total surrender to God, we know that we exist in Him and He exists in us. As faith deepens and wisdom accelerates we begin to climb up, step by step, level by level, the religions left behind in this pure ascension, the path of revelation in the presence of God.

Sufi

THE DIVINE ATTRIBUTES

At the heart of our mystery is the attempt to locate a point which is an intersection of the human and the divine, the place where form converges with formless. We who seem to exist in a spatial-temporal configuration, our limits defined by the elements composing this corporeal existence, nevertheless, know we are not our body, and yet we are required to function in that body. How do we discover the ray of light, the soul giving life to this body, and how do we find the source, the origin of that light? Since no one has seen the soul and no one has seen God, where are we supposed to look for evidence and indications, the clues overriding mere sensory information which we know to be unreliable in any case? The confidence we have in signs which appear to us through revelation alone depends on the strength and depth of our faith when something resonates and confirms, this is the truth, this is the truth. It is not something which can be proved or verified like an equation, it can only be conveyed by the resonance of a response vibrating sympathetically, precisely in tune with the source of that truth. Truth alone confirms truth.

God is a formless power we cannot see but can come to know in the highest states of wisdom, we can come to know by observing the manifestation of His attributes which are the actions of His devotees, His saints and good people everywhere. We cannot suggest that we even partly comprehend the extent and range of a single divine quality among the three thousand tradition assigns to Him, we cannot because nothing is above Him, nothing is below Him, nothing is beside Him. There is neither definition nor verbal ascription which completely characterizes something in and of itself limitless in nature because description is limiting, confining. There is a dilemma here, the very act of description is a presumption of form in what we know to be formless, the very words themselves have only human relevance, yet we apply them to the divine as though they were relevant because we have nothing else to use. What it comes down to, we can only say something about God by saying something about ourself, we can only study His nature by studying our own, and that is a partial understanding of why they say if you want to know God you must first know

408

yourself. This is not a study of the body, this is a study of the light and beauty in the human soul.

What distinguishes a human being from the animal kingdom are the qualities of God which encourage us to love, protect and comfort other living creatures, the seven levels of wisdom He has placed in each human heart and the special connection to Him He has also placed there as His mystery, His kingdom. It is our responsibility to discover His qualities, develop them in our own heart and put them into practice in the things we do and say. The process is quite simple, when we see a good quality in someone else we imitate that quality until it becomes our own, when see someone do something we recognize to be good we make that act something we do too. We cannot say we have identified any quality or attribute until we have made it our own, until the life of the senses, desires of the mind and desires of the body have died. Religion and philosophy can only address the lower levels of wisdom, levels we have in common with the animal kingdom, because we cannot approach any higher levels without the commitment to and experience of exchanging our baser qualities for His three thousand divine attributes.

He has these qualities although He has no form, He exists as a pure power with specific characteristics revealed in every part of His creation, in the sun and the stars, on the earth and seas, in every living and inert thing in all the worlds. Since God Himself is without form we need to adopt His qualities to work for Him, we need to give form to His existence by becoming the means through which He carries out His duty to us, to all of us, yet when we make forms and ikons of our thoughts and emotions, of all the invading forces and energies surrounding us, these are the forms which block His qualities from taking shape in us, these are the obstacles we place between God and ourself. Our true form is not the body, not the images we construct to fulfill certain misconceptions about who we really are, our true, original form is the light form composed by God's qualities and actions, by the three mystical letters, the *alif*, *lam* and *mim* which stand for Allah, Muhammad and Muhaiyaddeen, God, the light of His creation and the light of His wisdom.

Once we accept the need for change we have to realize that it will take time to eradicate the thoughts, habits and assumptions we have already accumulated and entrenched deeply in our life. Sometimes change will be glacial in speed, the real inner changes in the landscape, the soil giving rise to the crop of our qualities will need time for its chemistry to reassemble, but there will be moments of pure revelation that change us at once, forever. For the most part, change will proceed slowly keeping pace with the rate at which we release ourself from the hold of desires, from the confinement of attachments and the dictates of mind. This is easier to do while we are younger— we're more flexible and open to change when we are under forty because we are less likely to be set irrevocably in patterns of thought and action that habit alone makes hard to disengage, let alone comfort and disinclination. It gets harder and harder to believe we are less than perfect as the years drop their weight upon us, although it is not impossible if we keep remembering that the only things we have to give back to God are His loving qualities and our absolute faith.

If we fill our heart with inner patience and His divine attributes, if we do the duty that presents itself without thought of reward or congratulation and see our faith as the strength in our life, we will have the peace and stability which become the source of pure happiness underlining all experience. If we polish our life with modesty, reserve, sincerity and the restraint imposed by concern for behaving correctly, by the fear of doing something unacceptable to God, four qualities we examined earlier, and if we establish, along with that inner patience, the undeviating contentment, surrender of responsibility to God and absolute praise of Him for whatever comes, we have the map of purity for this world and the next. With these three thousand divine attributes what we construct is a changeless home for the soul in both worlds, a home which is nothing but His light, His love and endless wisdom where we can pray in bliss forever, one with the totality of all that exists.

If we try to acquire the qualities of God and accept the guidance of a perfected being who exemplifies this grace and beauty, we find the path lying open and clear before us, we have no uncertainty about method or technique or prayer, it is all revealed for us. Once we know that unflinching surrender and praise without end, His qualities are the basis for all that we say, all that we do. We offer our love, we do our duty without attachment, we advise with wisdom, we pray in purity, we treat all human suffering as our own, and in this way we learn the service to God and the human family, we learn to see everyone as part of this family without any sense of race, nation, language, religion, any of the arbitrary distinctions we impose to keep us apart. When we act with the qualities of

God, when we live with the qualities of God we live in the sweet scent of His presence, we live in heaven and detect His fragrance everywhere, we see Him in all His creation.

Of the three thousand qualities tradition uses to describe the aspects of God we have some hope of knowing, ninety-nine are recited frequently as the ninety-nine beautiful names, the *asma'ul-husna* in Arabic. But just to announce the names without some approach to the profound significance each name represents is not enough, we have to find the name and its meaning in the wisdom and truth of our heart. When we dig into ourself deeply enough to acquire these exalted states they serve us, these states protect our heart with light, they give us the peace we have searched for and their light gives peace to those around us, our wisdom and qualities generate a radiance which surrounds those close to us. If we discover the pure attributes of that One who has no anger, no greed, no hatred or arrogance, no lust, fanaticism or attachment, if we can find the purity of that supreme Lord who is our truth, our grace, our wisdom and all our good, the darkness, the sorrow, the karma, inherited and acquired, are all erased. When we eradicate the darkness embedded in the bad qualities of our heart, qualities which have flourished in the life of the senses, the life of the

413

world, of mind and desire, when this darkness obscuring the buried treasure is gone only light remains.

We can make this world His divine kingdom if we have the qualities of God in a heart merged with Him, with His love and unity among us, His presence illuminating everything, everywhere. Using these qualities ignited by wisdom, we build the inner house of prayer within the heart of His kingdom, the only true place of worship, an indestructible shrine not subject to the decay of the elements or the indifference of the congregation. We build our own inner site which we furnish with our own altars and prayer mats, although we continue living in the world too, happily fulfilling the obligations we have there without hesitation, recognizing both sides of the veil while keeping the point of focus on that inner house as He reigns supreme. It doesn't matter where we come from, it doesn't matter what language we speak, whether we're black, white or yellow, nothing matters but that one God and that one prayer rising from His qualities in the Ka'bah of the heart. A true human being who has perfected himself or herself in the divine qualities lives this way.

Replacing our own dark qualities with the qualities of God means transcending death, a life which has no end, the genuine worship of the soul because that austere black cube we circumambulate outwardly is not the true Ka'bah, it is merely an externalization for our understanding. The focal point of our life is inside where there is no form, only the things we need to be rid of and the beauty of His qualities, the grace of His light. When we come to the end of our earthly life we no longer have a body composed by the elements, the body we use here—the only form we have then is the form we create with our qualities, either a form of light or of darkness, the form that is questioned about our life on earth, what we have learned and the things we have done, or what we failed to learn and do. To build a form of light we need His truth, His wisdom and His qualities; should we fail to develop this beautiful form, should we be seduced by the dark satanic mills however, we carry the darkness with us to the world that lies beyond.

The story of our life is the script we hand over which we have written with our thoughts, our qualities and actions; we hand it in and whatever we prescribed for ourself, heaven or hell, is what we are given. When the elements return to the elements, earth to earth, fire to fire, water to water, air to air and space to space, if the soul has established a genuine connection to God, the soul goes back to Him. We have two important things to

415

help us prepare the transition from light to light, we have prayer and forgiveness. The immensity of His compassion and forgiveness is what we have to look at carefully: His willingness to understand and forgive is so great, if we try we succeed. When we pray to be forgiven for the things we did in ignorance, even the things we did knowingly, He listens and expunges the mistakes of the past from our record with the performance of the present, we are forgiven and we know we are forgiven.

Compassion which supercedes even love is the quality which looks at someone else's suffering as our own, which sees the predicaments and mistakes of another person with the understanding if we found ourself in a similar situation, we would probably do the same thing; compassion is both the root and lining of forgiveness. When God looks at the misconduct we are responsible for in our ignorance, He looks with the indulgence of a loving parent, He sees us as three-year olds at play, corrects and chastises us firmly while secretly amused and filled with love. The mistakes we make when we know better are dealt with swiftly, God sees our every tiny imperfection and admonishes us to correct such flaws, it is not appropriate for a devotee, a lover of God to behave that way.

416

But He opens the gates of forgiveness wide, encouraging us to come in because He prefers to forgive, He is so willing to forgive, just as we forgive a playful child. The love and deep affection for all His creation which flow naturally from His compassion are easier for us to grasp as models of the love and affection we also experience, although His love is so pure, so untouched by longing or desire it wants nothing in return, we know it quite simply as the grace of His existent perfection.

The wisdom igniting this love is the supreme understanding, it is the totality that knows the beginning and the end of everything, everywhere, this wisdom is the totality itself which we cannot begin to measure, as great as the mercy He extends to all living things. This wisdom is the lord and sovereign of all the worlds, inner and outer, whose mercy and justice are beyond our capacity to calculate, this wisdom is the holiness of all creation, it is the essence of purity, the essence of peace which He extends to every open, melting heart. He is the keeper of faith and the guardian of our safety, His grace and light are the ultimate protection in times of danger because He is might and strength beyond anything He has created. This beloved friend who restores what is lost and repairs every injury makes the imperfect perfect, and in His exquisite majesty is the creator and sustainer of all living things. This Lord, the hidden essence of power has created everything from nothing, has given physical form to each entity in existence, bestowing gifts freely upon them, providing their sustenance and nourishment, inwardly and outwardly.

Our God is the opener of hearts fulfilling the deepest longing in each one, relieving the pressure and tension in them with His omniscience which is absolute, while at the same time restraining the excesses He finds there as well. He extends His love and makes it available, spreading it everywhere when He is asked, but when we forget Him He humbles us until we remember Him again, then as our faith deepens He raises and exalts us once again, giving strength and honor to those with pure faith. If we turn away from Him and look instead at bad things and wrong ways until our last breath, He will humiliate us, degrade us and send us to the hell of our own making, and He knows all this because he is both all-hearing and all-seeing, inwardly and outwardly. He is the judge who pronounces the final verdict on our life in a way which is totally just, but completely unbiased and compassionate.

This gracious Lord who is subtle, kind, mysterious and gentle puts His immense goodness into the inner heart. He knows the hidden secrets of all His creatures, yet He is mild and forbearant, conferring patience, contentment and gratitude upon us in the splendor of His wisdom. He is the most exalted, the greatest power, the preserver and sustainer, the supporter and strengthener of everything in creation, He is the glorious and resplendent One who also calls us to account on Judgment Day. Generous and bountiful, He keeps watch over all the beings He has created, listening to their prayers and answering them in the most comprehensive and understanding way with endless wisdom and love. As the supreme ruler of every created being, He has the power to take away life from the living and restore life to the dead, He is the witness and the truth, the reality nothing can dislodge, He is the advocate and trustee. With infinite might and clear determination, the best friend we have exalts our truth and wisdom when we offer all praise to Him, then He wraps the heart of those who love Him with His grace, protecting this purity.

He is the beginning and the origin, the source of everything, restoring life again and again, bestowing life and causing the death of every created thing; with the in-breath we are born, with the out-breath we die, but He is eternal, without beginning or end, subsisting in and of Himself. This planner and creator of all that exists, this noble and generous God of infinite compassion is the One, unique, incomparable, the only One, the secret of grace, the secret of unicity, eternal and absolute. He is the power and the possessor of power who reveals His grace through every being filled with pure faith; He is the existent, before and after, deterring our inclination to be wrong and do wrong, to pursue darkness. He is the first, the beginning, He is the last, He will remain when the rest of creation has ended. Both the manifest in a way that is evident and obvious, and the hidden, the secret, He governs as a friendly, protective ruler in a most exalted manner, just and pure, taking nothing for Himself. In His mercy He causes and accepts our repentance, while requiring something from those who damage the purity of His creation.

Our God who is the great pardoner in His forbearance is kind and indulgent, merciful and consoling; our God who is the supreme Lord of every state or nation is the Lord of majesty and perpetual abundance. His protective justice is for all created beings, a justice that will be evident when He gathers us all together with love and compassion at the end of the world. He is inherent richness, independent, the One who grants wealth and takes it away, restraining our ignorance by removing the darkness, preventing us from going astray with His grace and love, yet ready with the difficulties of Judgment Day for the corrupt who ignore the blessings and benefits bestowed on every created being. As the light, the radiance of complete perfection, enlightenment and plenitude, He is the guide, the incomparable leader who has created an extraordinary variety of beings. He continues forever, surviving beyond all His creation, the imperishable inheritor, the unswerving director to the path of truth in a state of patience, absolute and pure.

Sufi

COMMUNITY

The community we belong to and pray for is the whole human community, no one is excluded because we were all born into that state of purity we call Islam, and we are all given the choice to find it, to know it again. Most of the people in the world at this time however, do not dedicate themselves, their lives to the search for God, they do not necessarily respond to a hunger for the truth because the distractions of the world consume their resources and their attention. In the search for answers to the pressing questions we have to ask if we are to understand the nature of our existence, the reality which is the essential structure, the home for our existence, it is helpful to find companions in the search, to spend time with others who have detached themselves from the demands of the world, at least enough to have a perspective on truth and wisdom which resembles our own. Then there is also the quiet necessity of finding the right yardstick to assess the rate at which we are actually changing, of finding people to engage in the daily business of life so that we can identify our successes and failures: yes I don't get as angry as I once did, but I still do get angry; yes I am more compassionate and loving than I used to be, but my heart is still hard—an introspective examination of how far we have come and how far we still have to go.

The solitude we need for prayer, meditation and reflection is appropriately punctuated with helpful fellowship and societal warmth, a diversity of race, gender, profession, trade, position, rich, poor, young, old, education, east, west, north, south, thin, fat, dark, fair reflecting the peoples of the world because God wants us all, the variety in the flower garden an expression of its strength and beauty. The prophet Muhammad, may God's peace and blessings be upon him, commenting on his own following, observed that the strength of his community lay in their diversity, and paradoxically, that strength is found in unity, a word nicely tucked inside the word community itself, meaning with unity; and that word unity comes from the idea, the word one, one God, one prayer, one family, this is the true significance of community.

We can't do the work at the foot of the mountain alone, first we need a wise being, an instructor who can explain and demonstrate the equipment we need to make the ascent, he has to show us where and how to assemble the things that will be useful in our backpack, and he also has to show us what we have to throw away, what is only a burden and not worth carrying around. Then as we make the climb we do depend on others, above and below, to help us steady the ropes and gauge our progress until we come to the treacherous places at the top of the mountain where there is only room for one and we have to go alone. It's not easy to do the necessary work, it's not easy for some to be comfortable with solitude and learn the hard lessons of truth and wisdom, and so we are given two forms of companionship, one is marriage and the other is community. In marriage we are given an intimate association with the person who knows us probably better than we know ourself, with whom we establish a connection that produces the best and the worst in us, and with whom we have the greatest opportunity to understand unity, oneness, an emblem for that merging with the divine which is the only thing to quiet the hunger, the longing of the soul which cannot stop weeping for the Beloved.

The other form of companionship is the intimacy of a close community where everyone knows everyone else, everyone has observed the lives of those who are connected in their love

425

and search for God, observed each other through fortune and misfortune, watched each other succeed sometimes and fail sometimes, noticed the changes or inability to change. In this tightly woven situation we are not impressed by the accomplishments any more than we are deeply critical of the errors, at any rate we have the ideal of not finding fault with each other and not attributing praise or blame no matter the situation. With the understanding that our personal shortcomings must be eliminated because our good qualities, the qualities of God we so earnestly try to develop, are the only sustaining supports and props for our absolute faith, this community, this diversity of energy and capacity is the playing field for the game of perfection, the reclamation of who and what we are. In our daily interactions, a proving ground as exacting as marriage, we have the opportunity to examine ourself in relation to the perception of ourself we generate, wittingly and unwittingly.

There are always surprises here, usually the unpleasant kind, but with the knowledge that this pathless path is not for the fainthearted we must discover the strength, the persistence to endure the things we must endure and carry on. No one is immune to the vicissitudes of conflict, whether it involves the performance or failure of duty, the performance of prayer or the social engagement of human relations in a context which is neither usual nor normal. The problems in this kind of community might take on the guise of doctrinal differences, how do we pray, when do we pray, what do we pray, or what is the best way to carry out the objectives of the community, what is the correct representation of the community to the outside world, genuine enough issues to a certain extent, but often used to cloak the real issues, the predilection for dominance and authority which tends to surface over many situations, small and large.

The blessings of diversity include always having someone around to help us out of whatever personal difficulty might arise; conversely, always being ready to help someone else out of his difficulty. The blessings of unity mean we are all one in the search for truth and love of God, an understanding which helps us soar above the collective and individual difficulties which necessarily come up from time to time in every life and every group. If we who profess this love and proclaim this search, if we cannot manifest a decent facade, where then on this earth will we find a place to live in accordance with the requirements for His kingdom, where else will we be able to establish His kingdom? Communities all seem to suffer from time to time, fall short of the aspiration, the ideal, but at least the ideal is a constant. The unity of the friendships formed in service and love of God has a special characteristic resonating with a permanence we can only identify as His. If we are never to give up individually, how much greater is the imperative that the community persist and survive, a version of paradise if only we knew, where the distractions and demands of the world are set aside for the grace and beauty of the divine world.

If we can't build a home for unity in this world, then what is the point of everything we have studied and learned, if we can't put this much into practice in this world, haven't we wasted our time here? Everyone talks about unity, nationally at the level of politics and government, locally at the level of schools, teams and sports, privately at the level of our individual organizations, but each of these defines a unity that is exclusive rather than inclusive, like the religions, my way not yours, my unity not yours. Or perhaps it's the unity which comes from burying differences of opinion temporarily, in wartime for example, an artificial unity which is put aside as quickly as the conflict or crisis ends. This is not the unity we try to learn in a community, this is the unity in which no sense of difference is

428

seen or recognized, whether it's difference of race, religion, gender, taste, opinion, it is the unity of the human family which cannot leave anyone out, one family, one prayer, one God, One. God belongs to us all equally, in unity, and we belong to Him, equally, in unity. This world of unity has no time, no season, no night and no death, this is the world of our emancipation, a freedom which is the release, the liberation of the soul.

Greeting each other with the traditional *salams*, saying *as-salamu 'alaikum* to each other, looking into the other person's eyes with an open, melting heart and saying may the peace of God be in your heart now and always, is that unity. When the response is given with the same purity and depth of sincerity, *wa 'alaikumus-salam*, and may that peace also be with you now and always, this is the confirmation of that unity because in the exchange we hear the sound of that One resonating His praise in the heart. The giving and receiving of *salams*, after prayers or meetings to promote wisdom and understanding, or upon chance meetings are part of the unifying glue of a community defined by its purpose and its love, its essentially Islamic foundation in unity. Islam means unity, the pure understanding of *la ilaha illallahu* which sees the essence of all the religions as one, which lives in the belief that there is nothing other than God, He alone is the reality we accept.

The unity of His truth is the true definition of the community we forge in His name; a Sufi community with this understanding can do the individual work of personal reformation and prayer, as well as the collective work of making this truth known, inviting others to taste the sweetness and clarity we have been given. This is a difficult balance to maintain, preserving the privacy, the solitude necessary for meditation and reflection while developing at the same time the public muscle for not only making ourself available to newcomers, but also actively searching for those who have that hunger to know, wherever they come from, whatever their background because all paths lead to One. True Islam obliges us to love everyone equally, to offer His message equally to anyone who loves God and rejects only the wrongs that God Himself has discarded, not any religion, any group or individual. What the community has to offer is a place to correct ourself, eliminate the mistakes of the past and find peace, be rid of our arrogance, our selfishness and the karma tying us to the inessential and impermanent, then in their place establish those blissful qualities of God, the love, compassion and pure contentment which give us and all those near us peace. The community can be an example of this peace and freedom for everyone, showing a better way to live, a better way to navigate the difficulties of this world, a better way to contemplate a life which goes from before our reckoning until after our journey is done. The community can show the world the qualities of God in action.

Of course if we have absolute faith, if we have that determined purity we can live anywhere and be a source of light, yet we have to know how easy it is to be distracted and disengaged, the human condition is such that we can lose everything we have worked so hard to learn until the very last breath. The community offers an invisible cloak, the protection of being good and doing good, the protection of loving and being loved, it encourages and inspires us when we falter or are uncertain. It is a refuge for our good thoughts and qualities, a place where our love and goodness can grow, where we can put the precepts taught by an infinitely wise being into practice: we offer the inner patience and absolute contentment, the trust in God by surrendering everything to Him, we offer praise of Him for whatever happens to us. Here is a place where we can make our faith deeper and our compassion grow, here is a place where we can realize our faults and eliminate them, where we can learn the equality of each member of the human family, where we can learn selfless duty and recognize the pain of another as our own, where justice and conscience become a living shield.

But we do not worship the community or believe it is unique; we can see that it certainly is not perfect, it is merely an illustration of the purity and wisdom we are entitled to and can claim, if we devote ourself to God correctly, if we serve each other in unity. Then there is no duality, there is compassion, tolerance and the recognition of God's existence everywhere, in all living beings, in all animate and inanimate existence, then the darkness dissolves in the radiance of His light. If we do not discover the unity which exists among all beings, if we do not find the unity of prayer here in this life on earth we are separated from God, and instead of living in radiant light, His plenitude, we live in the darkness of hell and illusion. God's light emanates from our gnostic eye, He resonates in an explanation that becomes the light of His throne at the crown of our head, He exists imperishably in our inner heart, a central point, the meeting place of the human community, all those who are purely focused in absolute faith.

This meeting place is the inner church, the mosque within the heart we are to construct individually and visit communally, as one. When we unite to worship here we find the love and grace of Allah shining with irresistible brilliance, when we use the key of His divine wisdom to push the gate open and fling the doors wide, we find the community of His prophets, *quths* and saints praying together with us, reciting His praise, glorifying His name, His attributes and actions. The *la ilaha* of the world, the elements and the body have all been discarded and nothing but the *illallahu* resonates through all the worlds, the world of souls, this world and the hereafter, the affirmation that only God exists. He alone is reality, truth and permanence.